ENDURING HILLS

limit ⟶ ⟶ he R ⟶ ., Ho⟶
in the Army ⟶ ⟶ ly t⟶ ar⟶ ⟶erouai
freedom.

Then the war and Mary. . . . Later
the city, marriage, an important job,
easy living, success. Attained were the
goals he had set years before, but now
he found himself harried, ruthless, discontent. He had come far from the
barefooted mountain lad, but had he
come into his own place? Who was
Hod Pierce, anyway? . . . Suddenly
he knew the answer.

The story is as endearing as the Kentucky hills and the people who love
them. Its appeal is in the author's
insight into human nature and her
ability to create sympathetic and wonderful characters out of simple people,
to vest them with dignity and stature,
and to express herself in language that
is often only a shade removed from
sheer poetry.

THE AUTHOR

Janice Holt Giles has led a very active
life in the field of religious education,
writing and directing children's work.
Until recently she was secretary to the
dean of the Louisville Presbyterian
Theological Seminary. Now Mr. and
Mrs. Giles are living on their farm on
Giles Ridge, at Knifley, Kentucky. The
people and Piney Ridge which the
author writes about in *The Enduring
Hills* are similar to her neighbors and
Giles Ridge. With projects such as
"making" a garden, remodeling the
house, and canning—a new experience
—Mrs. Giles finds herself busier than
ever before. Her city ways are still
considered "quare" by the neighbors,
but she has come to understand and
love the Ridge, and plans to use it as
a background for two new books.

The
Enduring
Hills

JANICE HOLT GILES

The

Enduring

Hills

Philadelphia

THE WESTMINSTER PRESS

1230

To HENRY, of course,
and to
LIBBY and NASH —
my three!

~~~~~~

FOREWORD

It is impossible to reproduce the speech of the hill people exactly as it is spoken. There is no way to put it down in black and white. You have to hear it. I have therefore not attempted to use their forms with every word. I have, however, tried to do justice to the most common usages. But even so, a word of explanation seems necessary.

The people themselves are not consistent in the use of words. Much depends upon the emotions, the strength of feeling, the length of a sentence, or the vowel and consonant sounds immediately preceding or following a word. For example, the aspirate " hit " for " it " is practically always used at the beginning of a sentence. And it may be used any place in a sentence, but when it is, the speaker has paused for breath, as at the beginning of a phrase or clause. So it is not true that hill people say " hit " and " hain't " consistently. And the word " if." Where it is euphonious, and if the speaker is not hurried, it becomes " ifen." Otherwise it remains " if." The possessive " your " is expressed two ways. " Yer ma," or " yer pa." And again, " Ifen it's yore intentions." One is quick, the other is slow.

Some words are almost pure Elizabethan in origin. " Seed " for " seen," for instance. And " afeared " and " heared." The contractions " e'er " and " ne'er," come, of course, from " ever " and " never." They are slurred into " ary " and " nary " in some places.

Remember that it is a lazy speech, softly spoken, with no wasted motion. Remember that it is so euphonious that it is as liquid as song. It falls from the lips with a honey sweetness. Take the phrase, for instance, "Hit's been a time an' a time." Is there a more lovely way of saying it's been a long time? Or, "forever and endurin'." Is there anything more eternal-sounding?

All the characters in this book are fictitious and all the events are imaginary.

CHAPTER ONE

THE EARLY MORNING SUN edged hesitantly up the first few inches of the sky. Each time Hod looked up it had risen a little nearer the tip of the trees that rimmed the far side of the cornfield. The long fingers of light meshed through the tops of the trees and shredded a pattern of lacy shadow halfway across the field. In a shy breeze the pattern rippled and broke, and wove a new pattern. It bent past the young corn and marked Hod's hoe with dark crossbars. It slanted off his blue work shirt and ran ahead of him in a thinned, pencil line.

The whole June morning was soft and easylike around him. The field was a rampart on the edge of the ridge, bold against the cresting sun. The corn was ankle-high, tender and green, and the faintly ribbed leaves rubbed a sigh down the long rows. It was caught and held for a moment here, then passed on there, only slightly diminished. It reached the farthest edge of the field and fiddled through the needles of a pine; it set a frenzied quaking among the leaves of a silver poplar, and then a wood thrush in an old hickory nut tree picked it up and let it tremble from his throat.

" Hod! H-o-o-d! O-o-o-h, Hod! " The round, high call split the air, curved high over the slope of the ridge, and dropped flute-like in the cornfield. Hod shifted the hoe to his left hand and straightened his back.

" Here," he yelled back. " I'm on yon side the field! " And he listened as his own voice was sent out of his chest full into the air, unseeing, but trumpeting out the sound. It was thick and hard and it sped, without partition, cleanly. Like as if I blew a silver note, he thought. Just like as if I blew on Grampa Dow's huntin' horn!

"Here," he called again, and he threw back his head and blew the sound high. "This here's Hod Pierce ablowin' his horn!"

"Horn — horn — horn — horn," came back the sound from the cliff across the holler, the echo making its own echo and sending it back into a cavern of space until at last it was only a piece of sound, flattened and spent.

"Horn," Hod whispered, and completed the cycle. Something went away from me and was gone and came back, and I am all together like I was before. Something was given and something was given back. It's a thing to think on. It's a thing to make a body wonder.

Hod let his arms go loose from the shoulder and let his fingers curl around emptiness, as he watched his sister step high and lightly through the green corn. She came hopping over the furrows with an uneven gait that brought her up to the place where he was standing, breathing fast and shallow. He noticed how red her hair looked in the sun, and how brown and smooth her face was. He wondered afresh at the clear green of her eyes and the queer slant at the outer corners of her mouth — like a smile was forever and endurin' tucked away there. He saw the faded dress molded tight and sharp across her thighs. He was surprised. "She's growin' up! Why, Irma's growin' right up!"

Hod let the hoe handle slide down his hand. "Breakfast ready?" he asked.

"Hit's ready an' waitin'! Did you fergit it's Saturday? Comin' on out to the field thisaway!"

Saturday was the day he took the corn to the mill at the Gap, and made the weekly purchases at the store for his mother.

"No, I didn't forget," he said, shouldering his hoe. "But breakfast wasn't ready, and I thought I'd have time to finish up that row I left last night."

"Never thought somebody'd have to come git you, I reckon," Irma grumbled.

Hod pulled a twig of her hair and grinned. "I don't reckon anybody minded very much," he teased.

Irma glanced cornerwise at him and stuck her chin up in the

air. Then she burst out laughing. "Race you to the house," she challenged, and was off like a flash. Hod followed, heels glinting in the morning sun.

Piney Ridge is the backbone of a group of knobby, stony, almost barren hills, lying in a remote and neglected section of South Central Kentucky. These hills ram each other so closely with their interlocking horns that the country around and between them is well-nigh inaccessible. A graveled pike winds through their jutting lower slopes, but the roads back into the hills are little more than trails.

Green River cuts a deep gash in the hills, but for a space after it leaves the hills it flows gently and placidly, and in the rich bottoms the land stretches black and loamy on either side. Piney Ridge rises like a hogback from the litter of the low, clustering hills, and broods timelessly over old Green.

Clinging to the rocky ledges, the thin level tops, and the deep-scarred hollows of Piney Ridge are the descendants of a resolute man who pushed past the great wall of the hills and settled himself and his wife behind it.

If Thomas Pierce was disappointed when he first looked on the six hundred acres granted to him in payment of his services in the Continental Army, no one knows about it. If he had hoped, when he and his wife Amelia packed their household plunder into one lumbering wagon and drove out of Virginia through the Cumberland Gap into the dark and bloody wilderness — if, then, he had hoped that the tract of land toward which he had turned his face would be fair and fertile, it is not recorded. That proviso which caused the dark hills and Wandering Creek to be peopled read only that "in payment of loyal service rendered the Continental Army from November, 1777, to January, 1779, by Thomas Johnson Pierce of Amelia County, the Congress of the United States deeds to him and his heirs 600 acres of land near and about Wandering Creek, in the territory of Kentucky." The grant was dated February 1, 1805.

Nothing was said about the hills and there was no way Thomas Pierce could know that practically the entire six hundred acres would be covered by their rambling, rocky ridges; because

11

Wandering Creek wanders, as lazy and easy as its name implies, all around and between the hills.

How often he must have thought of home and Virginia and the level fields beside the placid little river there! How bitterly he must have regretted leaving them! How like the drinking of the cup of hemlock must have been the tilling of these thorny acres! But he stayed. To him and his heirs had been deeded the land, and while Thomas Pierce has long since been forgotten, his heirs still till their thorny acres.

Along the saw-toothed lip of Piney Ridge runs a road. In the winter it is axle-deep in mud, and impassable except, perhaps, for a sure-footed mule. In the summer the hard-caked mud is churned to a thick dust which, when stirred, drifts lazily off into the holler like an acrid fog.

About halfway down the ridge the road is bisected by another narrow, rutted road, which, eastward, leads off over Blain's Ridge to Goose Creek and the little settlement of Pebbly. To the west lies Knobby Gap, where there is a post office, a blacksmith's shop, two general stores, a gristmill, and perhaps a dozen drab houses. A church raises its dingy, scaling spire between the two stores.

But all that lies between is Piney Ridge, and on the road running the length of the ridge live the numerous descendants of Thomas Pierce on what is left of his six hundred acres. A few have been ambitious enough to add to their holdings, but most have been content with their meager share.

None of the Pierces care how they came to be on the ridge. Piney Ridge has belonged to them as far back as they can remember, and beyond that they have little curiosity. Sometimes Grampa Dow, the oldest of the tribe, and getting long-winded in his old age, tells about his father, Jeems, who could remember when the deer, bear, and wild turkey would walk right up to a man's cabin. But for the most part the familiar pattern of today is all that matters on the ridge. The Pierces only know that this land is theirs, that Pierce feet have always walked it, and that Pierce feet will always continue to walk it.

Grampa Dow was Hod's grandfather. He had three sons — Gault, Lem, and Tom. As each married, he gave him a parcel of land, and when Tom, the youngest, married, he gave him the home place and moved himself and Annie down to the log cabin in the holler which Jeems had built. Lem took the piece down on the pike, and Gault settled on the middle eighty down the road from Tom. Tom was Hod's father.

And there were great-uncles and uncles and first and second and third cousins scattered the length and breadth of the ridge. Farther down the road, toward Wandering Creek, big Wells Pierce and Hardy Pierce divided Great-Uncle James's place, Wells taking the old house with fifty acres and Hardy building him a cabin on the far forty. Hardy's wife had died many years before and he had lived alone until he hurt his back; then his oldest girl, Matilda, who had married her own first cousin, Little Wells, had come to live with him and keep his house. Little Wells tended the forty acres for Hardy, along with his own, and they had a house full of young'uns which, some said, nearly drove Hardy out of his mind.

Still farther down the road was Great-Uncle Frank's place, and then Great-Uncle Tim's place was the last bit of level land before the ridge dropped off to Wandering Creek. Frank had seven sons to heir his hundred acres, and Tim had five.

Uncle James, Uncle Frank, Uncle Tim, and Grampa Dow had had sizable holdings in their time, but the land had been divided among their sons, and soon it would have to be divided among new sons. And so it went. There was no new land to buy without leaving the ridge, and few Pierces ever left the ridge. They could not seem to live away from their thorny acres.

Occasionally — only occasionally — was there born to one of the Pierces a son or a daughter with a trace of the vital spirit of Thomas Pierce who had cut a trail to this gaunt land. Grampa Dow was one. Once he had studied on being a preacher. He even got him some books and pored over them. Hod didn't know why Grampa hadn't finished his studying, but Gramma had always laughed about it and said, "The sperrit was willin' but the flesh was weak." Grampa Dow didn't rightly know what had happened to the books, either. "The young'uns must o' took 'em," he said. "I ain't seen e'er one in a coon's age."

And then there was Aunt Dorcas, Grampa Dow's sister, who somehow had got enough learning to teach the Big Springs school. Of course she didn't teach very long. She married one of

13

her pupils, a big, strapping hulk of a fellow, who was ten years younger than she, and went with him to live over in Bear Holler.

But the fact remains that occasionally there was a Pierce with a will to lift himself out of the general inertia that was characteristic of the clan. The will may not have been sufficient to lift very far, but it stirred a faint spark of hope and yearning which flamed for a brief moment before it sputtered out.

Such a will was part of the heritage of young Hod Pierce when he was born on a hot July day, to this land and to these people. He was seven generations removed from his pioneer ancestor, but in the strange, unfathomable way of nature Hod was endowed with qualities that made him the old soldier's spiritual son.

This may have been because both Grampa Dow and Hod's father, Tom, went off the ridge to find their brides. Grampa Dow married Annie Hobbs from Pebbly, and Tom had gone to Peachstone, near the Gap, for pretty Hattie Byron. Fresh blood may have offered a freer channel for the transmission of the stancher and nobler qualities of the line. However that may be, young Hod was destined from the start to chafe and pull at the pattern of his life, trying first to make his dreams fit the pattern, and then trying to make the pattern fit his dreams. The pattern of Pierce lives was the very warp and woof of his soul, but it couldn't stifle the spark of his dreams. From childhood he looked at his world with clear, judging eyes, and with a heart torn between what he loved and felt and what he saw and judged.

Hod was born in the home place and his childhood varied little from that of his father before him. His bare feet stepped out of the low kitchen door onto the same wood block that had been worn down by Tom's feet. He ate with the same bone-handled knives and forks, at the same oilcloth-covered table in the dark corner of the kitchen, from the same old ironstone plates. He took the milk down the steep, rocky hill to the same cold spring, and struggled back up with heavy buckets of water for his mother. He swung on the same sagging garden gate, and ate the spicy, short-core apples from the same gnarled old trees.

From July to February he went down the road past the church, turned off on a dim path through the woods and over the edge of the hill, and down the holler to the same school to which Tom

14

and Grampa Dow had gone. His father's initials were cut on one side of a giant beech tree in the edge of the clearing and Grampa Dow's initials were still plain on its other side. Hod cut his own there one day, fresh and bleeding, under his father's, and stood off to admire his handiwork.

It was at school that the Pierce pattern changed. His father and most of the others had suffered in the schoolroom as in a prison; had felt bewildered by the steady stream of facts and uninspired to open the door of knowledge. They were like birds released to fly again when each long day was over. But Hod's eager young mind soaked up knowledge and was ever thirsting for more. History and geography flamed with color and passion for him, and the precise accuracy of mathematics and science enthralled him. He loved every day of the short school term and raced through his books until the teacher was sore tried to keep him supplied.

"Why do you keep running ahead of the class, Hod?" she asked. "If you will study only the lesson assigned to you, you won't finish your books so fast."

"I don't aim to bother you," he answered, "but I can't seem to quit when I get to the end. I allus want to know what comes next."

"But you'll find out when we come to that part."

"Yessum, I know. But I can't seem to help it. I know it's there and I want to learn so bad I have to keep right on." And then he burst out: "Miss Bertha, I want to read all the books I can get a hold of. I can go faster'n the other kids, and if I can go faster without botherin' you none, why can't I? Seems like I can't go fast enough to learn all I want to, and I get afraid the books won't last me out."

After that Miss Bertha had let him move along as he could. She tried to find books for him, and even dug down in her trunk and brought him those of her college days. He seized joyfully on anything she brought him — history, fiction, poetry, even the dull stuff of theology, for her father had been a minister and she still had some of his seminary volumes. He read anything and everything she gave him. He seemed spurred by some frenzied need to keep forever reading.

"Hod," his mother said one night when he had forgotten to

15

chop the kindling for the morning fires the second time in a row, " I'm plumb wore out with you havin' yer nose stuck in a book all the time. Hit's the beatinest thing ever I seen how you go to school all day an' cain't git enough o' books. A body cain't git a lick o' work outen you if they's a book handy. I don't know what's come over you, an' you ain't even ahearin' me talkin' to you now! "

The strident voice brought Hod back from King Arthur's Court and he blinked in the dim light of the familiar room. " I'm sorry, Ma," he said, laying the book down. " I didn't aim to forget the kindlin' again, but I cain't seem to remember anything when I get to readin' a book like this."

" What's it about? "

" It's about knights and ladies that lived across the ocean. And about a girl called the lily maid of Astolat. The knights had to be very . . . very — " he groped for the word — " very gallant, and fight for the king and the ladies."

" Humph! Sounds plumb crazy to me! You better git out there an' fight that choppin' block or there'll be no more readin' to-night. Cain't burn the lamps much longer, noways. Hit's a pure waste of oil."

Hod, who had been making ready to go out, stopped at the door. " Can I have a candle in the loft room, then? "

" No, you cain't have you no candle in the loft room. Someday yer goin' to burn the house right down to the ground, an' us with it, aburnin' a candle up there with them straw ticks. You'll go to bed an' go to sleep like you'd orta, young man, an' now git goin' on that kindlin' 'fore I smack you."

Hod hadn't really expected to be allowed to read later. Seemed like Ma almost always said no. Like that time he had wanted to have a garden all his own. " Ma," he'd said, " kin I have me a little garden over here in the corner an' have me some radishes an' onions o' my own? "

" No," not interrupting her own hoeing.

" Why? "

Smack! The thin, calloused brown hand was likely to reach out surely and swiftly for his face. " Git to yer hoein' an' quit pesterin' me with yer why's! You ain't big enough to have you a garden, that's why! Besides, you'd fergit to take keer of it, an'

16

it'd jist be good seed wasted." And Hod never argued. Life was easier if you didn't argue with Ma. Things went smoother if you just did what you were told to do.

Hod set the lantern down by the chopping block and methodically went to work on the kindling. With sure, clean strokes the hatchet stripped the slivers from a pine log. Doggedly he worked in the winter cold, and doggedly his thoughts kept him company.

"I'm gonna" — he corrected himself — "I'm going to go away from Piney Ridge someday and see the whole world. I'm going to Louisville and California and Europe, and maybe to China too; and I'm going to see for myself what the rest of the world is like. I'm going to eat off of a white tablecloth with shiny knives and forks and I'm going to have good clothes and sleep in a real bed, and I'm going to *be* somebody. *Someday I'm going to be somebody!*"

This was Hod when he was twelve. By the time he was seventeen he had finished with the little country school. It went only through the eighth grade and Hod had gone as long as Miss Bertha was there, but when she left, there was nothing more for him in the schoolroom. He wanted to go on to high school, but that would have meant boarding in at the county seat, and Tom and Hattie could see no use in any further schooling. Money was too scarce, and his help was needed on the place.

Hattie said: "You've learned how to read an' write an' do a little figgerin'. Why would you need to know any more? 'Twon't he'p you none growin' tobaccer."

So now he was free of the schoolroom, for his father to shift most of the heavy work of the farm to his thin shoulders. Not unkindly. It was the way of the ridge. Sons took over the hardest work as soon as they were able.

Hod was up at first light in answer to his mother's call: "Hod! Git up!" Never was it softened. Never once did she climb the steep little stairs to the loft room to touch him and wake him gently.

He would tumble out of his straw tick and dress hurriedly, for the loft room was bitterly cold in the winter and stiflingly hot in the summer. In the summer, dressing consisted of pulling on his overalls and putting on his shoes, for he wore neither underwear nor socks, and he slept in his shirt. There was something faintly

17

repulsive to him in this, for his shirt always smelled of his own sweat and he shrank, fastidiously, from its contact. But he wouldn't have thought of asking his mother for a clean one. He put on the clothes she laid out for him, when she laid them out, understanding all too well that there wasn't enough money for him to have more than two pairs of overalls and three or four shirts. Since he carried the water from a spring on washday, he knew he couldn't have fresh clothes every day. At that he was cleaner than most boys he knew, for Hattie was a cleaner mother than most. But a bath once a week, with fresh shirt and overalls for him satisfied her standards.

Dressed, he stumbled down the steep, dark stairs to the kitchen, splashed warm water from the iron teakettle, which always sat on the back of the stove, into a tin washbasin, and washed the sleep from his eyes. Then he ran the snaggle-toothed comb, which the whole family used, through his hair two or three times, and his toilet was made. After that he was usually off to the barn, where his father had preceded him, and silently they fed the stock and milked the cows.

Breakfast was ready when they returned to the house. It was a meal that rarely varied: fried, home-cured bacon or ham; fried eggs; hot soda biscuits; milk gravy; scalding, black, boiled coffee; and homemade jam, jelly, preserves, or sorghum molasses.

Such a breakfast waited for Hod and Irma now. As they came through the door, Hattie speared brown pieces of meat and piled them high on the platter. Breaking eight eggs into the large iron skillet, she fitted the lid down and left them to simmer.

"Irma, you kin set the things down," she said sharply.

"Yessum," Irma said, flying to take up the hot biscuits, to pour the coffee, and to set a small pitcher of cream in the center of the table.

Hattie took the cover off the eggs and poured them into a warm, shallow bowl. She dropped a handful of flour into the hot grease in the skillet and stirred vigorously until it was blended. Then she filled the skillet with milk and gently moved the creamy mass back and forth until it thickened.

Hod sniffed. "Cream gravy, Ma?"

"I declare, Hod! You had cream gravy nigh onto ever' day o' yer life, an' you allus act like it was somethin' brand-new! Don't you never git enough of it? "

" Never have yet! Just be sure you make enough. I'll need it to pass the day at the Gap."

Irma drew her mouth down at the corners. " I wisht I could go to the Gap with him today."

" Now, Irma," Hattie said, " we got a sight o' work cut out fer us today, hit bein' Saturday an' all. I cain't noways make out here by myself. Likely the meetin'll start tomorrer night too. Hit's powerful early to be startin' a meetin', but them White Caps, they allus have the first 'un. But White Caps or whoever else, I ain't aimin' to miss the startin', an' they's more work'n I kin make out to do. You'll have to he'p today."

Irma sighed and slid down the bench along the wall to her regular place, and Hod slid in next to her. When Hattie sat down, the family bowed their heads and waited for the blessing. She smoothed back her hair. She always smoothed her hair back before the blessing, as if she must be neat to approach the Lord. She then cleared her throat and murmured rapidly: " Lord, we thank thee for what we are about to receive. Keep us from sin and save us in heaven. For Jesus' sake. Amen."

The blessing over, each one filled his plate, sprawled his arms along the table, bent his head over his food, and shoveled it in as fast as he could swallow. It was an insult to a good cook to talk when a body could eat. As each finished eating, he shoved his plate back and left the table. Hod and Tom moved out into the yard.

" Reckon I better git on down to Grampa's," Tom said, moving the toothpick in his mouth from one corner to the other. " I give him my word I'd he'p in his corn today."

" You sure you wouldn't rather go to the Gap today yourself? "

" No. You go on. Ifen yer ma don't remember to put a plug o' tobaccer on the list, don't you fergit it."

" I'll not. And I'll be home in time to help with the evenin' work."

Tom's eyes twinkled. " Mebbe," he drawled, " ifen that Lily Mae gal ain't down at the Gap today too."

Hod flushed and kicked the toe of his shoe against the wood block. " I'm not aimin' to tarry with any Lily Mae girl," he muttered.

"I dunno, boy. Ifen I was yore age, I'm afeared I'd be bound to tarry some."

"Well, I'm not actually talkin' to her, yet."

"No? Well, don't be like them molasses in there agittin' started. Happen somebody else is agoin' to notice them blue eyes o' her'n first thing you know."

Hod grinned at his father and poked at him with his fist. "You better be gettin' on down to Grampa's, and I better be headin' for the Gap." He started toward the house.

Hattie had laid out clean denim pants for him, and a fresh-ironed shirt. As he pulled them on, Hod thought of Lily Mae. It would be something, now, wouldn't it, if she should happen to be at the Gap today too. He remembered her wheat-colored hair, and the bold, strong look of her eyes. The other night when he walked her home from the singing, was she mocking him when she said she liked bashful boys, or was she saying it for true? A thin silver stream ran through him and set his legs to quivering. He stared strangely at his reflection in the cracked mirror hanging over the chest of drawers. He looked closely at his own straw-colored hair, springing thickly from the scalp, pushing back in one high wave. He examined his eyes, blinking them rapidly and widening them to see exactly how they looked. They were hazel, there was no doubt about it. He pulled his lips away from his teeth and looked carefully at their strong, even whiteness. He looked at the deep dimple in the middle of his chin. He screwed his head from one side to another, looking at his jaw from first one angle and then another. It was lean and ruddy, but he wasn't much to look at, he thought. If a girl like Lily Mae took a fancy to him, it wouldn't be on account of his looks.

What, then? What drew a man and a woman together and lifted their eyes to each other shyly? What, across the face of the earth, pulled the male and female into pairs? This thin silver stream of loneliness? This emptiness inside of him in the night? This need to stand on high places and look beyond the hills? What, in all time, was the way of man on the face of the earth? And how was a man to know, and what was he to know? His thoughts ran vaguely, without definition. There was only a feeling of deep nostalgia . . . for something that eluded him.

"Hod?" his mother's voice recalled him. "I've done fixed out my list. You 'bout ready?"

He tucked in his shirttail and went into the kitchen. "I'm ready."

She handed him the list, written in pencil on the cheap, blue-lined tablet paper she always used. "Hit ain't so much today, an' they's no real heavy things to pack, so I reckon you better not take the wagon."

He folded the list and slipped it into his shirt pocket.

"Now, mind, Hod," Hattie went on, "an' don't fergit nothin'. Don't mislay that there thread, fer I'm plumb outen it, an' I've got to git Irma's dresses sewed next week fer shore. An' you watch the miller on the toll real keerful. Matildy was tellin' me he uses a awful heavy hand ameasurin', an' we ain't got no corn to spare to fatten up his hogs with!"

"Yessum," said Hod. "Anything else?"

"Ifen you see Brother Jim, you might tell him we're all well. An' ask him how Frony is. She ain't been very stout this winter, an' it wouldn't surprise me none to hear any day she's been took with another spell of her heart."

Hod moved toward the door. "Find out fer shore if the meetin's goin' to start tomorrer night, an' who's goin' to do the preachin'. But don't go givin' him no invite fer dinner tomorrer, though. I don't aim to kill e'er nother chicken till my little 'uns come on."

As he went through the barnyard gate, Hattie called once more. "Hod! Uh, Hod! Better git Tom a plug o' tobaccer."

He waved to let her know he had heard and went on. He led old Buck to the fence, slipped the bit between his teeth and threw the saddle over him. Then, turning back to the barn, he hefted the bag of corn onto his shoulder. Under the load he hunched over to Buck and threw the sack up back of the saddle. He took a double hitch around the bag of corn, making it fast to the saddle, and then he swung up and moved down the path toward the road.

As he turned into the road, Irma came running out the front door. "Here's the money, Hod! Hod! You done fergot the money!"

He reined up the horse and waited, laughing, while Irma

caught up with him. She handed it up to him and said: " That was about the foolishest thing I ever knowed of! What was you aimin' to use fer money? "

" Wasn't thinkin' about money one way or another. Just plumb forgot about it."

Irma stood, fingering the saddle strings. " Hod," she said, her voice low and her head down. " Reckon you'll see John Walton down at the Gap? "

Hod grinned at her. " It's possible."

" Well, ifen you do, an' don't go out o' yer way none, but jist ifen you do, an' ifen you find out fer shore the meetin's goin' to start tomorrer night, jist let it drop like that we'll all be goin'."

" How does a body go about just lettin' it drop like? " he teased.

Her face flamed. " You know what I'm meanin', Hod Pierce! "

" Now, just smooth down your red hair! I wasn't meanin' anything. I'll find a way to let it drop like if I see him." He slapped the reins against Buck's neck and the horse moved slowly away. " And if he's at the Gap I'll see him," he promised. The dust between them rose in a thick cloud and Irma went back into the house.

Buck stepped off the distance lightly and quickly, following the meanderings of the road. When they came to the crossroads, Hod took a path through a pasture, into the woods, and eventually came out at the road that went down off the ridge to the Gap. Hod loved that little place in the woods. It was always cool and quiet, except for the squirrels and birds.

This morning the sun sprinkled the ground with gold dust, and sprayed the leaves with shining lacquer. The birches stood whitely in their cleanness, and squirrels fretted childishly among them. An old mockingbird trilled high up next to the sun, and a jay scolded him from a sumac bush. Hod leaned out and stripped a sassafras twig from a young tree; and peeling it, stuck it in his mouth to chew on.

" You old jay," he teased the bird, " nobody's botherin' you! You go on about your business! "

He eased Buck on down the hill, smelling the clean June morning and the warm sun and the bright blue day. It was a fair day, for sure.

CHAPTER TWO

Horses, mules, and teams were hitched to the long rail in front of the mill, which on Saturday was the gathering place of farmers from the whole countryside. They came in from every direction, bringing their bushels of corn, whetting their gregarious appetites with anticipation of a full, unhurried day of male company. Here the wine of man's talk was distilled afresh each week, and mulled voluptuously over each tongue.

Hod pushed past the knot of men lounging in the doorway and eased his load of corn into the line of sacks on the floor.

"Howdy, Hod," said the miller.

"Howdy, Uncle Billy. Reckon I'll have time to do Ma's buyin' before you get to me?"

"Plenty o' time. Plenty o' time. Be another hour yit 'fore I kin git to you. Go 'long an' don't be in no rush. How's all yer folks?"

"Well as could be expected, I reckon. You seen Uncle Jim around today?"

The miller spat tobacco juice on one of the sacks near his feet and looked slowly around. "No," he said finally. "Come to think of it, I ain't. An' he don't hardly ever miss a Saturday, neither. Could be Frony's puny again, but I ain't heared no one name it if she is. Want me to tell him yer lookin' fer him ifen he comes in?"

"I'd be much obliged to you," Hod said, and moved out the door.

He crossed the road to the store, went up its three rickety steps and inside. When his eyes had become accustomed to its dimness, he walked diffidently back to where Miss Ettie, the storekeeper, sat crocheting. Hod always dreaded this moment, for the store was usually full of womenfolks and he felt out of place among them. But Ma's list burned his pocket until he had made her purchases.

As he threaded his way through the women, he nodded shyly to each, noticing who they were so that he could tell Hattie. His heart pumped suddenly when he saw Lily Mae Gibbs standing over by the counter. He could hear Hattie's tongue clucking now. "So Lily Mae Gibbs was in town, was she? You'd think she'd stay home oncet in a while an' he'p her ma. She does a sight o' runnin' around fer a girl her age."

Maybe he wouldn't tell her Lily Mae was there after all. She'd been upset when she found out he walked Lily Mae home from the singing last time. Wasn't any need to tell her everything.

Among the women gathered at the counter Hod took note of Matildy, Little Wells's wife. She was a short, plump little woman, with crinkling brown eyes, and a good, hearty laugh. It rang out now and filled the store, and Hod smiled as he heard it. He had always liked Matildy. He would ask her about the meetin'.

Miss Ettie heaved her vast bulk up from the rocker and rolled her crocheting into a neat ball. The womenfolks always had to gossip awhile and look around until they made up their minds, but she knew Hod would have a list and wouldn't want to linger long.

"Howdy, Hod," she said, moving to meet him. "You got yer ma's list, I reckon. How's Hattie, an' all yer folks?"

"We're all tol'able, thank you. You all well?"

"Purty good. Ma's been ailin', but, as I tell her, when yer eighty-five year old you got to expect a few aches an' pains. She's right peart fer one her age. Lemme have Hattie's list."

Hod fished in his pocket for the list and handed it to her. "Ma said git Pa a plug of tobacco too. It's not on the list."

Miss Ettie nodded and went about filling the order. White thread, a bottle of Black Draught, a large can of baking powder, a box of pepper, a paper of pins, and Tom's cut plug. As she gathered together the articles, Hod listened to the women's talk.

Becky, Gault's wife, was telling Matildy and Lily Mae how she made her famous spiced peaches. "Hit's the way you make the sirup that counts," she was saying. "Ifen you bile it jist a mite too long, it hardens 'em. I never even let it spin a thread."

Matildy laughed. "I reckon yer right, Becky. But with that flock o' young'uns round my feet I'm lucky if I git e'er peach in a can, much less foolin' with sich fancies as spicin' 'em."

Becky, who had no children, looked wistfully at Matildy. "Air the young'uns all well?" she asked.

"Oh, tol'able. But with four you cain't never tell. I'm hopin' they won't come down with ever'thing till the meetin's over."

Lily Mae giggled and lowered her voice, but Hod could hear the clear whisper: "Ifen they ever' one had the whoopin' cough an' was coughin' their heads off, don't reckon you'd miss the meetin'."

Matildy's big, hearty laugh rang out again. "No, that wouldn't frash me none. I ain't aimin' to miss out on the meetin' fer nothin' like that!"

They bunched their heads together and Hod knew they meant to exclude him. This was hushed and intimate woman talk, meant only for a woman's ears. Self-consciously he kept his eyes away from them. He studied the canned goods on the shelves, whistled tunelessly under his breath, and stuffed his suddenly awkward hands in his pants pockets. When Lily Mae laughed too loudly and too meaningly, his glance was drawn to her like a magnet. He wanted desperately to talk to her. He thought of how it would be to walk boldly up to her and ask her whether she knew for certain the meeting was going to start tomorrow night and if she was going. He could feel how he would swing his shoulders back, uncaring, before all the women. How he would say for all to hear, "I'll be walkin' you home tomorrow night."

But he made no move except to shift from foot to foot uneasily. Miss Ettie handed him his purchases. He paid her and put the change in his pocket. As he walked past the women, Matildy spoke to him. "Hod, e'er one o' the folks come in with you?"

He stopped. "No," he answered. "Pa had to he'p Grampa today, and Ma and Irma cleaned house. So I came in by myself." He ran the rim of his straw hat around in his hands. "Say, Matildy, is the meetin' goin' to start tomorrow for sure?"

"I was aimin' to tell you," Matildy slapped her hand down on the counter, "and I plumb nigh fergot! The tent's all set up in the schoolyard at Big Springs, tell Hattie. An' Dan Wilson's goin' to do the preachin'. I ain't never heared him, but they say he's really got the sperrit, an' kin expound somethin' wonderful. Big Springs ain't as handy fer Hattie as 'twould be at Piney Chapel, but I reckon it's clost enough fer her to go real often."

"Well, much obliged, Matildy," and Hod turned to go.

"Tell her," Matildy added, "that he's goin' to take dinner with Lizzie tomorrer, an' if she figgers she kin take him e'er time durin' the meetin', she kin let me know."

"I'll tell her," he promised, and turned on his heel. He swung sharply into Lily Mae, who had moved back of him as he talked to Matildy. The girl gave no ground and lifted impudent, mocking eyes to him. Her face was only a few inches from his, and her bold, blue look held him brightly. His heart skipped a beat and then started pounding crazily. He felt paralyzed and rooted to the spot.

She tossed her yellow hair back and laughed. "I'm goin' to the meetin' tomorrer night," she said. "You aimin' to go?"

He swallowed hard and felt his voice cracking around the knot in his throat. "I reckon," was all he could manage to get out.

She leaned slightly forward so that for a brief moment her body brushed against him. Light as a moth's wing it was, but it sent an instant shock all over him. Even his finger tips tingled. She was so close her breath fanned his cheek when she said, "Ifen you do, bring yer gittar!"

He lifted his eyes to hers, and her shining, confident look darkened with promise. His tongue stuck to the roof of his mouth, and he thought wildly that his knees were going to give way. He could bear no more. He ducked his head and fled, hearing the women laugh as he stumbled down the steps. Lily Mae's laugh was loudest of all.

His nose burned with the depth of his indrawn breath, and he forced himself to walk away slowly. But his heart pumped loudly and there was a singing in his ears. Lily Mae liked him! She moved over on purpose so he would bump into her! He felt a joyful surge of exhilaration again, and he lifted his head high. She wanted him to come to the meetin'! Tomorrow! Tomorrow! Tomorrow was so fair a day!

"Ye-ay! Hod!" a voice hailed him. "Wait up!"

Coming around the corner of the store were two of his cousins, Wade and Sandy Pierce, Lem's boys, about his own age. They were handsome boys, taller than Hod, more solidly built, with brilliant curls and flashing, perfect teeth. Hod had envied them all his life, not only because they were so carelessly good-looking, but also because they were so wonderfully free. Lizzie was an easygoing mother, who showered love and affection on her young'uns and spoiled them out of all reason. She kept a slovenly house whose doors were open to everyone, and lived and let live as best she could. Her house was a scandal to as good a housekeeper as Hattie, and the way she was raisin' her kids was worse. But to Hod, Wade and Sandy seemed blessed by Providence' own kind hand.

He was proud of Hattie's smart ways and neat house, but he wished it didn't hedge him in so. Folks said Hattie Pierce had been as gay and purty as a bird when she was young. But ever since she was converted that summer, long before he could remember, she had been strict and, most times, joyless. Religion sometimes did that to a body. But folks all said that Hattie Pierce was a woman who really had the faith, now. And there was never a tongue set against her. She would die before she'd lift her skirts to a dance tune, and if a deck of cards had darkened her door, she would have burned them quicker than a flash, and her tongue would have taken the hide off him that brought them. Seemed like sometimes her religion was mostly don'ts, but one thing you had to say: she never talked one way and did another.

But Wade and Sandy, now. They could go swimming in the river whenever they liked; they could go hunting when they wanted to; they could have the horses to ride on Sunday; they could build martin boxes right in the house and Lizzie didn't say: " Git that stuff outen here! Yer jist makin' a mess fer me to clean up! "

They were even allowed to have a deck of cards at home, and Hod had seen Lizzie sit down with them, laughing just as hard as they did over the game. And they had a fiddle and a victrola in their house, and some mighty lively tunes they played on that victrola.

" We been wantin' to see you," said Wade, who was the older. " Pa said we could go over to the lumber camp this summer till the tobaccer's ready, an' hew ties an' make us some money. Reckon you could go? "

Hod's eyes brightened. What wouldn't he give to go with them! Why, he might make twenty-five or thirty dollars! It was a couple of months yet until tobacco would be ready to cut. He might even make fifty dollars! With fifty dollars he could go to Louisville. Maybe he could get a job there and work and go to

27

school. He could hew ties! Why, hadn't he just last winter split enough hickory to fence the pasture along the road?

"When you goin'?" he asked.

"Monday mornin' bright an' early. Pa's goin' to take us over in the wagon, an' we kin stop by fer you easy as not," answered Wade.

"We're goin' to stay over at the camp too," spoke up Sandy. "Ain't no use to come home 'cept on Sundays."

An uneasy feeling crept over Hod. He didn't know what Hattie would say to that. She had always held that the lumber camp was a godless place. But surely she would want him to earn all that money. If he could make as much as fifty dollars, he could give her half of it and still have enough to go to Louisville.

"Well, you all stop by," he said, "and if I can go I'll be ready."

Wade nodded and turned away. Sandy followed him and Hod started toward the mill.

"You goin' to preachin' tomorrer night?" yelled Wade at his back. Hod swung around.

"I reckon Ma'll want to go."

"Betcha a dollar you go . . . fer the singin' anyhow," teased Wade. Hod flushed.

"What do *you* know about any singin'?"

"Oh . . ." Wade laughed, "news gits around. I hear you like the color of Lily Mae Gibbs's eyes."

Uncomfortably Hod pushed his old straw hat back on his head. "I couldn't even tell you the color of her eyes," he lied intensely.

"Well, what *was* you lookin' at when you was talkin' to her over at Smiths' the other Sunday?" howled Sandy, and the two cousins fled down the road, whooping and yelling.

Hod kicked angrily at a pebble in the road. This is the meanest place in the whole world for talking, he thought. Just because I looked off the same book at singin' with Lily Mae Gibbs, and then walked down the road a piece with her, the whole ridge has got me married to her!

Piney Ridge found nothing strange in a seventeen-year-old boy's thinking of marriage. Many boys on the ridge married at sixteen or seventeen and had families before they were twenty. But no such thought was in Hod's mind. The girl Lily Mae was exciting. He didn't ferret out his feelings beyond that. His skin

28

prickled when he thought of her. But he forgot her when he thought of the lumber camp Monday. And maybe the big city this fall.

At the mill he looked around for John Walton, but not seeing him, settled himself on a sack of meal on the fringe of the circle of men who were chewing and spitting and ruminating. Little Wells was there, a short, sawed-off little man with merry, winsome ways. He and Matildy were cut from the same piece of cloth, Hod thought, fitting together like the pattern from one bolt of goods.

Ferdy Jones was in the group. Ferdy was a tall, skinny fellow with a nervous Adam's apple and a sharp nose that was always smelling gossip and talk, most of it scandalous and obscene. Ferdy liked to drink too well, and the talk was that Corinna had a bad time with him.

Lem was there, tall and stooped, and Gault; and thin, wizened little Old Man Clark, who lived in the tenant house on Gault's place. Matt Jasper sat over in a corner to himself, tobacco juice making twin lines of dribble down his unshaved chin. None of the Jaspers was very bright, but Matt had fits, and while he could work a farm all right, his eyes had a staring, vacant look.

Other men drifted in and out the door from time to time, but these men were the hub of the wheel. Hod knew they would sit here several hours. He listened and watched as they talked. Funny, he thought. You can tell the strength of a man by the way the others listened to him. Lem is like a stout oak tree in a forest. When he talks, the others heed him. Little Wells will be a stout oak tree someday too. But the sap is still green in him. Gault is strong, but it's like his strength had frozen in him. He's brittle. Maybe if he and Becky had had children, he would have been warm and gentle. Having no children seemed to dry up a man.

Ferdy Jones was a windbag, and, like the wind, his words passed over and were hardly noticed. Old Man Clark they humored, knowing his strength was past. They pitied Matt Jasper, but their pity was mixed with something like shame. He had the form of a man and the manner of a man, but there was something rotten and sick and unclean in him, and spiritually they isolated him and his disease fouled them. Are men like this the world over, thought Hod. Or is it the ridge makes them so?

The talk drifted lazily from one subject to another. Little Wells was speaking when Hod noticed. "That rain last week shore freshened up the tobaccer," he said. "Ifen we kin jist have a little spell o' rain along, we'd orta have a right good crop this year."

"How much you figger to have, Wells?" asked Gault.

"Oh, round seven, eight hunderd pounds, I reckon. What you figgerin' on?"

"'Bout the same. Mebbe a little less."

"I doubt the price'll hold this year, though," spoke up Ferdy. "What you think, Lem?"

Lem pulled at his chin and pondered. "Hit's untellin', but they's no real good reason to think it'll go down too fur. As a usual thing it builds up two, three year, an' then it'll start taperin' off. Ain't quite due to drap off much yit. But the tobaccer market's somethin' I ain't ever hopin' to figger out."

The miller came up behind Wells and laid a dusty hand on his shoulder. "Wells, how's that little Jersey I sold you awhile back doin'?"

"She's all right, Uncle Billy. A good little milker. 'Course she's dry right now, but she's due to come fresh in about a coupla months. I ain't got e'er thing to complain about in that cow. She's gentle an' she's easy to milk. You done me a favor when you sold her to me."

Ferdy Jones snickered. "That ain't the only thing that's due to come fresh over at yore place, is it Wells?"

Wells chuckled. "Well," he said, "I'm ahopin' Matildy an' the cow don't run too clost a race." The men laughed together, comfortably.

Hod saw John Walton come in and saunter over toward the hopper. He unfolded his long legs and drifted over toward him.

"Howdy, John."

"Howdy, Hod. Looks like nearly ever'body come in to the Gap today. All yore folks come?"

"No. Nobody but me."

The Waltons were one of the few outside families who had

settled in the ridge country. Old Man Walton had bought a little piece of land from Hardy Pierce and had brought his family from Tennessee. He had acquired more land from time to time from various other Pierces and now had one of the biggest farms on the ridge. Folks said he drove himself and his boys mighty hard, but they had to admit he made a showing for it.

John was an easygoing, quick-laughing young man. Hod knew him to be a diligent and dependable worker; and in that fraternity of quickening young men he knew him to be decent. He knew John would make Irma a good and faithful husband.

"You all aimin' to go to the meetin' tomorrow night?" he asked idly.

"They aimin' to start fer shore?"

"Matildy was just tellin' me they are. Tent's on the Big Springs school ground. She said Dan Wilson's goin' to do the preachin'."

"I've not heared of him."

"I've not either, but Matildy said he was a man with power."

John ran a thin stream of fresh-ground meal through his hands. "You all aimin' to go?"

"We'll be there."

"Well, I'll be seein' you then."

The word had been dropped like, and Hod could tell Irma that John would be looking for her. He turned back to the men, raising his hand to John.

CHAPTER THREE

Home looked good to Hod as he came in sight of it. It was always thus when he had been away, even for so brief a spell as the trip to the Gap each Saturday.

The house Grampa Dow had given Tom Pierce when he brought Hattie home as a bride hunched low by the side of the road. There were four rooms now; two across the front and two in the lean-to across the back. A narrow porch with a railing around it hemmed in the two front doors, and at the back an old wood block served as kitchen stoop.

The house was built of rough lumber, battened vertically, and it had long since weathered to a soft, mellow gray, like the sky

31

on a rainy day; and the white-oak shingle boards of the roof were curled at the edges. Days the wind blew hard they slapped noisily against each other and occasionally one would wrench itself loose from its bindings and scurry end over end across the yard.

The yard was closed in with a paling fence, weathered like the house, and a tired gate swung between cedar posts. Honeysuckle matted the fence to the right of the gate, and a brilliant scarlet rose climbed thickly down the left side. A bronze bush stood at either end of the narrow porch, and cinnamon vines followed thin wires to the roof in between. Roses were dotted about the yard in tight little clumps, and just by the chimney at the end of the house was Gramma's little yellow rose. It was said the first Tom Pierce's wife had brought a slip from Virginny, and Pierce yards ever since had always had a yellow rose. It clambered valiantly up the old stone chimney, and each summer its green spikes were softened with pale, buttery buds which opened full into a brilliant, extravagant gold.

Hattie had not planted any of these pretties. She didn't have much of a hand with blossoms. But she did her best to keep the grass from choking them out, and she kept the yard as tidy as her house and garden patch would let her. Tom too was neat about the place. He kept his barns and sheds mended, his tools where they belonged, and his fences clean. Tom and Hattie Pierce had a pride in themselves and in all they owned. Gramma had planted the blooms, but Hattie tended them faithfully.

Hod stabled the horse and went toward the house, sorting over in his mind the doings of the day. He was elated over the encounter with Lily Mae, excited and flooded with eager hope. Bring yer gittar! Now, what did she mean? And he had good news for Irma. First off, he'd tell her he'd seen John Walton. He nodded his head approvingly when he thought of John for Irma. They'd make out fine together.

But it was when he thought of the lumber camp that something took him by the throat and shook him hard. He could hardly swallow past the knot of excitement that tightened there. But he must be sure to pick the right time to tell Ma. He'd promise to be careful, and with the work caught up she surely couldn't care for him going.

When he stepped through the door, the familiarity of home closed round him. Since he could remember, it had looked the same. The house was oblong, with a big and a little room across the front and another big room and little room across the back. The big front room was the heart of the house, with the great fireplace at one end, and Hattie's bed across from it in the corner. Her sewing machine stood against another wall, and a dresser with cracked and peeling varnish completed the furnishings. A steep stair wound up from the corner by the fireplace to the loft room, which was Hod's.

The kitchen was back of the big front room, so that Hattie had only to step from one part of her domain to the other. A huge, black wood stove took up one corner; and hanging all around it were the pots and pans, skillets and pails, and stretched on a line kitty-cornered the dish towels always hung drying. Across from the stove was the dough table, which Grampa Dow had made. No one else had a dough table whose tray slid so smoothly in its groove; and Grampa had thought of the clever little shelf in the corner of the flour bin to hold the soda and salt. It saved many a step to the shelves over by the window. Grampa Dow was always studying ways to fix things up.

In the far end of the room the long table stretched down the wall. It sagged in the middle and it had been scrubbed until it was splintery, but a heap of Pierces could sit around it for Sunday dinner, and it would hold a sight of victuals.

The little back room was a storeroom. Times when the house overflowed with company some folks had to sleep there, but mostly it was a store place for Hattie's jars of garden truck and dried apples, and old trunks and broken-down furniture, and all the other things a family had need to hide away.

In the little front room there was a neat iron bedstead spread with a patchwork quilt. Gramma had made the quilt for Irma on her fifth birthday, and when Irma was old enough to have her own room, she put it on her bed. It was called a crazy quilt, because its pieces were put together any size or color. But Irma loved its bright colors and its queerly shaped pieces. This piece was from a dress Gramma had had when she first came to Piney Ridge with Grampa. This piece, fitting so lovingly here alongside it, was from a little shirt of Pa's. This piece, now, was from the

33

dress Ma wore the day she was wedded, and this one was from one of her own baby aprons. It all went together, however the pieces were cut, and in the end it was square and true.

In Hod's attic room was an iron bedstead like Irma's. Gramma had given him his coverlet too, but she hadn't made it. She said Abigail Pierce had made it long years ago on her own loom. She had carded the wool herself, and then she had woven the coverlet. And now Hod had a coverlet for his bed, soft and white and worn.

An old chest with several drawers, and a table with two shelves nailed above it, completed the room. Hod's clothes hung on nails in one corner. He spent little time in his room, and gave it less thought. It was where he slept and changed his clothes. It was a part of home, without having any significance of its own. It bore no mark of him, boy or man. Hattie kept it as spotless as she did the rest of the house, and it had the immaculate austerity of a monk's cell, swept, aired, and virginal.

To this home Tom Pierce had brought young Hattie Byron twenty-two years ago. Gramma had already worn off its newness in her years of homekeeping there, so when Hattie took it for her own, it had the smell and the feel and the look of a place where folks lived.

Hattie was ironing when Hod reached home, but she pushed the irons to the back of the stove and set about fixing him something to eat. "I wasn't lookin' fer you till midafternoon," she said. "You nearly allus stay as long as you kin. But I kin fix you a snack that'll do you till supper, I reckon."

"Don't bother," said Hod, heaving the sack of meal to the floor. "Just give me a glass of milk and some corn bread and I'll make out."

She set the glass of milk and a plate with a chunk of cold corn bread on the table and placed a spoon by it. When he had finished washing, he sat down at a corner of the table and began crumbling the bread into the milk. Hattie drew up a chair and buttered a piece of bread for herself.

"Didja git my things?"

Hod nodded, and put his spoon down to unload his pockets.

Hattie laughed. "Ifen that ain't jist like a man! Man or boy, if they've got e'er thing to pack, they'll squeeze it into a pocket! Anything to keep from packin' a sack. I recollect one time when you was little an' I sent you down to borry some eggs offen Becky. You come home with a egg in ever' pocket!"

Hod grinned sheepishly as he laid the articles on the table before her. "How could I pack a sack ahorseback?" he asked

Hattie laughed again and settled back for him to finish eating. Sometimes when they were alone like this she seemed more relaxed and quiet. Her busy hands would lie still for a time in her lap and her voice would be gentle and soft. Hod loved such times with her.

"Didja see Jim?" she asked.

He shook his head. "He wasn't there. I asked the miller if he'd seen him and he said he'd not been in. Promised to keep an eye out for him, but he never did show up, I reckon."

A little worried frown appeared on Hattie's forehead. "I jist know Frony's been took with another spell. Ifen I didn't have that there sewin' on my hands this week, an' my garden to clean out, I'd git Tom to take me over there an' see."

Hod reached for the last of the corn bread. "If Frony's had a spell," he said, "Jim'll be over here after you. I wouldn't worry about it if I were you."

"Well, a body'd orta keep up with their own kin," she replied, "an' Jim's the last o' mine. I'd hate to think o' Frony down in bed over there with not e'er soul to take keer of her."

Hod was silent. Ma was always quick to go when someone needed her.

"Who all was in town?" Hattie went on.

He named the women he'd seen in the store, leaving out Lily Mae. As he'd expected she clucked her tongue over Matildy. He named the men who had been at the mill, and he told of seeing Wade and Sandy. But he didn't say anything about the lumber camp.

"What about the meetin'?" she prodded him.

"The tent's already set up on the school ground, and Dan Wilson's to do the preachin'."

Hattie sighed. "I was afeared they'd have it down there. Hit's jist too fur to go ever' night. An' I love to go so good too. But I

35

reckon they had to have it there this time. The last 'un was at Piney Chapel. Who tole you?"

"Matildy."

Hattie rocked her hickory chair back on its legs and smoothed her apron. "You aimin' to he'p out with the music any?"

"If I'm asked I might," he answered. "Where's Pa?"

Hattie was raking the crumbs off the table into the palm of her hand. She shook it out the door vigorously. "He's not come back from Grampa's yit."

Hod started toward the front room. "Where's Irma?"

"She went up to the mailbox. She'd orta be back here too."

As he went by the fireplace, Hod picked up his guitar and ran his fingers lightly over the strings, ear bent intently to catch the tone. Folks on the ridge said Hod Pierce could pick the heart right out of a guitar. He only knew that whatever he was feeling could find expression through his fingers on the strings, and that something wild and yearning inside of him was stilled when he played.

"Ma," he called, "you know where those strings are I got last week from the mail order?"

"On the clock shelf," she called back.

"Think I'll restring my guitar. Might need it tomorrow night."

"Bring yer gittar!" "Bring yer gittar!" The words sang in his mind while his hands worked lovingly with the instrument. When he had finished, he tested the strings, tuned first one and then the other. He plucked a few chords, and then settled his chair against the doorjamb.

> "'You git a line an' I'll git a pole,
>   Honey!
> You git a line an' I'll git a pole,
>   Ba-a-abe!
> You git a line an' I'll git a pole,
> I'll meet you down at the crawdad hole,
>   Honey, Sugarbaby, mine!'"

Hattie came to the kitchen door. "Git it fixed?"

Hod nodded and let his fingers pick lightly at the strings.

"Sing me the one about the great speckled bird," Hattie said. Hod found the key, thrummed a rich chord, and his voice deepened to the opening words.

36

    " 'What a beautiful thought I am thinking,
        Concerning a great speckled bird.
    Remember her name is recorded,
        On the pages of God's Holy Word.

    " 'With all other birds flocking 'round her,
        They watch every move that she makes.
    They try to find fault with her teaching,
        But really they find no mistakes.

    " 'I am glad I have learned of her meekness,
        I am proud that my name's on her book;
    For I want to be one never fearing,
        On the face of my Saviour to look.

    " 'When he cometh descending from heaven,
        On a cloud as he writes in his Word;
    I'll be joyfully carried to meet him,
        On the wings of that great speckled bird.

    " 'Now she's spreading her wings for her journey.
        That she's going to take by-and-by.
    When the trumpet shall sound on that morning,
        She will meet her dear Lord in the sky.' "

Hattie sighed. " I've allus loved that song." Her eyes dreamed
beyond Hod into the past and her memories. The song made
her slender and bright and beautiful again. It went back down
the years to the tent meeting where she had first seen Tom, and
where she had sat on one of the back rows with him night after
night, letting her fingers lie warmly inside his. For the moment
she felt again the new and exciting tingle his big presence by
her side had brought her. At first he had said, " Miss Hattie,
could I walk you home tonight? " And after that he had simply
found his way to her side, and soon everyone knew big Tom
Pierce was talking to Hattie Byron.

There was a night when the moon was up, and her waist was
small to his arm and her mouth was soft to his kiss. And shortly
after, Hattie Byron was Hattie Pierce. Forever and enduring
Hattie Pierce. So brief the years. So long the time.

When Tom married Hattie, she had been as bright and beautiful as a dream. Her eyes were brown, speckled with green, like
the trout pool down in Wandering Creek. And her hair lay back

from its center part as smooth and black as a raven's wing. A man's hand reached for those smooth wings as naturally as it curved around a hoe handle. And a man could lose himself in her trout-pool eyes.

In twenty-two years Hattie Pierce had borne eight children. Six of them had died. Only Hod and Irma had lived. Hattie's beauty had been glossed over by grief and the hard passage of the years, and when Hod looked at his mother these days, he saw nothing of the brightness Tom's young eyes had beheld. The eyes were still fine and true, but the trout pool had long since dulled and dimmed. The hair was still parted severely down the center, but now it was streaked and gray. She had lost most of her teeth early, and her shrunken mouth had given her face a pointed, peaked look. Her shoulders were rounded and her stomach paunched.

She was worn and she was weary, but she was not defeated. A woman married her man and she bore him as many children as the Lord sent. That was a woman's life. There was no fretting in Hattie against the will of the Lord, nor any question of it. She tended her house, bore her children, buried them if they died, fed and clothed them and compelled their obedience if they lived, and lay by her husband's side at night. A woman's life was bound to be hard, but Hattie didn't feel her lot was any harder than the next, and she went through her days with determination.

She had not been " saved " until she was a grown and married woman. Hod was a baby that summer when she had been converted at the revival. She shuddered when she remembered how sinful she had been, but she felt certain the Lord had forgiven her. She had been like the heathen who didn't know any better until that night when the light had shone through on her. Since then there had been a zealous dedication of herself and her family to the Lord. She had purged herself of much of her gaiety and expunged all the innocent pleasures of vanity and worldliness. Her tongue had become more astringent since then and her judgments were sharper and more impatient. Tom and Hod and Irma tried to let her sharpness roll off their backs unanswered. She was Ma, and Ma's ways were her own. But Ma herself was the fixed and true pole of their existence.

38

For a moment after Hod stilled the quivering strings Hattie stood still. The stillness was all through her. Then she briskly came back to the present. "You better start bringin' some water up from the spring so's we kin all git a bath tonight."

Hod put his guitar down and followed her to the kitchen. He sniffed. "Something smells mighty good! What's for supper?"

"Squirrel an' dumplin's. Tom found two down in the holler this mornin'. But you don't git e'er bite till supper, so don't go sniffin' around! Git a move on, now."

He picked up the two buckets which sat on the narrow wash shelf by the door and swung off down the hill.

> "'You git a line an' I'll git a pole,
> I'll meet you down at the crawdad hole,
> Honey, Sugarbaby, mine!'"

"Bring yer gittar!" "Honey, Sugarbaby, mine!"

On the way back he saw Irma waiting for him in the road. He grinned at her, and hurried, sloshing water over the buckets in his haste.

"I saw him," he assured her at once. "He was at the mill, and I talked to him a minute. First I asked if they were goin'. And he wanted to know if we were goin'. I told him we were, so he said — and these were his very words — he said, 'I'll be seein' you then.'"

A flush started at the base of Irma's throat and slowly spread up her neck onto her face. She bit her lip. "You never said nothin' to Ma 'bout seein' him, didja?"

"Of course I didn't!"

"Well, don't."

"Doesn't Ma like him?"

"Ma likes him all right, but she'd change her tune ifen she thought I did!"

"You and John talkin'?"

"Not yit, we ain't. When would we have the chancet? That's why I was hopin' he'd be at the meetin'. I'll at least git to see him."

"Maybe something'll work out so's you can sit by him, or talk to him a little. But I sure don't know any way you could let him walk you home! "

" Oh, they ain't a chancet o' that! I don't even hope fer sich. But ifen I kin see him an' jist feel him alookin' at me, it'll make me happy."

They walked slowly around the corner of the house, and Hod lowered his voice as he spoke. " I'm not much better off. Ma hasn't hardly quit sulkin' yet over me talkin' to Lily Mae the other Sunday. But I'm aimin' to walk her home tomorrow night, come hell or high water! "

" Oh, it's some different with you, anyhow! You're a boy! All she does is pout an' quote Scripture to you. But it's untellin' what she'd do ifen she thought I was even thinkin' about a boy. An' me nearly seventeen too. She's done fergot her'n Pa was married when she wasn't more'n my age! "

Hod shifted one bucket of water to open the kitchen door. As he stood with the screen thrown wide, the far cry of a whippoor-will came low and tender across the holler. It sifted through the screen and seemed to mourn a lost love. In a sudden, luminous moment Hod could see Irma bent and old like Ma. Married. Skirts dragged by the hands of kids. " Maybe," he said slowly, " maybe that's just what she's not forgotten."

CHAPTER FOUR

It's ALWAYS COOL and damp down here, thought Hod as they walked through the holler going to the meeting Sunday night. The mist curled and drifted from the narrow creek, and he shivered as he felt its moist fingers on his throat. The high walls of the hills boxed in the ancient creek bed and he could hear the echo of their footsteps against the old cliff as they moved along the stony path. In the pools of the creek the frogs gar-rumphed, and from tree to tree the whippoorwills called that there was " cheap-butter-in-the-white-oak."

Hod lifted his head. There must be a million stars tonight, he thought. Like someone with an open hand had sowed a field of silver seeds. The Milky Way was a narrow, sifted band that arched the holler and rested on the hills. It's like being down in a deep, dark well, he thought, open only at the top. He stumbled.

"Mind the lantern, Hod," Tom warned. "You'll bust it agin a rock if you don't take keer." Hod shifted the lantern and set his eyes on the path.

The holler widened as the hills rounded off, and came out in a low, level valley. The creek, released from the imprisoning walls, slowed, paused to catch its breath, swelled in freedom, and threaded a more genteel way through the valley.

Hugging the last hill, in the wide mouth of the holler, was the Big Springs schoolhouse. A tent had been pitched on the grounds, its sides rolled up to permit the circulation of air. A platform had been built at one end of the sawdust-covered enclosure, and a pulpit stand of rough lumber stood about midway of the platform. The preacher's Bible and a stack of paper-backed songbooks rested on the pulpit. Seats, made of the same rough lumber, fanned out from the platform in three staggered sections. Strung inside the tent, and suspended at intervals outside, were dim, tired lights which flickered with the asthmatic breathing of a sputtering old engine.

The family joined the gathering crowd and said their howdies to all. There were no strangers here. At any gathering on the ridge or in the valley the people were the same closed group, kith and kin of Pierces or their in-laws, except for the little knot of White Caps who stayed to themselves usually.

Tom and Hattie seated themselves on one of the back rows. It would be cooler there. Hod propped his guitar against the end of the seat and went out to find the group of boys milling around the hitching post. John was in the crowd and Hod drifted over to stand by him. In case John missed seeing Irma in the bunch of girls he would know she was here when he saw Hod.

Irma joined the girls who were sitting, giggling, on the schoolhouse steps. Now was the time when the girls flirted their bright dresses and careful curls most enchantingly, parading their charms before the sidewise glances of the boys. After the meeting the two groups would merge and pair off, each boy seeking out his special girl to walk home. He might have to walk her whole family home at the same time, but over the rough trails and paths, in the dimness of lantern light, he would have a chance to slip a bold arm about her waist, or even to steal a kiss if they could drop far enough behind.

41

Out of the corner of his eye Hod saw Lily Mae in the circle of girls. He kept his eyes lowered, although he knew she was aware of his presence. His hands started sweating and he rolled a cigarette to occupy them. He dreaded the moment he would have to step up by her side and somehow find the voice to ask to walk her home, and yet, restlessly, he longed for it too. It would be an enduring shame if she turned him down. But she'd as good as promised! Well . . . he'd brought his gittar! Now let's see what she made of it.

He saw his mother looking around, seeking him and Irma. Other boys and girls might be allowed to sit on the ground outside the tent in the semidarkness, but not Hattie's. Hattie's children would sit by her side in decent respect to the Lord. He crushed his cigarette under his heel and walked over to take his place on the bench. Hattie nodded at him approvingly and leaned over to whisper, "Where's Irma?"

He caught a glimpse of Irma moving toward the tent and he motioned to her. "She's comin'," he answered. No, there wasn't a chance for Irma to have John by her side tonight.

Hod looked around the tent. It was comfortably full. The meeting was going to get off to a good start. Most of the ridge folks sat to the middle and back, the White Caps crowding the front. After all, it was their meeting.

Hod remembered the story Miss Bertha had told him about the White Caps — how, back in 1770 an old Mennonite preacher, one Jacob Engle, had grown desperate under the religious persecution of his people in his native Switzerland, and how he gathered together thirty Mennonite families and by might and main had secured ships to transport them to the new world. Miss Bertha had said one of the ships had not weathered the storms, and had gone down in an angry sea, taking all aboard with it.

The remainder of the small group settled in Lancaster County, Pennsylvania, and, because of their peculiar habit of baptizing in the river Susquehanna, had become known as the River Brethren. In time, Miss Bertha said, they had quarreled among themselves, mostly over small differences in their doctrinal beliefs — such a little thing, for instance, as whether in the washing of the saints' feet the one who washed should dry or whether another should stand by with the napkin and have the privilege.

42

They had split up into little bands, and some of them had migrated southward, into Ohio and Indiana and Kentucky.

Miss Bertha said their real name was Brethren in Christ, or "River Brethren," and their history went clean back to the Pietists of the Reformation days. But few, if any, of these people knew that. Here in the Kentucky hills they were called White Caps, because of the sheer little starched white caps the women wore at all times. The women also wore nunlike dresses, all made from the same pattern, ankle length, with long sleeves, high round neck, and a prayer bib. They wore neither jewelry nor make-up, and they were usually of quiet and modest manner.

Equally simple was the dress of the men. Their suits were dark, plain, and simply cut. In the old days they were home-made, but now the men were allowed to buy them in stores. Ties were prohibited, as were rings and other forms of worldly vanity.

The doctrine of the founding fathers had included several unique beliefs, such as that of trine immersion, and the efficacy of the prayer veil. On Piney Ridge folks watched the queer baptism, face forward three times, with curiosity; and occasionally a Pierce connection married a White Cap. He became less a Pierce when he did that, withdrawing from the clan solidarity and becoming one of a closer knitted band.

Hod's attention came back to the meeting. Little Wells was standing in front of the platform now, songbook open in his hand. Hod liked for Wells to lead the singing. He kept time with a firm, sure lead and never let the tunes lag. Books had been distributed, and while Wells held a last whispered conference with the preacher, an air of expectancy settled over the crowd. The meetin' was about to begin!

Little Wells walked back to his place and raised his hand. "Folks, we're goin' to start by singin' number sixteen . . . 'Joy Unspeakable.' An' I want ever'body to join in. Don't be bashful. You all know this song, so jist open yer mouths an' let 'er roll!" He spied Hod on the back row. "Hod! Hod Pierce! Bring that gittar o' your'n up here an' he'p us out. Hit ain't goin' to do you no good back there on the last row!"

Heads turned. Folks craned and laughed and whispered neighborly as Hod, flushed, made his way up front. Hattie modestly kept her eyes straight ahead. It would be unmannerly

43

to appear prideful, but even her rigid back bespoke her complacent satisfaction as Hod was singled out.

"All right now," said Wells as Hod tuned his instrument. "We'll take it in 'G,' Hod, so's the womenfolks won't have to reach fer that high note up there. Let's all stand up, an' don't nobody hold back! This song's a good 'un, so come on an' sing! "

It was a good song to start the meetin'. Five long stanzas and a chorus that was full of glory! Rapid, clean, four-four time, with powerful, exciting words. And the people lifted up their voices and the joy unspeakable coursed through their veins!

"Jist stay on yer feet, now," Wells commanded when the song was over, "an' let's sing number fifty-four . . . 'God Put a Rainbow in the Cloud'! The rainbow's a promise to all of us, so let's sing it like we was glad fer it."

This was still rapid, four-four time. The kind that made folks lift their faces to the hope and the promise. The kind that made them shout and rock on their toes! Yes, Lord! God put a rainbow in the cloud!

Wells kept the crowd on their feet for still another song — 'That Will Be Glory' — before he let them be seated, panting and hot. But the tempo had been set; the ice had been broken; and emotionally the people had been lifted joyously to a rainbow in the cloud and the glory road! Little Wells was an expert at opening a meetin'.

Ferdy Jones came forward now for his turn at leading. And Hod knew the tempo would change. Before the preacher took over, the mood must be shifted to sin and guilt. The probing finger of fear must dig into scared hearts, scavenge certain secret sins, and invoke judgment. Out of the clouds Ferdy's bellowing baritone would pluck them and remind them that the rainbow and the glory road were theirs only if their lives were pure and stainless. His right arm, pumping like a piston rod, would drive the pitiless rhythm before them. He would charge them with their sins.

"Amen," shouted Old Man Clark from the front row at the end of the first stanza. Amen . . . Amen . . . Amen, a chorus of voices fervently echoed. Have mercy, Lord, on me a sinner! Lord, hide me in the darkness! Let not the light shine! Lord, remember me, a sinner!

Ferdy led them into another warning hymn: " Hide Me, O My Saviour, Hide! " And the masochistic ecstasy of guilt and grief mounted. The flailing arm whipped accusingly, rising and falling relentlessly like the flagellant lash of a monk's rope on bare flesh. I went to the rock, but there's no hiding place there! Woe unto me! Ferdy's really got 'em goin', thought Hod. Now it's the preacher's time.

The preacher rose and lifted his chin to the sky. He spread his arms tenderly. " O God," he prayed, and his deep, full voice spread like a sheltering cloak over the people: " O God, we are as worms in the dust. Stained, spotted, and sinful. Our hearts are hard. We come to the throne of grace knowing we are not deserving of thy redeeming love. We have lived in sin and darkness in this weary world so long we have lost our way. We have hardened our hearts against you and followed the ways of the sinful world. We are doomed men and women. Yes, doomed, Lord, unless you remove the scales from our eyes and let us see the light again. Turn our feet from the paths of sin and lead us in the narrow way. Soften our hearts to see the error of our ways, Lord, and lift us up out of the mud and mire of the world. Lord, we are but poor pilgrims wandering in a world of woe! Take our hands and lead us home."

Amen . . . Amen . . . Amen. Take our hands and lead us home.

A general stirring and settling of the people followed. Song-books were laid aside, fans began to flutter, small children were bedded down against the long sermon, heads in their mothers' laps; the flock made ready for the shepherd.

The preacher spread his hands on either side of the Bible and leaned forward. " Brethren," he began, " brethren, I have taken my text tonight from the book of Revelation. That's the book that tells us what awful things will be in the last days. And, brethren, I say unto you the last days are upon us, and we can't shut our eyes from those things. The bridegroom cometh, and no man knoweth the hour. Repent and be prepared! "

For an hour the lush, sonorous voice rose and fell majestically. He spoke of scorpions and seals and death and hell, and he charged the people with black sin and the lusts of the flesh. His face flamed and his voice roared as he pictured the fiery furnaces and the everlasting torment waiting down below. Fear, awe, and dread trembled visibly on the faces of the people, and the tension mounted until it seemed to Hod as if the very roof of the tent would rise to give them breath. An hour of the exhorting, threatening voice left him feeling limp and wilted.

At last the voice softened, rich and full, sweetly pleading. This was the signal for Little Wells to start a pleading hymn: " Softly and tenderly Jesus is calling, Calling for you and for me. . . . Calling, O sinner, come home! " Folks rose and stirred restlessly and began to shift and filter through the crowd, stopping to talk earnestly with man or woman, boy or girl, who had not yet been to the bench. The preacher's voice never ceased its entreating pleas, and Little Wells followed expertly with one petitioning song after another.

One by one persons were answering the call. They came forward to fall on their knees at the long bench in front of the platform. Some silently buried their faces in their hands; others moaned and sobbed and sang. The preacher's voice rose above the tumult as he went from one to the other, placing his hand upon them, encouraging them, and urging them to lay their hearts bare. The noise of the moaning voices and the hot odor of sweaty bodies fused into one purgatorial overtone and Hod felt himself sway unsteadily. His eyes focused again on the mourners' bench.

There was Becky, Gault's barren wife, at one end of the bench. Her thin, black-draped figure looked fragile and lonely as it kneeled apart from the others, and hunched over her hands. She surely doesn't need to get religion again, he thought. What drives her to the bench time after time? Does she think God has hidden his face from her? Does she think if she abases herself often enough, the Lord will give her life, like Sarah, in her old age?

Matt Jasper was there too, and beside him was Lutie, his wife. Hod closed his eyes, but couldn't keep out the sight of Lutie Jasper, forever hopelessly weary, forever bearing one thin, sickly baby after another; laying them in their graves within a few weeks, or a few months, or a few years. Or if they lived,

46

tending their hopeless minds and bodies drearily. What were they praying for? Did they think the Lord would stop Matt's fits maybe? Or let the new baby live? Or not send any more? Even as Hod watched Matt, the shriveled, bony shoulders began to jerk convulsively. The big head on the thin neck swiveled grotesquely and stiffened, frozen at an angle. A high scream rent the air.

"He's got it," shouted the preacher, " he's seen the light! He's got the old-time religion in his heart! Praise the Lord! A soul is saved tonight! " And he raised his hands high over his head.

He's got a fit! thought Hod, and started toward him. Little Wells was quick before him. Together they carried him outside and laid him on the grass.

"He'll be all right, kid," said Little Wells. " These fits don't last long. They look a heap worse'n they are. Hit's a good thing it come right at the end of the goin's on, though. Preacher'll close up now."

" You reckon the preacher actually thought Matt had religion? "

" Why, shore. He wouldn't have no way o' knowin' 'bout pore old Matt's fits. An' what he don't know won't hurt him none. Hit'll mebbe encourage him some to have one take it so hard the very first night."

By the time Matt had revived, the meeting was breaking up, and Hod left him for Little Wells to handle. He had to get his guitar and hurry to find Lily Mae. Already some other fellow might be ahead of him.

In the tent Lem had crawled up on one of the benches and was shouting to make himself heard. "All them that lives up Piney way is welcome to a ride home in my wagon. I've got a bed o' straw in it, an' as many as kin pile in is more'n welcome to load on."

Hod saw Lily Mae talking to some girls at one end of the platform. He grabbed his guitar and started toward her. She saw him coming and laughed loudly and self-consciously. In the hurry and intensity of his purpose Hod forgot his shyness and blurted out, " Would you care to ride home in Lem's wagon? "

She tossed her curls back from her face. " Why, shore," she answered. " That'd be swell, ifen we kin find e'er place."

" I'll find us a place," promised Hod, and taking her arm

47

he steered her toward the wagon. It was already filling. Hattie and Tom and Irma were settling themselves; Lizzie and her children were finding places. Gault and Becky were waiting, and one or two others.

Hod placed his hands under Lily Mae's arms and swung her up into the wagon, letting them linger a moment and sliding them slowly and sentiently down her sides as he released her. How warm and soft girls are, he thought. "I'll be back in a minute," he whispered. "Don't let 'em go off without me." And he disappeared in the crowd.

He searched around the edges, and then he spied John standing disconsolately in a group of boys. He hailed him. "Hey! Hey, John! You wanna ride up the ridge in the wagon with us?"

John came to life. "I shore do!"

"C'mon then, Lem's about ready to pull out!"

When they came back to the wagon both boys vaulted up onto the end of the wagon bed and settled into the straw. Hod called to Irma, "C'mon back here and sit with us."

Irma scrambled over legs and bodies and Hod reached out to steady her. "Look who's here," he whispered.

John took her arm and pulled her down beside him. "I been awaitin' fer a chancet like this," he said. "I jist been hopin' an' prayin'."

Irma put her hand in his. "I been awaitin' too, John."

Hod settled himself by Lily Mae, and they pulled the straw up close around them and let their legs dangle out the back. By the time they were settled, Lem called from up front, "All set?" and clucked to the team. "All set," they called back and in a moment they were swallowed in the leafy tunnel of the road.

Lizzie spoke across the children to Hattie. "Well, whadja think o' the preacher?"

Hattie temporized. "Hit's too early to say yit. He seems like a powerful exhorter, though, if he kin jist hold out. We'll all have to uphold him an' he'p him ever' way we kin."

The talk flowed gently on, and Hod and Lily Mae were silent, feeling its edges curl about them. For the moment Hod was content, his fingers laced with Lily Mae's. It was good, and this was enough. Lily May swayed against him. "Where's yer gittar?"

"Right here."

"How 'bout a song?"

Hod hesitated. After the meetin' Hattie might not like a fancy tune. But he pulled the guitar around in front of him and thrummed the strings experimentally. Lizzie laughed and called to him: "That's a good idee, Hod. You play 'em an' we'll sing 'em."

"What'll it be?"

"'Buffalo Gal,'" called Lem from the spring seat. Hod's fingers trilled a run up the strings. "'Buffalo Gal' it is," he sang out.

> "'Buffalo gal, won't you come out tonight,
>   Come out tonight,
>   Come out tonight?
>   Buffalo gal, won't you come out tonight,
>   And play by the light of the moon?'"

"'Down in the Valley,' Hod," said Becky. Hod shifted the key, and the voices followed him. "Barbry Allen." "Lord Lovel." From one old song to another they went, melody lifted high in the night.

"'Crawdad Hole,'" whispered Lily Mae.

> "'You git a line an' I'll git a pole,
>   I'll meet you down at the crawdad hole,
>   Honey, Sugarbaby, mine!'"

"Are you my girl, Lily Mae?" Hod laid his forehead against her cheek.

"I'm yore girl tonight," she said.

Hod threw back his head and looked at a million stars. He laid his guitar aside and slipped his arm loosely around Lily Mae's curving waist. It was as soft and warm as a baby lamb's. He tightened his arm abruptly and pulled her close, turning her slightly against him. Lily Mae let her head rest against his shoulder and in the soft night breeze her hair blew across his face. It filled him with a gentle tenderness. His mouth, searching, found hers and clung for a long, still moment. Her lips were moist and slightly parted, and when he lifted his head he was breathing hard. This had been his first kiss. Lily Mae caught her breath and laughed, then, reaching back of his head, she pulled his

49

mouth down upon hers again. " Yer sweet," she whispered, " Hod Pierce, yer plumb sweet."

"Bring yer gittar!" So this is what she meant!

He felt warm and good. It was a fine thing to be ridin' in the back of an old jounce wagon with your girl. The wagon bumped and jogged along the rough road and the swaying motion threw them often together. The pliant, breathing softness next to him drooped and leaned against him. This was Tomorrow, his fair day!

Suddenly and impulsively, out of his warm feeling, he spoke. "Listen, Lily Mae," he said, "someday I'm goin' to leave Piney Ridge. I'm goin' to work and make enough money someway or another to get away. And I'm goin' to have a better life and see the world and get more learnin'. I don't aim to be a Piney Ridge farmer all my life!"

"What's wrong with bein' a Piney Ridge farmer? Ain't nothin' wrong with it as fur as I kin see. You eat an' sleep an' work anywheres, I reckon."

"There's nothin' really wrong with Piney," he said slowly, hunting for the right words. "There's nothin' wrong except it can't see any further than its nose, and it doesn't ever want to. If you get through the eighth grade you've got enough learnin'. If you raise enough corn to make do, there's no need to frash yourself raisin' more. Your grandpap raised tobacco and he cut it and stripped it a certain way, and what was good enough for Grandpap is good enough for me. If there's a drought and the tobacco's ruined, there's nothin' to do but tighten your belt and do without, because tobacco's the only way to get cash. If times get hard, you sit around and talk about it and hope something'll turn up so's you can make out. Lily Mae, there's a whole world out there where people don't wait for something to turn up. They make things happen. They don't stop goin' to school at the eighth grade. They go on and get a college degree."

"I don't see as a college degree would he'p you grow tobacco here on Piney any better."

"Yes, it would. That's just the point. Maybe it wouldn't grow tobacco any better, but maybe tobacco oughtn't to be grown on

50

Piney. This land is poor and washed out. Maybe tobacco's one of the reasons. There's schools where they teach you about that. They teach you nearly everything in those schools."

Lily Mae laughed. "Tobaccer's been growed on Piney as fur back as I kin remember, Hod, an' I reckon hit allus will be. You've got too high an' mighty notions, I'm athinkin'."

He shook his head. "No. I've not. I'm goin' to amount to something someday."

"Well, jist be shore an' let me know when you do," she said pertly.

They were quiet for a time, rocking comfortably against each other. "Wade an' Sandy's goin' to the lumber camp tomorrow," he went on after a while. "They're goin' to hew ties until tobacco's ready to cut. They say the pay's real good. I'm thinkin' of goin' with 'em."

"Ifen you go to the lumber camp you cain't go to the meetin' no more," she protested immediately, straightening up.

"I know, and I hate to miss it too. But it's a chance to make some money, maybe forty or fifty dollars, and I could easy go to Louisville on that and see about a job."

"Well, of all things," she sniffed, "all the time you been aplannin' to go off an' jist now ast me to be yer girl! What do you expect me to do while you're gone? Set around an' hold my hands an' be yer girl till you git back? That's not my way o' doin', Hod Pierce! There's many another fish in the sea, an' don't think I won't ketch a few!" She jerked out of his arm and bounced angrily away from him.

"Now, Lily Mae, I wasn't thinkin' that at all," he protested. "I was just tryin' to tell you . . ." For goodness' sake, how had this ever got started? In a sudden burst of confidence, born of his feeling of closeness to her, he had only meant to try to tell her something of what he wanted out of life. How could she take it wrong and how did it ever get so mixed up!

"You don't understand . . ." He was miserably hunting for the words to explain.

But abruptly Lily Mae leaned across him and called to Becky, just as Lem pulled the team up in front of Gault and Becky's house. "Becky, kin I take the night with you?" She was scrambling down even as she asked. "I kin walk on home in the mornin'. I wouldn't want to disfurnish nobody to see me home to-night." Her words were dipped in acid.

Becky said she would be glad to have her, and Lily Mae walked toward the gate without another word. Hod could think of nothing to say or to do. The turn of events had been too rapid for him. What in the world had Lily Mae got her back up about! He sat motionless as Lem pulled back in the road and the wagon jounced into the ruts again. Let her go, he thought bitterly. Just let her go. There's many another fish in the sea. But his arm remembered the warm, firm flesh around which it had been pressed, and he felt empty and tired.

The next stop was home, and Hattie and Tom and Irma piled out. They called their thanks for the ride to Lem and Lizzie, and groped their way into the dark heat of the house. Hattie briskly lighted a lamp, and Hod could see that her lips were set in a thin, firm line. She's mad too, he thought. Probably saw me kissin' Lily Mae, and I'll either catch the devil or she'll sulk two or three days.

He set his guitar in the fireplace corner and went outside to smoke. Hattie wouldn't have it in the house. He drew deeply on his cigarette and settled his shoulder against the post. The moon rode high and there was a halo around it. He counted three stars within the circle. Three days of rain comin', he thought. And he hadn't told Hattie about the lumber camp yet. How was he goin' to bring it up with her lookin' like she could bite a nail in two! He flipped the cigarette into the grass, his eyes following its glowing arch. Maybe in the mornin' would do. Better be turnin' in now. The loft room would be like an oven tonight, and he dreaded going up there. He'd like to bring a pallet down and sleep right here on the porch. But he knew Hattie wouldn't hear of it. "Poor white trash," she'd say. The screen squeaked softly, and as he turned Hattie stood beside him.

"Out here moonin' agin, I reckon," she said.

"Just thinkin'," he said, leaning back lazily against the post.

"Yes! An' I know what yer athinkin'!" Her voice was vehement and tense. "I heared part o' what you was tellin' that Lily Mae . . . about the lumber camp an' makin' so much big money an' mebbe goin' off to Louisville!"

52

He started to speak, but she went on fiercely. "Yer not agoin' to e'er lumber camp, not now nor never! You hear that! You don't know e'er thing about hewin' ties, an' the first thing you'd do would be to hew yer foot right off! Yer so clumsy! An', besides, I'll not have you off over there away from home, up to no tellin' what mischief. Lem an' Lizzie kin let their boys go if they're a mind to, but I aim to see you stay as decent an' God-fearin' as I've raised you. You jist fergit it right now! They's plenty o' work right here where you belong, an' yer beholden to stay an' he'p now that you kin do a man's work!"

He could see that her hands were tight knots, held stiffly in front of her. "But, Ma," he argued, "I'd make forty or fifty dollars and I'd give the most of it to you to help out."

She turned on him and scratched at him with her voice. "Do you reckon forty or fifty dollars'd pay me ifen you happened to a accident, like you shorely would? You think it would pay me fer the nights I couldn't sleep aknowin' you was over there roisterin' around amongst a bunch o' godless men?"

He sighed and closed his eyes wearily. This was Tomorrow! Where had it gone wrong? How had he bungled it so badly? First Lily Mae and now Ma. He felt hot and smothered, and as if something were closing in on him. What is it they want me to do, he thought. Nothing. Just plain nothing. Do nothing, think nothing, be nothing but Piney Ridge. Plow and plant and sucker and tend and strip and cut and dry and sell tobacco! Go to mill on Saturday! Go to preachin' on Sunday! Marry and build a two-room shack on the far side of the pasture! Have a bunch of kids! Get up at daybreak and go to bed at dark! Sweat and struggle and starve! No! That's not for me! That's not for me! Life was meant to be sweeter. And I'll find a way! I'll find a way!

But tonight he was so tired. "All right, Ma," he said at last. "Forget the whole thing."

She turned back to the house and opened the screen. Looking back at him, she could see him silhouetted against the night sky, and she paused with the door half open. "Hod," she said, "Hod . . ."

"Yessum?"

But whatever tenderness she may have felt could not overcome the long years of stern repression. Whatever gentle thing she meant to say to this yearning son of hers remained unspoken. "You better git on to bed," and the screen slammed lightly behind her.

CHAPTER FIVE

Tom roused Hod before daylight the next morning. "Git up, Hod," he called. "Git up. We've aplenty to do today. Git movin', boy!" He tugged at Hod's hair and shook him until he rolled sleepily to his feet. "C'mon now. Let's eat an' then you do the milkin' an' feedin' whilst I go down to Grampa's. Agin you've done with the chores you better light into that corn patch an' git it hoed out. I aim to start work in the tobaccer today. But we ain't got no time to be asleepin'."

Hod struggled with his clothes and followed his father into the kitchen. Irma was setting the table and she caught his eye as he went by to wash. A motion of her head toward Hattie at the stove warned him. He came awake all at once. So Ma was still sore!

The air was sultry with Hattie's displeasure, and they sat down to breakfast in a smoldering silence. Hattie's mouth was a tight line and her movements were quick and jerky. Irma and Hod kept their eyes on their plates and ate without comment. Tom alone seemed unaware of the brooding cloud.

"Ifen you git done in the corn this mornin', Hod," he said, "you better git on down to Grampa's an' start his'n this afternoon. You kin stay an' do up his night work then, an' eat yer supper down there."

"*Ifen* he gits done!" Hattie's voice shrilled across the table. "Ifen he kin hoe e'er row fer moonin' over that there Lily Mae Gibbs, hit'll surprise me!" Hod ducked his head and his face went scarlet.

Tom said soothingly, "Now, Ma."

"Don't you 'now, Ma' me, Tom Pierce! I reckon I seen what I seen! Him an' that shameless Lily Mae ahuggin' an' akissin' right under my eyes . . . an' Irma no better! Ifen she didn't do the same, 'twasn't because her own brother didn't set her no example! An' you, missy! You needn't to think I won't have my

54

eyes open the next time! You both think you was purty smart aputtin' somethin' over last night! Hit'll not happen agin, I'll promise you that! Settin' there all cuddled up in the straw, alookin' at the moon an' asingin' fancy tunes, when the fear o' the Lord orta been in yer hearts! I don't aim to have sich goin's on, an' you kin both remember that!"

"A little huggin' an' kissin' never hurt nobody, Ma," Tom said gently. "An' I should think you'd a ruther had 'em adoin' it right before yer eyes than asneakin' behind you."

Hattie's hands were shaking. "They ain't no use you takin' up fer 'em, Tom! You'd ortent to go encouragin' 'em in sinful ways! I'm tryin' to raise 'em up decentlike."

"I know," Tom said quietly, "I know."

Hattie jerked her chair back from the table and picked up her plate. She stalked stiffly to the stove and splashed it noisily into the dishpan. Tom poured his coffee into his saucer and blew on it. He sipped it cautiously and looked across at Hod and Irma. Shaking his head at them, he sighed.

"Hello!" called a voice from out front. "Hello! You all up yit?"

"Now who's that abellerin' at this time o' day?" Hattie snorted.

"Sounds like Lem," said Tom.

Hod slid out from behind the table. "Must be Lem's atakin' Wade an' Sandy over to the lumber camp. They said they aimed to go early this mornin'."

"So?" Tom followed Hod out on the porch, with Hattie and Irma close behind him. "Git down," he called. "C'mon in an' eat a bite."

"We've done et," Lem answered. "The boys is goin' over to the lumber camp an' they said Hod here might want to go too. Thought there'd be no harm stoppin' to see."

"Hod ain't goin'," Hattie said flatly. "He don't know the first thing about workin' in lumber. An', besides, I'll not have him off over there up to no tellin' what mischief. Are you an' Lizzie plumb outen yer minds to let them two o' your'n go aroisterin' around amongst that bunch o' godless men over there?"

Hod looked wistfully at Wade and Sandy, who could nearly always go where they pleased. Wade closed one eye mischievously and grinned. Nervously Hod grinned back.

Lem was talking. "Hit's all a matter of opinion, I reckon, Hattie." He turned to Tom. "I jist come by Gault's, an' Becky was tellin' me Grampa fell last night outen the hayloft an' sprung his ankle. She said Gault was doin' up the work this mornin', but she reckoned we'd all have to he'p out till he's on his feet agin. I don't see as how I kin make out to go today, though. Takin' the boys over to the lumber camp an' all. Reckon you an' Hod kin go?"

"Shore," Tom answered. "Well, I declare! I've told Pa more'n oncet he orent to git up in that hayloft after dark. He's gittin' too old to go crawlin' around sich places." He rubbed his nose with his thumb. "I'll go on down this mornin', an' Hod kin go tonight. Hit works out jist the way I'd thought on anyhow. I been he'pin' him with his corn, an' I'd aimed fer Hod to finish it up."

"You better come go with us to the lumber camp, Hod," Wade prodded. "You git paid fer workin' over there."

"You shet up," said Irma fiercely.

"I reckon I better git ready an' go 'long, Tom," Hattie put in, "Gramma'll be needin' some he'p herself." And she turned back into the house.

Lem gathered up the reins and pulled the horses around. "Well, we better be gittin' on. I'll stop at Pa's this evenin' on my way back."

As the wagon wheeled into the road, Hod swallowed the hurting knot in his throat. There went his chances to make fifty dollars, or maybe more.

Irma gets the worst of these spells of Ma's, he thought, on his way to the barn. She has to stay in the house with her and hear it over and over again. Pa was always trying to stand between them and Ma. Like this mornin'. He was easygoing and hard to ruffle, but some days it looked like that just riled Ma more than ever. The best thing to do was to keep quiet and let the storm blow itself out.

He thought on the ways of Hattie. Nobody on the ridge kept a cleaner house, and nobody had the pride in washing and ironing and keeping her family clean that Hattie did. And her garden patch was always early and full. She took a pride in that too. Times she was in a good mood she was almost gaylike and

56

happy. And he remembered how soft and easy were her hands the time he had the fever. She hardly left his side, day or night, for weeks, and she tended him and made him broths and custards and egg dishes to tempt him. She was never too tired to do for those that needed it, either. Going out in all sorts of weather to bring a new baby, or to lay out someone who had died.

And then there was this other Hattie. This sharp and acid Hattie who clawed at them quickly and unexpectedly. This Hattie who pored over her Bible and strove to rid them of blemishes; who bound them so closely with tight wires of fear. This Hattie whose mouth was thin and whose hands were knotted and whose voice shrilled.

He sorted out all the ways of Hattie and tried to put them together smoothly. This one here. That one there. He set up the good ways and molded and rounded them, and he tucked the sharp and acid ways out of sight. Best to let them go. Let them prick and spear quickly, but let them hide darkly. Best not to mind. He was whistling when he reached the barn.

He worked in the corn all morning, his hoe making its steady way down the rows. His back soaked up the sun and he bent under it, taking the heat into himself. There was a content in bending his back to the sun, and in turning the earth beneath his hoe. It was porous and moist from the rain several days before. His feet were planted strongly, feeling the hot dirt and the looseness of the soil. He moved down the rows, feeling the earth give beneath his hoe; feeling it pull in his arms and back.

There was a way in which the warmth of the earth was like the warmth of the sun, all joined together and giving. The sun hot upon his back and the earth warm beneath his feet. The sun, day-giving, life-giving. The earth, absorbing and storing the warmth, and giving it back. This earth, strong and deep and loamy. This earth which sheltered the corn in seed, rooted it, bound and tied it, but gave it up to the sun. This corn, now, growing green and tender and ankle-high. He slid his hoe around a young green blade, and smiled at its brave upward thrust.

Irma came to the field at midmorning with a pail of cool water. He set his hoe against a tree and drank deeply. When he handed the pail back to her, Irma said, " I'm aimin' to take the night at Gramma's this night, Hod."

He made no answer. She went on. "I'm aimin' to see John Walton ever' chancet I git whilst this meetin's goin' on. I'm goin' up to the mailboxes now an' John'll be awaitin', an' I'll tell him he kin come by Gramma's an' walk with me to the meetin'. Ifen I kin work it out, I'm aimin' to stay at Gramma's ever' night. Long as Grampa's ankle is sore I'll have a good cause, an' this is my best chancet. But I ain't aimin' fer Ma to come between me an' John like she's done with ever' other boy I've looked at. I like him too good fer that."

Hod stripped a leaf from the tree and pulled it back and forth through his fingers. Irma waited quietly. Finally he threw the leaf down and picked up his hoe. "I'll help every way I can, Irma. You belong to know what's in your mind. I don't know why Ma's the way she is, but we aren't either one of us kids any longer to be kept under latch and cover."

"I don't look fer Gramma or Grampa to take no notice. But if they do, you reckon they'd feel called on to name it to Ma?"

"I don't reckon they would. Gramma's always been a sight easier on us than Ma. And I've never known Grampa not to be fair in his judgments. He'd likely give you a talkin' to himself. If I was you and they took notice, I'd just plumb out and tell 'em. My opinion is they'd likely think you were a big enough girl to know your own mind."

Irma picked up the empty pail. She ran her hand lightly across her hair which the wind had blown into loose strands. It curled redly in the sun. Hod watched her fasten it beneath a little silver clip. Now it was Irma and John Walton! She turned away, swinging the pail idly. "I know my mind, Hod," she said. And the sea of green corn parted and undulated in the wake of her passing.

Hod finished the corn by the middle of the afternoon and started down to the holler to work in Grampa's patch. He moved carefully through the thick grass, down the path to the road and down the road past the old church to the edge of the ridge where it dipped down into the holler. Here he forsook the road and took a thin trail which led off down the steep hill. Past the white birch, and around the big rock. Yonder was the last turn. Here was the creek, and he stooped for a drink before splashing

58

through its noisy chatter. Now he was in the meadow, with the grass to his hips, and it swayed and parted to let him through.

The house was on the far side of the meadow, but he angled off to the left and went on to the corn patch. Here the shade was already deep from the steep sides of the ridge, and the little creek rushed clear and bright over the white stones. The air was cool and damp, and Hod threw off his hat and pulled his shirttail out. He let the air wrap itself around him and lay chill fingers on his skin until he shivered in a transport of ecstasy. He felt the heat withdrawn from him and a fresh energy poured into him so that he worked rapidly and tirelessly until first dark. Then he left the field and set about doing up the nightwork.

When he had finished the feeding, he came up to the door and stepped onto the sagging old porch. Gramma swung around from the stove. "That you, Hod?"

"It's me."

"You fair frighted me! I've done got the milk pails ready, an' you better git on out to the barn an' git the milkin' done. I'm bound to git a snack o' supper here, but I'm behindst, what with tearin' 'round to Gault's, an' fetchin' fer Dow. Fortunate hit is it ain't winter time fer this to happen. There'd be a sight o' chores fer a body to do. The way it is, ifen you kin all take keer o' the milkin', an' feed the animals, an' bring me in a little mite o' kindlin' wood fer the breakfast fires, I kin make out."

Gramma's eyes were worried for all her tongue was wagging. She's talkin' to keep from lettin' on, Hod thought. Her little wiry body was as taut as a fiddlestring, and her hand kept straying to the knot of gray hair on top of her head. Her mouth was pinched in and a leader in her neck stood out hard and gaunt. She's worryin' a sight, Hod reflected. She's tuckerin' herself plumb out.

He picked up the milk pails, swung one from each hand, and made his way back to the barn. The pails clattered against the gate as he let himself through, and a cow threw back her head uneasily. Inside the barn he lifted the milking stool from its peg and settled himself beside the brindle cow in the near stall. He ran his hand down her side and talked gently to her. "So-O-o, Pet. Easy, Pet."

He drummed the first stream of milk into the waiting bucket. It made a thin, tinny sound, like a downpour of rain, but it swished around the edges. Steadily he pulled the milk down into the bucket, and as it filled the sound was changed from emptiness into fullness, and there was no longer the tinny drumming against the bucket. Now it was rich and thick and heavy, and soon there was hardly any sound at all except a faint hissing as the hard stream of milk, forced by his hand, joined the solid heaviness of the milk waiting in the bucket. There was a rhythm in the squeeze and pull and release which pleased Hod. Pet stood easily and gave down her milk under his gentle hands.

From Pet he moved on to Star, and when he had finished milking both cows, he took the milk back to the house and gave it over to Gramma. Then he went back to the barn to feed the horse and to pull down some more hay for the cows.

The feeding done, he went to the house to light the lantern. It was too dark to cut the kindling wood without light. Gramma had it ready for him, and he touched the lighted match to the circle of wick and watched the flame run around the circle. Light chasing itself until it's joined together again. He lowered the glass and went out into the dark, not needing to feel for the step now that he had a light.

The wood block was solid and the ax was wedged into it deep, just like Grampa had driven it there this morning. The place for an ax is driven deep in the wood block. Hod jerked it loose and felt its heft in his hand. He chose a piece of pine and swung the ax down. He let the feel of the pine splitting run clean up his arm. It was a good feel, a finished and completed feel. Something done. Something final. He filled the basket and swung it up onto his shoulder.

"There, Gramma. That ought to start you a right good fire in the mornin'."

Hod filled the tin basin on the wash shelf and plunged his face in the water. He sputtered and splashed and groped for a towel.

"Hit's right in front o' you! Right there in front o' you! Ifen it'd been a snake, it'd a done bit you! I declare, men are the unseein'est things that ever was! Now you come on an' set down here an' eat you a bite. I know yer bound to be plumb wore out. They ain't much to eat, but they's aplenty of what they is."

Hod slipped back of the table onto the worn old bench and

filled his plate. Gramma might not call it much to eat, but when Gramma set a table there was always plenty. Tonight she had beans boiled with fat meat, tender green onions from her garden patch, a slice of red ham, and steaming hot corn bread.

Irma came in from the next room while he was eating. He looked up. "I see you made it all right."

She nodded and set about straining the milk into the big crocks already scalded and waiting for it. "John'll be by about good dark, in a few minutes, now. I'm aimin' jist to walk right out an' go on down the road with him. You goin' tonight?"

"I don't know. Lily Mae got riled up about something last night, and I don't know's she's expectin' me. If I'm goin', I'll catch up with you time you get to the meetin'. You can wait up a minute on the edge of the clearin'."

There was a shrill whistle from outside. "That's him awhistlin', now," Irma said. She untied the apron and hung it on a nail near the stove. She ran to the wash shelf and looked at herself briefly in the mirror and ran the comb through her hair. "Reckon I'll do," she said. "We'll wait a spell fer you." She laughed quickly. "But if you come, Hod, you kin take yer time!"

His mouth was full of bread and milk, but he grinned at her and motioned for her to be on her way. If Ma ever found out about this, there sure would be a stir! But maybe Ma wouldn't find it out.

Now Gramma was back in the kitchen hovering over him. "Hod, I saved you a piece of this here chess pie. I knowed you love it so good, so I says to myself, 'I'll jist save Hod a piece.' Hit come out real good, if I do say so myself. I allus say that chess pie is the best pie a body kin have. Ifen you got butter an' lots o' eggs an' cream, it's about the best eatin' they is."

Hod washed the pie down with the last of his milk. Let her talk. She's afraid to cease talkin'. If she stops her talkin', she'll have to think about Grampa. How is it when two people are one flesh? How does it come to be that a man and a woman can be so joined together that if anything happens to one the hurt spreads out over the other? Gramma's hands were picking at a rough spot in the oilcloth table cover. The hurt was already spread over her, and her hands were seeking a quiet place. A great pity ran all through him — a pity for Grampa in the hay-

61

loft and for Gramma dragging him to the house, and for the pain in Grampa's leg and the fear in Gramma's heart. The pity began in his throat and he swallowed it down into his stomach, and then it ebbed into his thighs and down into his legs. The hurt spread over him from Gramma and Grampa, and he felt it in his bones and muscles, and it was a hurt and a pity for all pain and suffering everywhere. A pity for all mankind who must hurt and die.

"Hod," Gramma's voice brought him back, "he's hurt bad."

"No, he's not, Gramma. He's just got a sprained ankle. Why, a sprained ankle doesn't amount to anything. He'll be up and around again before the week's out. You'll see. A sprained ankle doesn't amount to a hill of beans!"

"He's past seventy, Hod. An' mebbe it's broke. Who's to know? He won't have the doctor. An' its swole somethin' powerful. An' old folks' bones don't mend so good."

"Pa said if he could move it, it wasn't broken."

"He cain't move it none now. Hod, he was jist pitchin' down some hay, an' 'fore he knowed it, he was flat of his back. Said he never rightly knowed what happened. The pore thing laid there it's untellin' how long 'fore I heared him acallin'. Time I got there he'd crept to the edge o' the loft an' was lyin' there amoanin'. How I got him down the ladder an' into the house I've no idee. A body's give strength to do what has to be done, I reckon. Then I run for Gault, him bein' the clostest. An' Gault, he come an' looked at it an' wropped his leg up, an' said he didn't figger it was broke. But it's swole somethin' terrible. An' it's all black an' darklike."

"Well, sure, Gramma. A sprained ankle always swells up and turns blue. It'll go down soon, if he keeps off it."

"You go in an' talk to him whilst I do up the dishes. He's twitchylike with the hurtin' an' all. An' he'll want to know how you made out with the work."

Hod moved into the other room of the house. The square logs this room was built of closed round Grampa's bed like a brown frame, smooth and shiny in the lamplight. Grampa was propped up in the old wooden bed with the high headboard rising almost to the ceiling. His bad leg rested on top of the coverlet. His massive shoulders spanned the pillows stacked behind him, and his great gray head moved restlessly from side to side.

" Hurt pretty good, Grampa? "

" Now, that's a fool question! Certain it hurts! Man cain't pull his anklebone clean outen place 'thout it hurtin'. Fetch ye up a chair, boy. Fetch ye up a chair an' set down. Reckon you kin make out to do the work fer a spell till I git back on my feet? "

" I reckon."

" How'd you make out in that there corn today? "

" Got a good start. But your patch is so shady and the ground's so damp the weeds are rank. It'll take me a right smart spell to get it done."

" Yeah," Grampa agreed. " That allus was the most trouble-some thing 'bout that there patch. But I've tried corn ever' other patch on the place, an' it jist natcherally grows best there. Same ground as makes rank weeds makes tall corn, I reckon. Ifen my leg gits better, though, 'twon't be long I'll be laid away. I'd orta be up from here agin another week passes."

" Well, I wasn't complainin', Grampa. You just rest yourself and we'll make out to get everything done." Hod dragged a chair over to the bed.

" I declare, Hod," Grampa said, " believe if you was to bring in my hickory strips an' them two frames in the shed I could be aworkin' on them bottoms. Mebbe you could sorta prop me up some higher here in the bed, an' lay one o' them frames acrost the bed, like. Ifen I could jist be aworkin' with my hands, seems like I'd be a heap easier."

Hod piled the pillows behind the old man's back and pulled him up higher in the bed. Then he went out to the shed and brought in two chair frames he found there, and the rings of hickory strips which had been soaking to make them pliable. He helped his grandfather get one of the chairs set before him at an angle that was comfortable for him to work, and then he loosened the circle of hickory. He watched the knotted, mis-shapen old hands test the texture of the hickory and then fasten it to the chair to begin his weaving. It went across, around, un-der, and back.

It was fascinating to watch how surely the old hands wove the strands together . . . how taut and firm the pattern was. Grampa was counted the best chairmaker in the whole of Adair

63

County. There were always three or four chairs out in the shed waiting to be bottomed, and folks came from all over to get him to make their chairs new from stout, dry hickory. Couldn't anybody hold him a candle. Folks said Dow Pierce's chairs never wore out. The bottoms maybe. You could sit out three or four bottoms of a chair during its lifetime. But if Dow Pierce made the frame, it would outlast a man. Hod ran his hand down the leg of his chair, and thought of how Grampa made it. With never a nail or spike. Just seasoned wood bored into green wood, careful-like and sure, and rounded and smoothed until it was shiny.

The lamplight wavered fitfully in a light breeze and made tall shadows across the logs. Outside, the burr of frogs was beginning and the whippoorwills were crying lonesomely. Hod reached out his hands. " Let me see if I can do it, Grampa."

Grampa gave over the chair frame and the strips and cautioned him, " Mind you keep the strips even, now, an' don't let no slack creep in."

The boy bent his head over the work. At first he felt clumsy handling the strip, and his movements were awkward. After a few laps, however, he found that the strips fitted into his hand naturally when he held them a certain way.

" Why, it's just all in gettin' the feel of it, isn't it? "

" Mostly," answered Grampa. " They's some couldn't never git the feel of it, though. They's some ain't the patience ever to mess with it. Hit's slow work, makin' chairs. An' ain't ever'body has got the turn fer it."

Hod ran his palm over the smooth, hand-rubbed legs of the chair frame before him. It was satiny to feel and the grain of the wood was finely etched. " I reckon I've got the turn, Grampa," he said. " I've always loved to whittle and make things out of wood, and I sorta love the feelin' of wood itself."

" Hit'd be natcheral to you. I reckon I got my turn fer it from Ma. Her that was Abigail Sawyer. She could make e'er thing you wanted outen wood. Right quare fer a woman too. But she was handy that way."

" How long you been makin' chairs, Grampa? "

" Why, I wouldn't rightly know, boy. Might' nigh all my life, I reckon. Hit jist come handy to me, an' the first thing I knowed

ever'body was bringin' me chairs to bottom, an' then I com-
menced amakin' 'em new. Over fifty year I've been makin' 'em,
that I know."

"There's something comfortable about makin' things out of
wood, isn't there?"

"Ain't no feelin' like it. Put a good piece o' whittlin' wood in
a man's hand, an' give him a good, sharp knife, an' ifen he ain't
content he ain't my kind of a man."

The boy and the old man bent together over the chair. Hod
finished the overlapping and Grampa fastened off the last strip
for him. Hod swiped his hands down the side of his pants. "Some
folks say the furniture places in Louisville make hundreds of
chairs a day. Would you think that could be so?"

Grampa's head jerked. "Mebbe. I've heared tell. But they
ain't turned by hand, an' they ain't framed of hickory. You
cain't hurry hickory none."

"I've not hardly been out of Adair," Hod said, his eyes pinned
to the dark square of the door. "Just over to Campbellsville, and
Ma said she took me to Liberty once to an all-day singin'. But
I don't remember about it. Campbellsville, now. There's a right
smart of stores and things there, but I reckon Louisville must be
a sight to see."

Grampa looked at Hod and there was a twinkle in his eyes.
"Yer feet's itchin', huh?"

"Maybe," and Hod laughed.

The old man pulled the quilt close around his shoulders and
settled his head against the pillows. "Well," he said, "most
Pierces is content to stay by their land. But I reckon there'll
allus be one or two yearnin' to git out an' see the world. Yer
great-grampa — him that was called Jeems — he was one. Had
him a good snug cabin here he built hisself, an' a good woman,
but he was allus agoin' off somewheres. I mind how he used to
tell about the Mexican War, an' all them fur places he seen.
Texas an' Mexico an' the like. But I mind mostly how he'd tell
how tired his feet got awanderin' over that strange land."

Hod stirred. He'd read about the Mexican War. He looked at
his feet, and they were Jeems's feet. They walked silently across
the ridge and they felt the stones and the sharp spine of the
ridge. They stirred the pine needles in the woods and splashed

65

through the creek. They tramped down the earth for a cabin to be built, and they searched the hillsides for stout oak and pine logs. They marched off to war, and they wandered the red dirt of Texas. They crossed over onto foreign land and were sore and cracked from the long marches over scorching sand.

But they came back to Piney Ridge and walked again behind a plow in cool, fresh dirt. At last they stopped and lay still, shod and boxed, and were lowered into the dirt to become a part of the dirt. The boy shivered and pulled his identity back into himself. This here's Hod Pierce!

"I'd like to see them places."

Grampa eyed him quizzically and hitched his quilt higher. "They ain't no place so homey as Piney Ridge."

Hod picked up his hat from the floor. He turned it round and round in his hands, and picked at the frayed edge of the straw. "Grampa, you been content most of your life?"

Grampa raised his arms and stretched mightily. "Why?"

"Just wonderin'."

The old man held the boy's eyes with a clear, straight look. "Hod," he said finally, "I reckon they's a time in ever' man's life when he hurts all over with discontent. I've had mine. An' only the good Lord an' yer gramma kept me from makin' a plumb mess o' my life." He laughed gently. "An' the time was when I laid most of the mess to yer gramma." He paused, and his look strayed toward the kitchen where Gramma was redding up the dishes. Then it came back to Hod. "Content? I reckon we wasn't intended to be content for too long at a stretch. But mostly I've liked livin'. I've had me a little piece o' land o' my own . . . an' a roof over my head that belonged to me . . . an' I've raised what I put in my stummick an' it set light there on account of it. I've had me a good woman to go along with me, an' kids that's pleasured me. I've had work to lay my hand to . . . work o' my own choosin'. An' folks around to neighbor with. Don't know what more a man could want. Livin' jist about biles down to that, I'd say. Ifen you take e'er thing away from it, a man ain't got full measure. Ifen you try to add to it, hit won't hold no more. Yes, I been right content."

Gramma darkened the doorway, smoothing down her hair and wiping her hands on her apron front. "You goin' now, Hod?"

66

" I better."

" Tell Hattie to come."

" She'll come. Pa or me one'll be comin' every day. Don't worry."

Hod opened the screen door and stepped out on the small porch. The stars were sprayed across the night, thick and yellow and hot. The hills closed all around him, tight, pressed down, closed in. " Livin' jist about biles down to that, I'd say. . . . I been right content." But what if you want to push the hills back? What if you have a longing so fierce it pulls and tugs inside of you? To stay where the earth is sweet and dark and familiar. Or to go where the boundaries broaden into wide skies. What if a man seeks himself back beyond the place where the sun rises? What if he must find other suns and other hills and other streams flowing swiftly? Would he then be content? Would he then come into his own place?

He stepped out into the night and took the path with long strides, his feet finding the way unerringly. The path dipped by the meadow gate, and swung down to the creek. Across the shallow water it rose sharply, and a man had to get a long breath for the climb. A slow mist was rising all down the holler, trailing in thin wisps around the trees and settling softly over the land. It twined itself around his legs and he pushed through it ghostlike and walking easy on a cloud.

The climb was long and steep, and he walked out of the mist halfway up. By the time he reached the top of the ridge he was winded, and he stopped by the white birch to ease his breathing. Up here there was a moon, and all down the ridge he saw the spiny humps and saddles of the trees. Back down in the holler the mist lay, blotting out the light in the cabin; blotting out space and the edges of space.

Across the holler was the cliff, white and shining in the moonlight. It scarred the hillside in austere purity, towering above the trees and free of them. Hod cupped his hands around his mouth. " Hey! " he cried. " You over there! This here's Hod Pierce ablowin' his horn! "

Feebly the echo made its way back across the holler. It doesn't carry as well at night, he thought, and stepped on down the road. He had forgotten all about the meeting.

CHAPTER SIX

THE HOT, BRASSY DAYS slipped breathlessly by. Hattie's old wood range in the kitchen had a fire in it from morning until night as she started the canning season. It was a point of pride with her that she never left an empty jar in the house. So the pots and pans simmered constantly on the back of the stove, which made the big, low-roofed kitchen steam like a boiler room. Tom grumbled: " Looks like you've a notion to can ever' blessed thing on the place. Want me to pick you a mess o' them dog fennel weeds? I seen some tall 'uns over in the fence corner."

Hattie, whose temper was short with the heat and the hard work, snapped at him, " You won't be the one that'll pass up e'er thing fitten to eat come winter, Tom Pierce! "

The long, hot, dry spell made the menfolks uneasy. It wasn't good for tobacco. Tobacco must have heat, but it must have plenty of moisture too. And a ruined tobacco crop on Piney Ridge meant no cash for a long, bitter year. So, daily, Tom and Hod and all the other ridge farmers scanned the sky for signs of rain; and they hovered anxiously over their tobacco fields, feeling the texture of the leaves and shaking their heads ominously.

Grampa's ankle stayed swollen and sore, and the long, hot days held him housebound and fractious. Irma was still staying the nights with him and Gramma, and she and John were holding tight to their stolen hours together. The meeting was coming to an exhausted close after three burning, passion-charged weeks. The preacher was worn out by the heat and the violent outpouring of his energy; the people were sated of their emotional hunger. Hattie was too tired after a long day over the stove to go many of the nights now. But Hod continued to walk the long way regularly.

Mostly this was to keep Hattie satisfied about Irma. For his own joy in the meeting had been short-lived. Lily Mae continued to ignore him, punishing him by laying her bold glance on the other boys and never once favoring him. Evening after evening he miserably saw her gather a group around her, toss back her sunburned curls, and let her laugh ripple like wind in the trees, sweetly, lightly, over her shoulder in Hod's direction. He stayed away from her. Not for anything would he have risked a rebuff. With a measure of dignity available to him through his hurt he kept to himself, quiet and contained. But she stabbed him afresh each night. He felt a possession of her which he dared not think another shared. But Lily Mae was so prodigal with the gift of her eyes and her smile that he was tormented with doubt. The long, dry days drew him taut, and he felt stretched and thinned. He had an uneasy sense of impending trouble, and he knew he would be glad when the meeting closed.

The morning of the last day of the meeting dawned as still and stifling as the ones that had gone before. Even the sun had a limp, fried look, like an egg cooked too quickly. By noon, heat waves shimmered in the blinding glare, and the whole world lay quivering under them. Hod sought the shade at the side of the house and hacked away with a long knife at the overgrown grass. Nothing could be done in the fields till it rained, and the time had best be spent in small chores around the house.

He heard the swish and slide of a footstep in the grass and leaned sideways to catch a glimpse of Becky coming down the front path. " Hi, there, Becky," he yelled, waving the knife at her. "Aren't you afraid you'll get a sunstroke out in the sun this mornin'? "

" Reckon my skull's too thick," she laughed. " You aimin' to scythe the hull yard with that there knife? "

" No, I'm not that lively. I'm just aimin' to clear the paths. Ma's inside quiltin'. Go on in."

He went back to his chore, stopping occasionally to wipe the sweat out of his eyes. Inside, there was the buzz of Hattie's and Becky's voices, and at intervals he could hear Becky's explosive, raucous laugh. It always startled him. Becky was a little, thin, frail-looking woman whose voice should have been soft and gentle. Instead it was deep and nasal, and when she laughed it was like the clanking of tin pans.

He heard them come out on the porch and heard Hattie say something about its being cooler out there. Then he forgot them and was not conscious of them for nearly an hour. Hattie's voice recalled him. " Hod! C'mere! "

There was something like steel in it, and a harsh hand squeezed his throat dry. He laid the knife down carefully and moved slowly to the porch. Becky was sitting, white-faced and scared, her hand to her mouth. Her eyes met his. " Hod, I never aimed to tattle nothin'. I never thought but what she knowed."

" Knew what? "

Hattie's voice cut in cleanly. " Becky's jist been atellin' me that Irma an' John Walton's been ameetin' ever' night down at Grampa's. I'm askin' you what you know about it."

Hod looked at his mother, and he saw her hands knotting and twisting. His eyes met hers steadily. " I just know Irma's a grown girl, mindin' her own business."

" Hit ain't her business to go meetin' e'er boy on the sly! "

" It's your doin' it has to be on the sly. And it's for Irma to say when she meets him and where." His eyes held his mother's without wavering.

" You don't know what yer sayin'! An' she don't know what she's doin'! But I'll git the truth one way or another. Ifen the whole countryside knows but me, they's aplenty to tell."

She went in the house and reappeared with her sunbonnet on her head. She stood for a moment tying its strings firmly under her chin. " I'm goin' to git Irma now," she said, and walked past them without seeing them.

" You've sure done it," Hod said bitterly to Becky.

" Hod, I never knowed she'd mind. I was right proud that Irma was atalkin' to sich a good boy as John Walton, an' it come over me to name it to Hattie. I swear, Hod, I'd cut off both hands 'fore I'd a caused Irma e'er bit o' trouble." Becky was crying now, and the tears rolled down the lined cheeks and dripped forlornly off her pointed chin.

" Well, never mind now. What's done is done. Irma'll catch it, and we'll all pay for it for a week or two. Worst is, Irma and John really love each other, and this'll go hard with 'em."

Becky wailed and threw her apron over her head. " I wisht I could cut my tongue right out. I wisht I was deaf an' dumb an' dead. Pore little Irma, an' it's me that's done brought this on her! I wouldn't a caused her no trouble fer nothin' in this world.

70

Oh, me! Oh, me!" And she rocked back and forth, moaning.

"Becky, you better go on home now. Ma's not goin' to be in any easy frame of mind when she gets back here with Irma. Everybody's goin' to be walkin' low. You best go on now."

"You tell Irma I never aimed to."

"Oh, if it hadn't been you, it would have been somebody else. Nothin' can be kept on this ridge. Don't go blamin' yourself too much. But you better get on out of the way."

"I'm agoin'. But you tell Irma I never aimed to."

"I'll tell her," Hod promised, and Becky shuffled down the road, stooped and weeping.

What Hattie said to Irma, Hod never knew. It had been said before they reached home, for when they came in they were both white and drawn and silent. Irma went directly to her room. The afternoon wore itself out and supper was a desolate meal. No one went to the meeting that night, and the first dark found them all in bed, weary with the tension of the day, and guarded against the spoken word which would bring on the storm.

At breakfast the next morning Irma appeared tight-lipped. She helped with the meal and ate silently, glancing at none of them. It was as if she had repudiated all of them. Hattie's face was a stone image, with lines frozen in place. She was remote and withdrawn, and her rounded shoulders sagged with a heavy burden.

Hod tried to find a moment alone with Irma, to proffer his help if she needed it. But she merely shrugged his words off and kept her face still and flat. Only once did she say anything. "This ain't the end. I promise you, Hod. This ain't the end of it."

This dreary day was Hod's birthday. This day he was nineteen years old. There was no mention made of it, nor any notice taken. But when Irma seemed to have no need of him, he thought he might give himself a present and go fishing. He put a cork, hook, and line in his pocket and set off down the road for the river. He felt an overpowering need to be alone. The house was dull with silence and thick with hidden quarrels. He wanted to be away from it. He wanted to be still . . . to be at peace.

At the river he cut a long reed and tied his fishing line to it, set the cork and hook, and threw it in. Then he settled himself in the shade on the bank. The river was low, but still the water swirled and eddied, as clear and green as an emerald. Green River. Rightly named, he thought. He stretched out and let his hands lie limp on the damp, spongy ground. One hand gathered a clump of the dark loam and crumbled it, letting it slip through his fingers. The earth is good, he thought. There's nothing wrong with the earth. Only people get mixed up. The earth is forever and enduring the same. It answers a man's need. If a man knows his need, that is. But supposing a man doesn't know his need. Supposing he only knows an emptiness. An emptiness that isn't always an emptiness, but is sometimes a fullness. How is he to know whether he is empty or full? Whether he's to go or stay? How is a man to know what makes him a man?

He sat up suddenly and shook himself. The cork floated placidly and undisturbed. I'm moonin' again, he thought. Believe I'll take a swim. He stripped and slipped into the cool water, thrashed and snorted and ducked himself, then swam rapidly across the river and back. This was the hole where he had learned to swim, he remembered. Right over there by the sand bar Little Wells had thrown him in that day and shouted, "Sink or swim!" And he had swum. This was the hole where he and Wade and Sandy used to try to touch the bottom. You had to bring up a handful of pebbles to prove it. You went down and down in the limpid depths until you could lay your hand against the cold white stones. In a second you scraped your hand full and shot back to the surface. "Touched bottom," you shouted, and held your hand aloft, the white stones sparkling in the sun.

He floated lazily on his back, squinting against the sun. He felt the inertia of time-space endlessness and was melted into the water which upheld him. He shifted his eyes to the gleam of his white body washed by the clean ripples. He thought of the words of a song he sometimes sang . . . lonely river . . . weary water. Old Green was a lonely river, but its waters were never weary. He lifted his hand and watched the drops flow in a thin, fine stream down his arm back into the mother water. These drops that touch my body, now, go on. They pass the Smith place and the Beaver hole, and the old covered bridge. They go

72

farther than I've ever been. They eat out the banks of the Ohio; they marry the waters of the Mississippi; they flow free into the receiving cradle of the ocean. O free and searching water!

The sun was tipping the trees when he crawled out, dressed, stripped his line from the reed pole, and set out for home. Supper was over when he arrived, but Irma set a plate for him and he ate cold beans and potatoes hungrily.

When she had served him, Irma said quietly, " Hod, me an' John is goin' to git married."

It struck him like a blow in the pit of his stomach, but he went on eating. " That's good," he said.

So this was what she meant when she said it wasn't the end. This was her answer to Hattie. He went on to think of her and John. Married, setting up housekeeping. She was so young and so little to be going away from home. Even Hattie's sharp tongue couldn't keep home from being a sweet place. Did she know what marriage was like? Did she know how it would be with her and John? He shrank from the thought of her shoulders bending so soon. He wanted her free of burdens yet awhile. But she was a woman grown, and if this was her choice, this was what he wanted for her. He said none of these things, however, and he kept his face impassive. " You sure? " he asked her.

" I'm certain," she answered steadily.

" What did Ma say? "

" I've not told Ma, an' I ain't aimin' to till it's all over."

" When you plannin' to do it? "

" Saturday. I seen John at the mailbox and we made it up fer me to go over to Frony's an' Jim's at the Gap tomorrer. John'll meet me over there, an' we'll go to the county seat an' git the license. Then ifen you'll come to the Gap Saturday like you allus do, we'll wait an' you kin stand up with us."

Hod nodded. They had it worked out and it ought to go off without any trouble. But Irma had always been a sturdy, independent little person. He didn't urge her to tell Hattie. In fact, he agreed that it would be best not to tell her.

Thus it was planned and thus it was consummated. On Saturday morning Hod took his half bushel of corn to the mill as usual. Later he stood by his sister's side in the spare, plain front room of the preacher's house and listened to the words that made

73

her John Walton's wife. "Forsaking all others, cleave only unto him."

Forsaking Ma and Pa and him; the clean-swept rooms and the slow-ticking old Seth Thomas clock on the shelf; the yellow rosebush by the chimney; the old dominecker hen that squawked when it rained; the sunset over the beech grove. Inexorably the words repeated themselves in his ears. "Forsaking all others." Now it was going to be Irma and John, forever and enduring. There was partition and creation. There was a dividing and a loss; and there was the making of a whole. No, he had the impulse to say. No. But he stood quietly and his face was calm, and he signed the certificate with a steady hand.

As soon as the brief ceremony was over, the young couple drove off in Old Man Walton's spring wagon. They would stay a week or two with John's folks, and then they were going to set up for themselves in the tiny, two-room tenant house on his father's farm. They would start with a bed, a stove, and maybe a couple of chairs. Friends, neighbors, and relatives would give them dishes, pots and pans, and bedding. Folks on the ridge always helped a young couple get a start.

Just before the wagon moved away, Irma slipped a note into Hod's hand. "Give this to Ma," she said.

She had written two short lines. "Dear Ma. Me an' John got married today. I will come when I can. Your loving daughter, Irma."

When he gave Irma's brief note to Hattie that Saturday afternoon, Hod expected her to grieve, to storm and rage, to weep and scold. But she did none of them. She read the note and folded it neatly twice over into a small square. She laid it carefully on the edge of the table, and walked past him to the door. Bracing a hand on each side of her she stood there, looking out over the fields to the hills beyond, with her shoulders straightened and her face lifted. Hod waited, feeling weak and a little sick. It was an interminable time before she moved again. But when she turned, her face was quiet. The deed was done. Irma was safe now. The God-fearing ridge mother's anxiety that her child might go wrong was laid. An' John Walton was a right good boy, folks said. A hard worker an' a decentlike man. Yes, she could rest easy.

There was a look of peace and even of happiness on her face, and an odd, strange, fleeting beauty. Her eyes were soft and her mouth was sweet. She smiled at Hod gently and reached out to pat his shoulder. "I'll have to git them quilts done now fer shore," she said. "Irma'll be needin' 'em, come cold weather."

CHAPTER SEVEN

IRMA WAS MARRIED and the house was empty of her walk and her talk and her bright laugh. To Hod the first week after she was gone was like a strange and bewildering dream. When he came in the kitchen to breakfast in the mornings, he expected her to be there helping Hattie. When he slid into his place on the long bench at meals, he was lonely, and the bench was now too long and empty. A dozen times a day he listened for her voice and waited to hear her call him. How can a family so quickly be less than a family? How can one who is part of home so suddenly become no part of home? What is there to prepare you for the cutting away of something dear, and how can you heal the gaping hole that such cutting away leaves? He had not thought he would miss her so.

They talked of her often. "Hit don't seem like I'll ever git used to her not bein' here," Hattie said fondly. The fact of the marriage had freed her love of the alloy of distrust, and it went out full and deep to this daughter who had now taken on a woman's greatest task.

John brought her home for supper one Saturday evening when they had been married about two weeks. The sun was easing its way down behind the hills when they drove up and John hitched his mare to the yard fence. Hattie pulled the curtain aside from the front window to see who it was. Her cry brought Hod and Tom from the kitchen. "Hit's Irma an' John!" she called. "I declare if it ain't! I knowed when that ole rooster stood on the back steps this mornin' an' crowed that somebody was acomin'. Hit's a good thing I set to right then an' cooked up some decent victuals. An' baked that there cake!" And then she was out the door running to the front gate.

"Git out," she called, "git out! Ifen I ain't the gladdest thing

75

to see you!" Irma crawled over the wheel and flew to her mother's arms.

Hod and Tom reached them, and Tom held out his hand, grinning at John. "Well," he said, "you takened on a man's-sized job, ain't you? Marryin' this girl right out from under her ma's nose?"

"I figger I'm a growed man, Tom," John chuckled.

"Well, you shore takened us by surprise, boy, but now yer in the family, yer shore welcome. As fur as I'm concerned, they's not e'er 'nother boy Irma could a picked would a suited me better."

Hod had gone around on the other side of the horse to unhitch the traces on that side. He stretched his head over the mare's back. "Reckon he must a suited Irma pretty well too. Leastways, she hooked him mighty fast!"

Irma wrinkled her nose at him. "You're jist awishin' somebody thought that much o' you! That's all's wrong with you!"

Hattie slipped her arm through Irma's. "You jist hesh, Hod. Hit allus takes two to make a weddin', I've noticed."

The men laughed. John handed Irma a bundle from the wagon, and she and Hattie went through the gate toward the house. "You jist come right on in now," Hattie was saying; "hit won't take me a minnit to git supper on the table. My, I'm shore glad you come!"

Inside, Irma laid her bundle on the bed and followed Hattie to the kitchen. "I brung you some quilt pieces, Ma. Miz Walton give me a heap, an' I knowed you was allus needin' some. They're real purty an' the colors is bright an' cheerful."

"Now, ain't that nice? I was jist tellin' Hod the other day I was aimin' to git yore quilt I started last winter done. Fer I know in reason yer bound to need it, come winter."

"Well, I was aimin' to take back some o' my things tonight. That coverlid Gramma made fer me, an' them summer quilts you give me, an' a few things like that."

"They're jist like you left 'em. Take e'er thing you need. Tom an' me, we was wonderin' ifen you wouldn't like to have yer little dresser. Hit's right purty, an' it would brighten up yer house."

"O Ma, could I? I'd shore love to have it. We've not got much

76

yit. Jist a bed an' a table an' cookstove, an' some chairs. John, he said when the tobaccer's in, he'd git me e'er what I needed, but I've allus loved that dresser so good. I'd ruther have it than a new one. Don't disfurnish yerself none now."

"Hit won't disfurnish me a bit! Hit's your'n. Hit was bought fer you, an' yer welcome to it. You think you'll like over there?"

"In time, I think. Hit's a little ole house. Jist two rooms. But John an' me aim to fix it up. He's agoin' to whitewash the outside, an' I thought to paper the rooms, an' paint the floors. John's folks has been right nice. His ma's a sweet woman, an' she seems real proud fer him to be married an' settled. She give me some o' her dishes. An' they was her best ones too, mind you. I told her we was goin' to git ever'thing like that soon as we could git around to it. But she let on like she was jist pleased to do it. An' John said I'd hurt her feelin's was I not to take 'em."

Hattie was bustling back and forth, but she nodded her head as she listened to the stream of Irma's talk. "I allus heared Susie Walton was a good woman. That ole man now. He's a hard worker, but I reckon work never hurt nobody."

"John, he works hard too. Seems like they work different from Pa an' Hod. Or even Grampa. I don't rightly know how it is, but seems like our menfolks allus went at things sorta easylike. I know Pa's frashed you many's the time with his ways, but he's allus been so good natured with it. John, he's good-natured like Pa, though. But he works hard an' don't never take no time off to go fishin' or huntin'."

"He'll be a good pervider, then. We ain't never went hungry here, but we been too clost to it fer comfort, times."

Hattie set the table and burdened it with the food she was dishing up. Green beans, tiny and tender, cooked with a piece of smoked side meat. Corn, heaped high on the platter, steaming and golden yellow. Small, round tomato preserves. Thin green slices of cucumber pickles. Jelly and jam and molasses. Proudly she opened a loaf of store bread and piled it high on the plate, with biscuits and great squares of flaky corn bread. She poured milk into a tall blue pitcher and set it at one end of the table, and then she set the bubbling coffeepot at the other end. Last of all, she brought out the chocolate cake, standing four layers tall on the old cut-glass cake stand.

When they sat down to the table, John and Irma slipped naturally onto the long bench at the back, and Hod took a strange place at the end.

Looking at Irma and John across the table, Hod had a strangely awed feeling. These two were now one. They looked the same, they talked the same, and yet there was a proud new assurance in their bearing. Irma laid a knowing hand on John's arm sometimes. And John bent an owning look on her bright head. Together they had explored a new land. Together they had come into the sweet knowledge that only those who are very deeply in love could know. And nevermore would they be without the touch of it. It would lie over their life, and give it glory. Irma took on a new growth to Hod. She was a little less Irma, a little more woman. And in her increased stature he relinquished his last hold upon her. The forsaking had taken place, and he, in turn, could at last forsake her, leaving her free to be wholly John's wife.

He thought of Lily Mae, and the familiar dull hurt went through him. She had looked the other way at the store last week. Pretended not to see him. How could she stay angry so long? Or did she mean to stay angry forever, never forgiving him? He could no longer say, "There's other fish in the sea." There weren't, for him. He hadn't thought a girl could hurt you so. He hadn't known how lost she could leave you feeling when she took her warmth away.

He didn't ask himself if he wanted with Lily Mae this belonging which Irma and John now had. He only knew that to look at them in their new belonging sent an ache down his arms and left them feeling empty and drained. And he came upon a truth then — that once a man has held a woman in his arms, they can no longer be satisfied to fold across the emptiness without her. Abruptly Hod pushed his chair back. No more would go down.

Hattie urged food on the others until they were stuffed, and then she made them go out on the porch while she washed the dishes.

"I'll he'p," Irma said.

"You'll do no sich! Yer company tonight! When you come agin, you kin he'p e'er way you kin, but you ain't goin' to turn yer hand tonight. You go set with the rest on the porch. Hit

78

won't take but a minnit, noways."

As she went through the front room, Irma picked up Hod's guitar from the corner by the fireplace. "Thought I might as well have it handy," she laughed. "I'm wantin' some music when yer supper's settled."

The night was beautiful with a still, languid beauty. A wash of silver stars was spread widely across the sky, and the trees across the road were massed in blurred and softened outlines. The katydids were fiddling, and down in the holler the old bull-frogs grumbled about a "jug-o-rum, jug-o-rum, jug-o-rum." Over in the pasture a cowbell sounded gently, mellow and golden and muted.

Hod sat on the porch step and leaned his back against the post. He soaked up the night sounds and let them thread quietly through his body. The grass around the steps was heavy with dew, and the cinnamon vines spiced the air with a pungent, heavy odor. He stripped the dew absently from a blade of grass. Dew was a funny thing, now. Some said it fell, like rain or mist. Some said they'd heard tell it rose. But all summer long, rise or fall, the dew was there . . . as wet as rain, but infinitely more personal than rain . . . more mysterious and more delicate.

Hod's eyelids grew heavy. The voices lifted and fell around him, as soft as a woman's waist. As slow as molasses. As sweet as the smell of the cinnamon vines. They faded to a hum, burred through with Tom's deep laugh occasionally. They made no sense at all, and he felt himself rising and falling on the gentle rhythmic waves that flowed around him.

Irma's foot prodded him awake. "How 'bout that music?"

Hod lurched and nearly fell off the step. Unkindly Irma poked at him again. "C'mon, wake up!"

"I'm awake!"

"Then let's have some music."

Hod laid the guitar across his knees and plucked lazily at the strings.

"What'll it be?" he asked.

"You know that there tune, 'Lord Lovel,' or somethin' like that?" John wanted to know.

"Yeah, but it's awfully sad and mournful," Hod said.

"I know, but hit's got sich a purty tune," John insisted.

"Well, all right," and Hod thumbed a chord and leaned his head against the post.

> " ' Lord Lovel stood at his castle gate,
>   A combin' his milk-white steed;
> Then along come Lady Nancy Bell,
>   A wishin' her lover good speed,
>   A wishin' her lover good speed.

> " ' Where are you goin', Lord Lovel, she said,
>   O where are you goin', said she.
> I'm goin', my dear Lady Nancy Bell,
>   Strange countries for to see,
>   Strange countries for to see.

> " ' When will you come back, Lord Lovel, she said;
>   When will you come back, said she.
> In a year or two or three at most,
>   I'll come back to my Lady Nancy,
>   I'll come back to my Lady Nancy.

> " ' He'd not been gone but a year and a day,
>   Strange countries for to see,
> When languishing thoughts came into his mind
>   And Lady Nancy he would see,
>   And Lady Nancy he would see.' "

The song went on and on through its long story. Lord Lovel rode and rode until he reached London town, where he heard the people all mourning. And when he asked who was dead, they told him it was Lady Nancy. He ordered her grave opened, and he kissed her grave-cold lips while the tears came trickling down.

> " ' Lady Nancy was laid in the old churchyard,
>   Lord Lovel was buried close by her;
> And out of her bosom there grew a red rose,
>   And out of his, a brier,
>   And out of his, a brier.' "

"I declare!" said Irma, when Hod stilled the last lingering quiver of the strings, "that song makes me plumb sad. I kin allus see pore Lord Lovel acomin' home an' findin' Lady Nancy dead an' buried."

"Well, he hadn't orta left her, seems to me," Hattie put in.

"Guess he must o' had a itchin' foot," said John.

"Hit says 'strange countries fer to see,'" Tom added.

Strange countries for to see! Hod knew how it must be when a man had to go, strange countries for to see. Home was sweet, and love was sweeter. But strange countries were like a hand in front of you pulling. The wonder of them never ceased.

"Sing somethin' gay, now, Hod. Sing the 'Crawdad Hole'!"

Hod laughed and swung into the swift rhythm. Irma joined him, and then John took up the tune with a pleasing, full voice. They rollicked down the verses to a breathless finish. "Lily Mae likes that one too," Hod said when they had ended the song. Hattie cut her eyes at him cornerwise and lifted her chin obliquely.

Hod sucked in his cheeks and pulled a brash chord from the guitar. "'Oh, they call it that good ole mountain dew,'" he shouted. "'They call it that good ole mountain dew'!"

"Now, that'll do, Hod," Hattie's voice sliced through the music. "Man or boy, I ain't aimin' to have you singin' no sich a song as that! Jist put yer gittar up now!"

"O Ma, it's jist a song," Irma protested.

"You heared me." Hattie was immovable.

Hod laid the guitar aside and rolled a cigarette. Somewhere down the road a dog barked.

"That's Lem's old Spot dog," Tom said. "Reckon what he's doin' up on the ridge."

They were quiet on the porch, listening. Soon they heard the muffled sound of voices. A smothered laugh or two came down the road and the shuffling of many feet.

"What in the world you reckon's goin' on?" Hod asked, puzzled.

"Sh-h-h," warned Tom.

And when a shot broke the air, all bedlam turned loose. The noise of pans being banged against one another, of iron bars clanging together, of cowbells and whistles, of a dozen shotguns being fired at once, of people screaming and yelling, deafened those on the porch. They sat stunned by the first impact of the drowning sounds, unable to move or to think.

Hattie recovered first. "Hit's a shivaree," she said, shouting above the din to make herself heard. "They're ashivareein' Irma an' John!"

Hod grinned in the dark. But his heart was pounding hard.

Every young couple who got married on the ridge hoped for a shivaree. It was the ridge's way of voicing approval of the marriage. It was a token of esteem. And here the folks were shivareeing his own sister and her new husband. And by the sounds of it, it was a bang-up shivaree! He slipped off the porch to take his place among them.

The crowd milled through the front gate and divided, half marching around the house one way and the other half going the other way. For fifteen or twenty minutes they marched around the house, the men shooting off their guns, the women banging their pans and ringing their cowbells, all of them shouting and laughing. The folks stood on the porch and waved and shouted as the lines went by.

Then suddenly the crowd converged on the porch. The women dragged Irma, who was laughing by now and enjoying the excitement, from John's side, and dumped her unceremoniously into a big washtub. She pulled her legs under her hastily as they lifted the tub, swinging it high between them, and carried her around the house.

At the same time the men had laid hands on John. John protested mildly and pretended to wrestle with the men, and it was Hod who seized him strongly and threw him from the porch. Then, setting him astride a rail, they took up their march again.

In a few minutes it was over, and the two were brought back to the porch, disheveled, panting, and laughing. John crippled across the porch, mocking his ride on the rail, and the men called crude jokes at him. Hod looked on proudly. If it was boisterous and vulgar, it still was hearty and neighborly.

When the crowd quieted, Hattie asked them all in the house and served them great cups of black coffee and the four-layer chocolate cake as far as it would go. There was a great deal of laughter and shouting at the young couple, and much merry singing.

Hod went out on the porch to cool off. He sat on the steps, and pulled his knees up under his chin. He sighed gustily. It was a proper thing to be shivareed so successfully. Irma and John had got off to a fine start now. He turned his face against the rough stuff of his jeans and rubbed his cheek against it. Then he straightened briskly. Fiddle! Everything started him moonin' these days! This was no way for him to be actin'!

He was startled when a pair of hands, smelling freshly of per-fumed soap, slipped over his eyes. He covered them with his own broad palms. Lily Mae! His heart jumped into his throat and then tunneled to his feet. Lily Mae! He pulled the hands down and turned to face her. " I didn't know you were here," he said softly, his breath coming quickly between his words.

" Did you think I'd fergot? "

She was so close, bending over him. And she smelled so sweet. Even as his senses dipped and swirled, he identified the odor. Honeysuckle! He swallowed. " The way you been actin' I didn't know what to think! "

" C'mon," she whispered, taking his hands and pulling him off the step. " C'mon, let's go out in the yard where nobody kin hear."

" Where nobody can see? " he asked hopefully.

" That's as may be," she giggled, and led the way around the house behind the yellow rosebush.

Eagerly Hod caught her and gathered her close. His arms folded round her softness and the empty ache was filled. He held her tightly against him, feeling her warmth steal over him.

" Hod, yer hurtin'! "

" I aim to! Don't ever treat me like that again! "

She raised his face in her two hands. " Silly," she laughed, " silly! Didn't you know I was yer girl! "

" I'll not let you forget it again," he promised, and he let his arms rest wearily about her waist. Something was at peace in him again.

CHAPTER EIGHT

THE HEAT DRAGGED ON, and the corn and the tobacco burned in the fields. The sun brought the day up by four thirty these mornings, dragging it gray-faced and heavy-eyed over the hills, sponging out as it went any stray clouds left over from the night. Then in hot solitude the great yellow disk whitened the sky with glare, and reduced the earth to a flaccid state of inertia.

The tension built up and up as the brassy sky fought to collect clouds and bank them against the rain. Each day the bank was thicker, heavier, in the west, and when the sun could not shred it into fragments, it sullenly hid behind the dark curtain. Each afternoon there was a far rumbling of thunder down the river valley, and when night had blown cool over the land, the edges of the ridge stood out starkly against the summer lightning. At last one evening the swollen, black belly of the banked clouds sagged and burst, and the rains came squalling out of the sunset.

For two days then it rained — a slanting, cold rain which soaked into the earth and packed it down, muddying the fields and streams. It traced a chill finger in the air and sent the thermometer shivering down into the forties. With stoves down for the summer, the raw, damp cold sent folks huddling around the kitchen ranges. Grampa built up a little fire in the fireplace mornings and evenings and hovered over it. His ankle was still sore and stiff, and he had been housebound now for over six weeks.

"Plague take sich weather," he fumed, "never seed sich a summer. First the sun nigh cooks you. Till you feel as parched an' dried out as shoe leather! Then it comes on to storm an' mighty nigh frosts! Even my bones is shakin' with ague!"

His old, thin blood was miserable with the cold, and the second night of the rain he was sneezing and Gramma was urging him to bed. "Dow, you'll take yer death! Git in the bed an' leave me kiver you up, an' make you a cup of tea! Ain't no use flyin' in the face o' nature thisaway! Hit don't change the weather none to act contrary!"

"Who's actin' contrary! I jist don't want none o' that there bed, an' I ain't aimin' to have none! I been layin' on it most o' these last six weeks, an' I'm plumb tard of it."

Gramma said no more, knowing it was useless, and she watched him come down with a heavy cold helplessly. She wasn't overly alarmed. A summer cold didn't amount to nothin', mostly. She dosed him and physicked him and listened to him fret. Even when the cold went down into his chest and he began to wheeze and shake with paroxysms of coughing, she wasn't too uneasy. She'd seed Dow cough the night through, many's the time. A cold allus had went to his chest.

He had been sick about a week when Tom came home from

doing the work one night, his face sober and quiet. "Pa's right sick," he said at the supper table.

"So?" said Hattie, pouring milk into the glasses. "His cold's bad?"

"Hit's settled in his lungs, I'm afeared. He's got a right smart fever tonight. Won't have the doctor, though. Says it don't amount to nothin'. But I thought I'd better go back down tonight an' do fer him. Ma's all tuckered out."

"I'll go with you," Hattie said at once. "Hod, ifen we don't git back 'fore mornin', you see that things git done."

"Yessum."

They returned the next morning, tired from the sleepless night. "Gault an' Becky's stayin' the day," Tom reported to Hod before going to bed, "an' Lem's goin' tonight."

"Is he bad off?" Hod asked. Seemed funny to think of Grampa really sick. As long as Hod could remember he had been a giant of a man, strong, burly, able to outwork nearly any two men on the ridge. It didn't seem real for folks to be watchin' up with him. He'd always been the one to sit up with everybody else.

"Well, he's purty sick." Tom bent to unlace his shoes. "An' he's agittin' old. Pa must be nigh onto eighty. Things goes hard when yer that old."

"Did you get the doctor yet?"

"No. But me'n Gault has decided ifen he ain't no better by night we'll one of us go after him first thing in the mornin'. He's past tellin' a body what to do now."

Hattie and Tom slept until the middle of the day. Hattie fixed dinner then, and kept the fire going to put up some beans that had been picked the night before. "They'll spile if they're left e'er 'nother day," she said. Tom and Hod worked in the tobacco, the rains having packed the soil to where it needed loosening. They worked side by side, their hoes mulching the caked dirt, saying little. Both of them were thinking of Grampa. Both of them were counting memories, a generation apart, but remarkably alike for all that. A great, spendid figure of a man had towered over their days, sweetening them and giving them the imperishable quality of himself.

A man wasn't ever by himself, then, Hod thought. He was himself, and his father, and his grandfather. Suddenly he had a clear vision of Hod Pierce stretching back in time, part of him Pa, part of him Grampa, part of him Jeems, and on back. All his days of living were before him, and he saw with certain clarity how he had been molded and made. Something of each of them and something of all of them had been poured into him. A man was a reservoir into which his people poured the stream of their living, and then it went on out of him, and through him, down on into time not yet lived.

Late that afternoon they were all sitting on the porch, waiting for the house to cool a bit before eating supper. Hattie had slipped her swollen feet out of her shoes and was fanning herself with her apron. Tom was whittling down the end of a new ax handle, curling long shavings on the grass at his feet. Hod was propped against the post, leaning occasionally to pick up a tendril of shaving and wind it around his finger. They were too weary and too hot to talk.

Tom looked up from his whittling suddenly. He leaned an ear toward the road. "Somebody comin' up the hill," he said.

They all listened and turned to look down the road. Hod stood up. "Whoever it is, he's comin' in a hurry."

Tom stood too. "He shore ain't keerin' none 'bout his wagon!"

They still could see nothing, but they kept watching the road. The heavy tunnel of trees ended at the old church, and within a few minutes they saw the wagon coming. The horses were running and the wagon was lurching from side to side on the road.

"Pa, that's Lem's team," Hod said, and started running toward the gate. Tom was right behind him, and Hattie began to struggle with her shoes.

"Somethin's shore wrong," Tom said. "Somethin's bad wrong!"

Hod and Tom were waiting by the side of the road when Lem pulled the horses up. He was standing tall in the wagon, his knees buckling to the sudden stop. Trouble was written all across his face.

"Hit's Pa," Lem said, "he's takened worse. I'm goin' fer the doctor!"

"I've been afeared o' that," Tom said. "Who's there? Gault?"

Lem nodded. Hattie was already turning to go into the house and get her things. She stopped and said, "Lem, you better let Hod go after the doctor an' you go back with Tom an' me."

"No," Lem said, "no. I'd ruther go myself. You all go on. I'll git back quick as I kin. Lord he'p us if the doctor ain't there." Even as he spoke he jerked the team into the road again.

Hod ran to hitch old Buck to the spring wagon. It would be too slow walking down the trail. By the time he drove around to the front of the house, Hattie and Tom were waiting for him. They climbed in and Hod whipped the horse into a fast trot.

"Keerful, son," Tom warned. "We'll not git there no quicker ifen you run a wheel agin a rock."

When the road dipped down the hill, they had to go carefully, and Hod was impatient of the time it took to ease the wagon down the steep, rocky slope. Then they had to wheel around the schoolhouse in the mouth of the holler and go halfway down the holler again. Hod whipped old Buck to a run the last half mile.

A group of men stood in the front yard, hushed and reverent. They stood aside to let Tom and Hattie and Hod pass through. No one spoke. Why, it's like he was already dead, Hod thought.

Gramma met them at the door and threw her arms around Hattie. "My pore Dow," she cried. "Oh, my pore Dow, Hattie!"

"Hush, now, Ma," Hattie said, patting the grief-racked shoulders and smoothing the hair back from the wet, swollen face. "Hush, now. We'll all do all we kin. An' Lem'll be back with the doctor, soon. You come an' lie down, now, an' let me do fer Pa."

Hod watched her lead Gramma to the bed and tenderly lay her down. She brought a pan of water and took a clean rag and bathed Gramma's face gently. Hod know how easy was her touch and comforting. He knew what strength would flow from those thin, brown hands, and how the bastions of hope and faith would be buttressed by them. He knew what calm would pass from them to Gramma.

Gramma grew still under the gentle hands, and Hattie laid the wet cloth over her eyes. "You rest yerself now."

She straightened and lifted the pan of water. "Hod, you kin empty this. I'll go in an' look at Grampa."

"I'll go in with you," he said. "This can wait."

At the door he had a sickening desire to turn back. He didn't want to see Grampa like this. But Hattie had already gone inside and he made himself follow her. Lizzie was sitting at the head of the bed. She looked up when they entered, and when she saw who it was she moved to let them draw nearer. She put a hand on Hattie's arm and said softly: "He's done fer. He's goin' fast."

Hod swallowed and looked at the bed. Only Grampa's white face could be seen. His great head moved restlessly on the pillow and a froth of bubbles blew in and out of his mouth as the slow, gasping breaths came and went. Hod closed his eyes. He couldn't look.

"You two go on out," Hattie said. "I'll stay with him till the doctor comes."

"I'll stay," said Lizzie. "You was up all night."

"Well, then, Hod, you'n me better go out. They ain't nothin' we kin do right now."

They left Lizzie with Grampa and joined the group that was gathering in the next room. Gault and Becky were there. They went in to see Grampa again, and shortly came out. Becky was sobbing, but Gault was dry and tearless. Hod watched, aching for Gault and Lem and Pa, and aching for himself because this was Grampa who lay in the next room. He felt the common blood stream that tied them all together and bound them in a common kinship. He felt it stretching from him to Becky and Gault, to Lem and Lizzie, to Gramma and Grampa. And it went on back to Abigail and Jeems. And it went into the soil of Piney Ridge, and the trees and the rocks and the river. It went into the corn growing green and tender. It went into fuzzy, pale tobacco leaves. It went out all over the ridge, into every morning's sunrise and every evening's dark. It went out and pulled tight and close all the ways of living on Piney Ridge, by all the people on Piney Ridge, and it came back inside Hod Pierce.

Gramma slept, and there was no sound except the whispers. People came and went. Neighbors stopped and sat for a while and murmured softly to one another and to Hattie and Tom and the others. Hit's too bad. He was sich a good man. We'll not know how to git along without him. Hit's untellin' how Annie'll take it when he goes. God knows it's hard to lose yer man. Seems like some o' yer own life goes into the grave with 'im. Pore Annie. Pore Dow.

Hod moved restlessly about the place. He drew fresh water

88

and drank deeply, but his thirst was not real and the water tasted bitter. When would Lem get here with the doctor? And then he had the hopeless thought, what good would it do, anyhow?

Hattie called him in and set food before him and Tom and the rest of the family. Gramma still slept, worn out with grief and worry. No one ate much, but everyone made a show of swallowing a few bites. No one talked much. It was as if by talking they might shut out the sound they were all listening for. What were they listening for? Hod listened too. What was he listening for? And then he knew. Grampa's labored breathing came through the door like a sobbing undertone of grief. It was a faint sound, dragged out long, dragged in long. It had been there all along, but he had not consciously heard it. Now he knew. They were all listening for it to stop.

He felt a sudden panic that it might stop while he was swallowing this bite of meat, and he wouldn't know. And then he had a deeper fear that he would hear it stop, and he would have to know. He pushed his chair back and went out in the yard. But he was still listening. He felt himself straining to listen. So he went back in the house and sought his chair in the corner out of the way.

Night came on, and Hattie lighted the lamps. Gramma moaned in her sleep, and Hattie and Becky washed up the supper things out in the kitchen. There was a muted waiting — a softened interval of suspense that had no relation to reality. Hod felt the minutes spin out into time, and he drew apart as if he were watching the scene from afar. He himself was a part of the unreality and yet he stood apart and looked on. In a moment now he would find himself at home, sitting on the porch tuning his guitar, or maybe just sitting there, and old Duke, the dog, would be scratching fleas under the floor, making a thumping noise against the boards. In a moment now he would be back, identified with the night and the earth and the stars. He would not be here, waiting on the edge of something intangible and vague and fearful. In a moment now.

And then it stopped. The sobbing, dragging sound through the door stopped. Becky was fanning noiselessly with a folded paper. The paper was caught at the end of its motion, and held, arrested. Her eyes went to the door, as if she could see beyond and, seeing, make the sobbing start again. Hattie lifted her hand toward Hod, but dropped it by her side. Gault was standing by the outside door, and he turned as if to hear better. Tom did nothing. He had been sitting there as still as a stone, except for his right hand which flexed, opening and closing, opening and closing, on his knee. The hand opened, and when the sound stopped, it paused in its flexing a brief second, and then it closed tight and hard. It did not open again.

Hod looked at Tom's fist on his knee. His breath choked in his throat. Open it, Pa! Open it! Open it! He was on his feet and he thought he had shouted the words. And then Lizzie opened the door and her face was wet with tears. "He's gone," she said. No one spoke. Gramma turned in her sleep and moaned once. The sound went inside Hod and shook him, and he stumbled outside into the thick, dark night.

He stopped at the rail fence back of the house and gripped the rough rail tight. He felt its roughness and he closed his hands hard upon it. This is the way death comes. You are breathing, dragging the air into your body and pushing it out again. You are real and warm and living. You can run and swim and laugh and sing. You are brown and lean, and you can swing a hoe in the hot sun. You can feel the tug of the plow in the earth. You can love all the good things of the earth and its seasons. There's all of life ahead of you. And then that sobbing, dragging sound stops, and you are nothing. The world turns and the sun and the moon and the stars are bright, but you are nothing. The corn grows and the fish leap in the river, and the rains fall, wet and silver. Flesh is hurt and bruised and loved. But you are nothing. You, pushed down, unknowing and nothing. You, Hod Pierce, unknowing, forever!

He beat his tight fist on the rail and rejoiced in the hurt. He wanted to feel the hurt deep and lasting. The hurt was real, and he was real if he was hurting. Who is Hod Pierce? A mote of dust on a whirling planet — a breath of air in a cosmic wind — a dust and a breath, lost in forever! The littleness and the awfulness of it pressed him down. This here's Hod Pierce! He pounded it into the rail fence, beating his identity back into himself. This here's Hod Pierce! But the voice inside pushed up and up. Who is Hod Pierce? Who is Hod Pierce?

Grampa was buried on a Monday. He was laid in the Pierce burying ground down in the holler. Abigail and Jeems had buried the first Pierces there, and it was the resting place of all the others who had followed. It was a sweet plot of ground, with honeysuckle and wild roses running rampant over it. And tall trees rimmed it in beneath the hills.

All the Pierces from all over the ridge were there. All were joined together in mourning. The holler was full of Pierces.

Hod stood with his eyes lifted to the hills while the same preacher who had married Irma and John consigned Grampa's body to the earth. Strange. A man of God must join people together, and he must also part them forever. He must begin life, and he must end it. In the beginning . . . Amen.

The preacher's voice was soft: "'While the sun, or the light, or the moon, or the stars, be not darkened, nor the clouds return after the rain: . . . Or ever the silver cord be loosed, or the golden bowl be broken, or the pitcher be broken at the fountain, or the wheel broken at the cistern. Then shall the dust return to the earth as it was: and the spirit shall return unto God who gave it.'"

The first clods of dirt tapped a knocking on the wooden box. Gramma cried out, a high, thin cry, and Becky and Hattie spoke softly to her. She leaned heavily on them, letting her head fall forward, and they supported her gently.

Hod lifted his eyes beyond the open wound in the earth. On a nearby tree a leaf, dried by the heat and wrinkled brown, swung back and forth in the fan of a light breeze. He watched it and shut his mind and ears to the filling of the grave. Back and forth the leaf swung, gaily, saucily. And then a gust of wind snapped the brittle stem. The leaf, free, floated soft as a downy feather toward the ground. The breeze caught it, turned it somersault, puffed it up again, and then ran away. The brown feather drifted into the open scar and lightly came to rest on a lump of dirt. It wavered and tilted, and then it slid a little to one side. The next moment a shovel was emptied, and the leaf was buried.

CHAPTER NINE

AUGUST CAME IN sticky and steamy. Grampa was gone, but life went on. The door of the old cabin was swung shut, and Hod helped the folks move Gramma up on the ridge into Irma's old room. He felt all her grief added to his own, and tenderly he packed the belongings which were so shaped by Grampa's ways and Grampa's living. The old mantel clock. The big wooden bed. The sagging chairs. The ancient, cracked dishes. Some of the things Gramma gave away. But she hugged to herself many more than she could ever use again. Hod knew she had to hold onto them, to keep for herself those things that were so much a part of Grampa. She was keeping a little of him. Hattie too was patient, never warning her there wasn't room for so many things. She set them around the room, and cluttered up the rest of the house with them, letting Gramma cluck over them broodingly.

Hod went to the mill the next Saturday as always, and it was good to sit with the familiar group of men and listen to their talk. They spoke briefly of Grampa. His great strength and his goodness. And his ways.

"Couldn't nobody make a cheer like Dow," said one.

"No, sir, they couldn't nobody tech him when it come to makin' cheers," the rest agreed.

"He'll be missed," another said. "He was a good man." And there was a silence which was a tribute to the big man who had gone on.

Then the miller spoke of other things. "I hear they got a bumper crop o' tomaters over in Indianny this year. Hear they need ever' hand they kin git aholt of."

"What're they payin'?" someone asked.

"I heared Jim Byron say the two Knight boys come home from there last Saturday night, an' they tole they was gittin' ten cents a hamper. He said they claimed they was makin' eight an' ten dollars a day right along."

The circle of men sagely nodded their heads. "That's a right smart bit o' money," they agreed.

"Feller could easy make a hunderd dollars clear in a month

over there," the miller said.

"I could shore use a hunderd dollars cash money right now too," said Jim's neighbor; "wisht I could go."

"Me too," said one of the others, "but I git down in my back so easy I couldn't noways hold up to it."

I don't get down in my back easy, thought Hod. I could hold up to it! I'll go! A hundred dollars! Why, that was a fortune! That much money would be the open door for him. His heart sang. This was the way, finally. He knew it was.

"You say the Knight boys came home last Saturday night?" he questioned the neighbor. "Do they come regularly?"

"Come ever' week," Jim said. "Ride down with Cooper, the produce man, in his truck. He's aworkin' over there too. Haulin'."

"What time do they go back?"

"Late Sunday evenin'."

"Reckon they'd have room for one more goin' back?"

"Don't see why not, ifen you don't mind ridin' in the back."

Hod waited for no more. He had to get out to the Knights' place and talk to someone about it. The Knights lived a scant mile from the Gap, on the Pebbly road, and Hod lost no time covering the short distance. Old Man Knight was sitting on the front porch mending a pair of plow reins as Hod walked up. "You Mr. Knight?" he asked.

"Yep," without looking up from his work.

"Johnny and Slim your boys?"

"Yep."

"They pickin' tomatoes over in Indiana this summer?"

"Yep."

"They come home on week ends?"

"Yep."

"Comin' tonight?"

"Fur as I know."

"Goin' back tomorrow?"

"Ifen they come, they will."

"About what time?"

"Five o'clock."

"Does Mr. Cooper pick 'em up here, or do they meet him somewhere?"

"Meet him at the Gap, front o' Weaver's store." The old man

looked up, spat tobacco juice expertly to one side of the step on which Hod's foot was propped. " Yer a Pierce, ain't ye? Offen the ridge? "

" I'm Tom Pierce's boy," Hod replied.

" Knowed ye wuz a Pierce the minnit I seed ye. Me an' Tom's coon hunted all over that there ridge, many's the time." The knotted old hands fretted with the leather reins. " You thinkin' 'bout goin' over to Indianny with the boys? "

" Yessir. I'd like to get me a job over there pickin' tomatoes too. I heard Johnny and Slim come home every Saturday night with Mr. Cooper and go back on Sunday. I'd like mighty well to go back with 'em tomorrow night."

" Don't know of e'er good reason why ye shouldn't. Tell ye what ye do. You be at Weaver's by four thirty tomorrer evenin' an' I'll tell Johnny to keep his eye out fer ye. Cooper, he won't mind havin' one more. He don't charge the boys nothin' noway. Says he has to come an' he allus likes company. Might be the boys kin git ye on in the same field where they been pickin'. They been doin' right good this year." He shifted his plug of tobacco from one cheek to the other and shot a thin stream of brown juice into the dust.

Hod mulled over the information, then took his foot off the step and straightened up. " Well," he said, " I'd sure be much obliged to 'em for the ride, Mr. Knight, and any help the boys can give me. You tell 'em I'll be there, ready to go." He shoved his hat back, scratched at his head, and settled the hat firmly in place again. " I better be goin', I reckon."

" You ask yer pa ifen he recollects the night him an' Blackjack Knight treed a jug o' moonshine 'stid of a coon, an' see what he says." The old man's stomach heaved as he laughed in recollection. " I could tell you things yore pa an' me done when we was sprouts that'd make yer hair stand on end, young'un," he went on. " Tom wuz allus a lively 'un. Couldn't nobody ever git him to take a dare. We shore had some high ole times them days." He sighed. " But I reckon it's best to leave the past stay dead an' buried. But you be certain an' tell him ye seen me."

" I'll tell him," Hod promised, and opened the gate. " Much obliged, and tell the boys I'll be ready and waitin' for 'em."

After supper that night he was restless, with his plans mulling through his head. He hung around the front porch for a while, then went out to the barn where Tom was mending a plow. He fidgeted awhile, wanting to talk and not knowing how to begin. Tom looked up finally. "Somethin' itchin' you, boy?" he asked.

Hod's breath sucked in. "Pa, I'm goin' over to Indiana to pick tomatoes. I'm goin' tomorrow with the Knight boys. I heard at the mill today they need hands and they're payin' good. I talked to Old Man Knight and he said I could go back with Johnny and Slim and maybe get on at the same place they work."

Tom put his hammer down. He took a plug of tobacco out of his shirt pocket and carefully pared a chunk off one end with his knife. He put it in his mouth and chewed methodically until it was softened before he spoke. "What does yer ma say?"

"I'm not goin' to tell her. She'd just fuss and take on. It'll be better if you tell her after I've gone."

Tom nodded. "She shore ain't goin' to like it none."

"I know she's not, but I've got to go, Pa. I want a chance to make some money of my own, and maybe go to a trade school in Louisville, or something. I don't rightly know just what I want to do. But I know I've got to get away from here and see for myself."

Tom looked at the boy steadily. A broad band of late sunlight lay between them, filled with sparkling dust motes. The barn smelled of hay, and the warm, steamy odor of animals. Tom spoke finally. "Reckon they ain't no way but fer you to go. This has been a long time breedin' in you. I been watchin' it. I don't want to hold you back none. I cain't say as I hold with it, but I've allus said that ever' man's got a right to decide fer hisself what he's goin' to do. Best thing to do is git it outen yer system, I reckon."

"Can you make out without me?"

"Oh, they's allus ways to make out. Gault an' Lem'll he'p with the tobaccer, an' in a pinch I kin allus git Matt Jasper or Old Man Clark."

"Maybe I could come back to help with the tobacco. Or maybe I'll have enough money to help out with."

"We'll make out. I cain't he'p you none with money, but

leastways I kin give you a chancet to make yer own."

Something light rose in Hod. Pa had always been easier than Ma to get along with. All at once he felt a man, a grown man, talking with another man — one who understood, just because he was a man. Hod grinned at his father. "Well, then. You'll tell Ma."

Tom picked up his hammer and hit a strong lick on the plow-share. "I'll tell her."

Hod lingered in the door. "Think I'll go over and see if Lily Mae's at home."

"Better not stay too long," Tom warned. "Tomorrer's goin' to be a big day fer you."

Hod whistled for old Duke and cut across the field back of the barn. The sun slid ponderously down behind the rim of the ridge, and stirred a breeze in its wake. The nightjars started whining, and a bird in the hedge of trees cheeped fretfully. First dark purpled into night as he went, and the breeze blew itself away. It was the dark of the moon, and Hod stepped lightly.

Outside Lily Mae's house he whistled softly. There was a light in the front room and he guessed Lily Mae was there. He whistled again, insistently. The door opened and Lily Mae stood framed in the lamplight.

"It's me," he called. "Can you come out for a while?"

She closed the door behind her and he heard her step on the porch. Then he could hear nothing as she felt her way across the grassy yard. But he could feel her nearness. He could feel it in the prickle of his skin and the familiar quickening of his senses whenever he thought of her or was near her. It poured over him now, and the heady joy of being with her took hold of him. Suddenly she was by his side, and then she was in his arms, pressed against him.

"What you doin' out tonight?" she whispered, when he had lifted his head.

"Tellin' you good-by," he answered, stopping her questions with his mouth.

She let herself go in his arms another moment, her lips soft and moist beneath his. And then she drew away. "Tellin' me good-by?" she asked, running her hand lightly over his hair, drawing one finger down the curve of his jaw.

96

"Don't," he moved his head restlessly. His hands were still on her waist and he shook her gently. "Don't do that."

She laughed and rested her arms around his shoulders, clasping her hands behind his head. "Where you goin', then?"

"To Indiana. To work in the tomato fields."

"When?" And she let her face rest lightly against his cheek. Her hair tickled his ear.

He laughed and pushed her. "Get away from me," he said, and his voice was rough. "You can't keep me from going that way."

"Who said I was tryin' to keep you from goin'? I jist asked you when you was goin'."

"Tommorow."

"Well, that's tomorrer. This is tonight, ain't it?"

"Yeah, this it tonight. But don't forget I'm goin' tomorrow!" He pulled her close, and their talk stopped for a while.

"When'll you be back?" she asked after a time.

"In about a month," he said. He didn't mention the possibility of going to school. No need to get her riled up about that until the time came. Maybe he would be back in a month, anyhow. And if he wasn't, it would be easier to write her the news than to tell her now and risk spoiling their last time together. First from Hattie, and then from Lily Mae, he had learned that with women there are times when it may be healthier not to be completely honest.

The time slipped by as they whispered together, and then the door opened and Lily Mae's mother called. "Lily Mae? You'd best come on in, now. Hit's agittin' late."

Hod let her go with one last, long kiss. "Don't forget you're my girl," he warned.

"I'll not," she promised, "but don't you stay away too long!"

The Knight boys came down the road at about the same time the truck drove up the next afternoon.

"Howdy, Hod," Johnny Knight said. He was a tall, brown boy, with thin flanks and long, lean legs. His shoulders were broad and swaggering, and his body tapered into the hips, coming down straight and powerful. He had a strong, bold face with good features, a clean-swept jaw line, and a nose that hooked slightly over

97

a long upper lip. His mouth had a quirk at the corner, as if he scoffed lightly at himself and the world. His reddish-brown eyes had a merry light in them, a twinkling gaiety which approved life heartily.

" Howdy, Johnny," Hod replied. " Your pa told you I wanted to go back with you, I reckon."

" First crack outta the barrel, he told us. He takened quite a shine to you. Said he wanted we should he'p you all we could."

" He used to know my pa, guess that's why," Hod said. Slim nodded at Hod and went around on the other side of the truck to join Mr. Cooper. Slim's nickname suited him. He was tall, thin, angular. Where Johnny had an easy, careless attitude of good will toward men, Slim was saturnine, inturned, quiet. He seemed much older than Johnny, although actually he was several years younger. Hod was not drawn to him, while instantly he felt at ease with Johnny. " You think I can get on over there? " he asked Johnny.

" Easy," replied Johnny. " They're beggin' fer hands. The to-maters is fallin' off an' rottin' on the ground account o' they cain't git 'em picked fast enough. We'll git you on with the same man we're apickin' fer, an' you kin stay with us. Rooms is hard to find, an' three in a room'll be cheaper on all of us. We'll git the landlady to put you up a cot in with us."

" I don't want to be any trouble, but I'd sure be obliged to you for helpin' me out," Hod said.

" Hit's no trouble. First time you go over to Indianny it's kinda strangelike an' different from home. But ifen you know somebody that knows the ropes an' kin kinda put you onto things, it goes a heap better. You got any money? "

" No."

" Didn't figger you did. Well, you won't need none 'fore you kin draw yer wages. We'll stand good fer yer board an' room till you git paid, an' Ma allus packs us somethin' to take along an' eat on the way goin' back. There's plenty fer you too."

Hod hadn't thought of all these details. He had started out without a penny to his name, his one goal being to get to Indiana, pick tomatoes, and make one hundred dollars. Rather humbly he realized that he was being befriended generously by two boys whom he knew only casually, and he was beginning to understand how much simpler they were going to make things for him. He felt chagrined that they should have to assume responsibility for him, but he was grateful for their willingness to do so.

"I'll sure do my part," he told Johnny. "I can work as hard and as long as anybody, and I'll see to it that the man you work for doesn't regret hiring me. And I won't be any trouble to your landlady, either. A cot in your room will be fine for me. I'd rather have it that way myself. I'm not lookin' for it easy over there."

"Hit's not so bad," Johnny said. "After you git used to it, the days go on all right. C'mon now, I think Cooper's 'bout ready to leave out."

They clambered into the back end of the truck and piled the heavy tarpaulins into one end to make a soft heap. Slim got in front wth Cooper, slammed the door, and the truck moved heavily onto the road. Hod felt a high, exultant singing in his ears and his pulse was beating like a trip hammer. Already the hundred dollars was in his pocket!

After they went through Campbellsville the way was new to him, and he sat quietly watching the country slide by. Fifty miles from the town he began to notice a distinct change in the lay of the land, the quality of the soil, and the kind and sizes of the farms. They were out of the hills and there was only a gentle, rolling swell which stretched off in greater distances than he had ever seen under cultivation. The soil was dark and rich-looking and the pastures were lush and velvety. He saw acres of such pastures, fenced in by neat, cross-board fences, and he saw immense barns and silos and beautiful, picture-book houses.

Johnny spoke. "Ever been up this way before?"

Hod shook his head. "Campbellsville's as far as I've ever been."

"This is good country," Johnny said. "Bluegrass country. All them big farms is rich land. A man makes a mort o' money on one o' them, I reckon."

Hod thought of Pa's stony acres, and the split rail fence around the thin little pasture, and the pitifully patched old barn. His young eyes looked far beyond the voluptuous blue-green grass, back to Piney Ridge. He let his memories linger lovingly on the ridges and the rocks and the thorns. And loyally he thought how the Pierces had come and compelled the ridges and rocks and thorns to make a home. But this was something of what he wanted to see now! This was part of his dream!

It was dark when they reached Louisville and they paused only long enough for him to write a post card to Hattie. Pa would tell her, but he wanted to reach out and lay his own touch upon her. It eased a trembling in him just to write her name. He still belonged somewhere.

To Hod the sprawling city at the falls of the Ohio was only a cacophony of blurred and fantastic sounds, and a mirage of hurrying traffic and neon lights. Then they were across the broad Ohio, leaving the glow of the city behind and spearing the dark of an Indiana highway with the lances of their headlights. Around ten o'clock they reached a little town, and the truck turned off the highway onto a graveled road. It rolled to a stop in front of a shabby frame house.

"Here we are," said Johnny. "Pile out."

Hod grabbed his parcel of clothes, crawled out, and followed Johnny and Slim into the house. "You wait here," ordered Johnny, "an' I'll find Miss Sadie. She'll be out back, more'n likely."

He went off down a narrow, dark hall and Hod stood at the foot of the stairs, shifting uncomfortably from one foot to the other. Mr. Cooper came in and went silently up the stairs. Slim followed him. "Johnny'll git you fixed up," he said as he mounted, "an' I'll see you up in the room."

"Sure," Hod answered. "I'll just wait here." He spoke casually, but he was feeling forlorn and lonely. He looked around as he waited and saw that while everything in the house was worn and shabby, it was also clean. That made him feel better, somehow. It was like finding something Hattie's hand had touched. He told himself: I'll make out. I'll make out fine here.

Johnny came back down the hall and behind him came Miss Sadie. Hod liked her at once. She was a round little lump of a woman, looking friendly and comfortable. She was wiping her hands on her apron. Johnny made a vague motion toward Hod. "That's him," he said.

Miss Sadie laughed a big, easy laugh. "What's your name, son?"

Hod told her.

"Johnny says you're goin' to pick with him an' Slim, an' you want a cot in their room."

" Yessum. If it won't trouble you too much."

" It'll be no trouble at all, if it'll do you. Fact is, it'll have to do you. There's not another room in the house, an' I couldn't take you no other way. But if it suits you, it'll suit me."

" That'll be fine, ma'am. I'll make out all right on a cot. I'd rather be with Johnny and Slim anyhow."

" Well, we'll call it settled, then. Johnny an' Slim pays me fifteen dollars a week for their board an' room, an' I reckon I can come out ahead if you'll pay me seven. You can pay me Saturday night after you get paid. If it's handy, you can pay me for this week and next week too. Johnny said you didn't have no money so I won't press you, an' I'll take their word you're all right. It don't pay to let your bills run too long." She turned to Johnny. " Johnny, you get a cot out of that closet under the stairs an' go on up. I'll bring some sheets up in a minute."

She waddled off, and Hod and Johnny rummaged in the dark little cubbyhole until they found the folding canvas cot. They took it upstairs to the room, where Slim had already gone to bed, and set it up under the windows on one side of the room. By the light of the single hanging bulb in the center Hod could see that the room contained a double bed, a big oak dresser, and two straight chairs. Johnny moved some clothes out of one of the dresser drawers and motioned to it. " You kin have this'n fer yer things."

Hod unrolled his parcel and put his clean shirt, the extra pair of blue denim pants he had brought, and two pairs of socks in the drawer. He slipped them out of sight hastily, aware of their meagerness, and somehow ashamed. He would get him some more clothes when he got paid, he thought.

Miss Sadie knocked and came in with an armful of blankets and linens. " If you'll fold these blankets an' put 'em under you, they'll make a right good mattress," she explained. " An' you'll get clean sheets once a week an' two clean towels. The bathroom's at the end of the hall, but there's no hot water except on Saturday. Johnny, you get him up in time for breakfast in the mornin'." She turned back to Hod. " I hope you'll feel at home here, son, an' I hope you do good with your pickin'."

Hod ducked his head. " Much obliged, ma'am. I'll make out fine."

She closed the door, and Hod set to work making up his bed. Johnny went down the hall to the bathroom and Hod undressed and slipped between the cool fresh sheets. They smelled airy, like Ma's, and he pulled the top one close to make the smell a part of him.

Johnny came back, and after asking Hod, " All set? " turned off the light and shoved Slim over to crawl into bed beside him. Out the window Hod could see the Big Dipper tipping its empty cup over the trees. That would be right over the beech grove at home, he thought.

" Johnny," he whispered hesitantly after a moment.

" Yeah? "

" How far is it home? "

" 'Bout two hundred miles."

The room was quiet and Hod let the full weight of two hundred miles press him flat against the curve of the earth and spin him bleakly into solitude. He was homesick, fiercely and terribly homesick, and he felt trapped and bleeding. This was one of those places he had wanted to see. But it was just a room. Less lovely than his own room at home, with two strangers in the bed a dozen feet away. He wanted to start putting his feet down the trail to the holler. He wanted to see Ma turning down the lamps and latching the screens. He wanted to hear Duke thumping at his fleas under the porch. He wanted the curves of his own straw tick fitting easily around him. He wanted to go home!

CHAPTER TEN

THERE WAS NO DIFFICULTY the next day in getting Hod signed on as a picker. Steady pickers were so hard to get that the farmer merely nodded at Hod and told him to go with Johnny and Slim. He helped them load the truck with empty crates, and then they were driven to the twelve-acre patch that had been assigned to them.

Hod learned that a crew of three or four pickers were assigned to a certain patch at the beginning of the season and they picked it over and over until the peak had passed. Four weeks was an average season. In a large field of tomatoes grown for the canneries the vines were not staked. They spread their growth close to the ground and carpeted the field with a mass of creeping vines and fruit. Every six or seven rows, two rows of vines were pulled together so that the truck could be driven down the field. Cooper drove his truck now down the first of these roads and the boys threw the crates out on either side. Later, as they picked and filled them, they would carry the full crates back to the same road where the truck would pick them up. For each crate of tomatoes, which held about a bushel, they would be paid ten cents. The farmer checked in a load of crates from ⚹3 field, and tallied them. The boys kept a tally too. At the end of the week the tallies were checked and the farmer paid off the ⚹3 crew. The crew kept individual tallies and divided the pay between themselves on that basis.

Hod and the others were at the field by seven o'clock, but by the time they had scattered their crates and settled down to picking it was usually eight, or after. They picked steadily, bent over the low vines, until noon. Then they took an hour in which to eat and get the kinks out of their backs before going back to crouch over the vines again until five thirty. Each man picked as steadily as his cramped muscles would allow, for the amount of money coming to him on Saturday night depended entirely upon the number of crates he could fill.

The first few days in the field were days of sheer agony for Hod. Lean and wiry as he was, and accustomed as he was to hard work, the stooped position welded his muscles into armor plate. To straighten was torture; not to straighten was worse. By midafternoon he was usually working in a semiconscious paralysis of mind and body.

The first day he picked fifty bushels. Five dollars! His board and room were going to cost him a dollar a day, so he actually made four dollars. He was satisfied that night as he eased his tired back onto his bed. He knew that within a week he could step up his picking to seventy or eighty bushels. And if he could clear six dollars a day, he could have his hundred dollars by the time the peak had passed.

About the middle of the week he wrote to Hattie, giving her his address. " This leaves me fine and hoping you're the same," he said politely. Then he told her he was doing fine with his picking and he would be home in three or four weeks. Well, he might go home for three or four days, he defended as he wrote it. It was a meager, skimpy little letter but he felt better when he had written it.

He tried to write Lily Mae too. But her image got in the way. You couldn't write to Lily Mae. You could only . . . well, you could only fill yourself from the fountain of her warmth.

He made thirty-six dollars the first week, which Johnny and Slim told him was good. Better than they had done, they said. He paid Miss Sadie fourteen of it, bought some underwear, another shirt, and a pair of blue denims, and hid fifteen dollars in his dresser drawer. " Now," he said. " Now, I've got started."

Gradually his muscles became accustomed to the crouched position and he learned to ease them without losing time to stop and straighten. Doggedly he whipped his aching back down one long row after another, and he was soon keeping pace with Johnny and Slim. He didn't know whether he would ever eat another tomato or not, but, by golly, he was sure pickin' 'em!

The little town was dirty and dingy and had little to offer by way of amusement. The canning factory was the heart and center of it, and it came to life only during the canning season. Then it was a busy, humming beehive during the day, and a tired, snoring mass at night. Johnny took Hod around the square the first Saturday night he was there, but he saw little to interest him. After all he had been used to the Gap and the blue-denimed farmers all his life. This canning factory crowd which milled the streets on Saturday night was only another section of the same thing.

Week nights the boys were too tired to think of fun. But Miss Sadie had an old banjo in the front room; when Johnny learned that Hod could pick it, he bought strings for it, and each evening, before going up to their room, Hod played and sang awhile.

" Sing ' Barbry Allen,' " Johnny would say.

And Hod would plink out the tune to the long, sad ballad. Johnny never tired of it. " ' Young man, I think you're dyin',' " he went around humming to himself. Hod grew weary of it, but he always sang it.

The second week Hod made forty dollars. He handed Miss Sadie seven and kept three for spending money. That left thirty dollars to bank in the dresser drawer. He counted the forty-five dollars over and over, loving the feel of the bills and exulting in the possession of them. He was feeling fine. He was feeling victorious.

As he was putting the money away, Johnny came in. "Hey," he exclaimed, "how 'bout let's ride as fur as Louisville with Old Man Cooper tonight! I don't feel like goin' down home. Slim, he kin go on if he wants, but I'd ruther see the bright lights myself. Want to?"

Hod's heart leaped crazily. Want to! More than anything he wanted to! But immediately he was sobered by the thought of the money it would take.

"How much'll it cost?" he asked cautiously.

"Five dollars'll do it," Johnny assured him. "C'mon, let's go. Cooper ain't gonna wait all night. He's ready to leave out right now."

Suddenly Hod decided. All right, it would take five dollars. He had allowed himself three for spending money the next week. He'd add two dollars to it and have one grand time in Louisville! And then he'd scrimp all next week. "Goin' just like we are?" he asked.

"Shore, ain't nobody knows us over there noways."

They were off at once. And almost before they knew it they were crossing the bridge into Louisville. Cooper let them off at the foot of the bridge on Main Street.

"This ain't the main part o' town, though," Johnny said. "Hit's further on down."

They wandered down Main to Fourth Street, and up and down Fourth, Jefferson, and Market. Not knowing, Hod thought this was all of Louisville that mattered. It was enough for him, anyhow. He was confused by the rush of traffic, the blaring street noises, the crowds of people hurrying everywhere. He clung tightly to Johnny to keep from being separated from him. He thought that if he lost Johnny he'd just curl up and die. He'd never know which way to turn.

They found a restaurant on Jefferson and had supper. Hod fearfully noted the prices on the right side of the menu. A dollar for his supper seemed terribly high to him. He wanted steak, but the price was too steep for him, so he followed Johnny's lead and ordered ham and French fries. They weren't too good, the ham being stringy and tough and the French fries soggy with grease. But it was something to be eating at a swell restaurant in the city.

When they had finished their supper, they wandered out on the street again, down Jefferson to the Haymarket. The big market square entranced Hod, and he idled down one aisle and up another eying the fine vegetables and farm produce displayed in the stalls. They spent an hour in the market. Then Johnny grew restless.

" C'mon," he said, " we never come to town to spend the time in a market. C'mon, let's find us a movie or somethin'."

If Johnny knew, he didn't tell Hod that the Haymarket area was said to be one of the most vicious in the city. They hadn't gone far before a man sidled up to them. " You boys just come to town? " he asked, his voice coming at them from the corner of his mouth.

Johnny took charge. " Yeah, but we know where we're goin'."

" Well, that's O.K. Just thought if you was strangers in town I could put you wise to a few things. If you want a couple o' drinks, or something, or if you'd like to sit in on a friendly little game, I can take you right there."

" Beat it," said Johnny curtly. And the man slid away down an alley. " He's in the business," Johnny said. " You don't never want to let one o' them git his hooks into you. Ifen you do, you'll wake up in the mornin' with a knot on yer head, all yer money gone, an' a mighty bad taste in yer mouth." And Hod tucked another bit of knowledge away into a corner of his mind.

They stopped at a little theater near Fourth Street and looked at the billboards. They took their time, eying the pictures judicially. Then they decided to go in. This was Hod's first movie. From the time they stepped into the darkness his eyes were glued to the screen. It was a Western and he watched it tensely, every movement being real and personal to him. He was tied in knots when the villain stole the rancher's money and threatened his daughter. And he felt a tremendous relief when the sheriff took the trail after him. He edged forward to grip the arms of the chair when the gunfire grew rapid and the outcome was uncertain. His breath came shallow and fast as the tension mounted, and he leaned back limply when finally right was vindicated and wrong was justly punished. That was the way things should be.

Johnny punched him then, and he pulled himself slowly back to reality. He was loath to leave, but Johnny was already stumbling up the dark aisle. It was difficult, after having projected himself so completely into another world, to come back down to earth. Outside they blinked in the light, and stood for a moment indecisively.

"We got to decide whether we're goin' back tonight or whether we'll stay all night. Ifen we're goin' back, we'd better be gittin' on down to the bus station," Johnny observed.

"Could we stay all night?"

"Shore. I've stayed two, three times. Know right where to git a room. Hit's jist around the corner. You wanna stay?"

"I'd like to. Like to see things in the daylight."

"Well, let's jist git a room an' then we kin scout around all we want to."

In less than ten minutes they had rented a room in the next block. Hod left all the details to Johnny. When the matter was settled, they went out on the street again and stood uncertainly on the corner.

"Reckon we could go to another show," Johnny said finally, tapping his thumb against his chin. "But I git tired settin' so long . . ."

Hod watched the flow of traffic and grew dizzy trying to count the cars. He didn't know how anyone could ever drive in such a mess. And he watched a neon sign advertising fish dinners. A fisherman pulled in a big fish on a taut line. Just as he landed it, the sign went dark. In a few seconds the fisherman started pulling in the same fish all over again. The movement intrigued Hod, and he wondered how the sign was made. But the perpetual motion wearied him, and he felt the pull and tug of the fish in his arm until it ached. It irritated him and made him restless. He shifted on his feet.

Suddenly Johnny grabbed his arm. "I got it. We'll go out to the park. The amusement park. Boy, it's jist like the Fair out there. Whyn't I think o' that sooner! Now we'll jist have a hour or two 'fore it closes, an' it ain't open on Sunday, neither. I don't know how come me to fergit it. C'mon, we'll have to ride the streetcar, an' the best I recollect it's a coupla squares down the street."

Fontaine Ferry was in a beautiful park in the west end of town.

107

Here the Ohio curved in the last loop of the great " S " which it traced around Louisville, and here one of the loveliest of the city's parks had been built. To Hod it was like fairyland . . . the luscious, deep green of the carefully kept lawns, the beautifully landscaped drives and walks, the sweep of the river beyond, the park lights shimmering on its rippling surface. He had been accustomed to the wild, uncontrolled beauty of the hills, but he had never before seen cultivated beauty, clipped and swept and controlled. Fleetingly he thought of the difference between a good huntin' dog and a house cat. Well, there's good in both, he thought. Depends on what you want them for.

The amusement park was off by itself, and it was all Johnny had said it would be. For an hour and a half they whooped and hollered on the roller coaster, the Ferris wheel, and the various other rides. Tickets were only ten cents then, and a dollar or two went a long way. Hod thought he had never had so much fun in his life. Johnny was a gay companion, willing to try anything, and Hod let himself go like a ten-year-old boy. He took into himself the brightness and the gay crowd and the laughter, thinking it would always be a part of him . . . a thing to remember over and over again.

Around midnight they stuffed themselves with hot dogs and ice cream and went back to their room. Hod was dog-tired and he undressed swiftly and crawled into bed. Johnny moved restlessly about the room, fiddling with the window shades, the light cord, an ash tray on the dresser, until Hod was in bed.

" Think I'll go out fer a while," he muttered then. " I ain't sleepy. If I don't git back right straight, don't worry."

" O.K.," Hod answered from the pillow, too sleepy to wonder, and Johnny clicked out the light and was gone.

When Hod awoke in the morning, Johnny was snoring on his side of the bed and his breath was faintly sour and acrid. Hattie's strictness had kept Hod pretty much at home, but he knew what morning-after liquor smelled like. Tom kept a bottle in the barn most times, and nipped along on it occasionally. Once or twice in his life Hod had seen him roll into bed pretty full, and he remembered the stale, sour smell of his breath the next day.

He wrinkled his nose now as he caught the odor from Johnny. So that's what he was going out for! Well, best let him sleep then.

108

He wouldn't wake of his own accord until around noon. That would give Hod a chance to get out and see something on his own.

He dressed quickly and went back to the same restaurant for breakfast. His money was running short, so he had doughnuts and coffee, which didn't fill him up but eased the emptiness in his stomach.

First he wanted to see the river. So he asked a policeman on the corner for directions. He was surprised to learn it was only three short blocks to the river front, and he coasted lazily down the hill, slipping on the cobblestones when he came to the end of the walk. An excursion boat was loading passengers for its first trip up-river. The fare was fifty cents, and the boat went as far as Ten Mile Island upstream. Hod counted his money. He had a dollar bill and a dime. Well, if he ran short he'd borrow from Johnny, or hitch a ride back to Indiana. He had to go on this boat!

The old *Island Queen* tooted its whistle one last time. The dock hands upped the gangplank, and the cumbersome, high-decked stern-wheeler backed laboriously away from the dock. Hod found a place on the deck near the wheel, where he could watch the huge paddles turn slowly, lifting their burdens of water and spilling them in a fall of sun-shattered cataracts. He was held rooted to the deck, feeling the surge of power trembling beneath him. It communicated itself to him, becoming part of him, tracing its quivering finger through his legs and up into his chest and arms. He lifted his head with sudden exaltation of his own oneness with the boat, the water, and the upward push against the current. His breath came deep out of his chest and a wave of sheer joy swept over him.

Downstream the river spread before him, widening to the Indiana shore. In his mind he traced the map. Down there, not too far, the Green slipped into the Ohio. The same Green that flowed heedlessly through the hills of home, and that gentled itself on the breast of the broad, low, flatlands around the ridge. He was sorry the trip didn't take him south, so he could ride buoyantly over the confluent flow of the Green and the Ohio. You couldn't tell one from the other, he thought. But he would know they were all there.

His questing mind then followed the stream on down the map

109

to Cairo, where it joined the Mississippi. So many times he had traced the course in his geography that he could see the twists and turns and looping bends the great river made, until finally it broadened and emptied into the sea. The sense of the mightiness of the water concourse gripped him, and made him strain his eyes to look far and hungrily into the distance. He was going to see it all someday. He felt the distance eating at him with a lonesome, homesick ache and his heart thumped painfully, until a comforting thought came to him. He would never really be far from home. For on whatever land he stood, if water from the eastern ocean touched its shore, a drop of Green River would be lapping, salted and transfused, but remaining yet unchangeably an emerald droplet that had known the hills.

That night, back in his bed at Miss Sadie's, with Johnny and Slim deeply asleep nearby, he went over the evening and morning in Louisville, and he sorted out the things he wanted to keep. The market . . . that was good. The thrill of his first movie . . . that too was good. The clear, sparkling fun of the amusement park . . . oh, yes, that was good. But the best was the river. High above everything else flowed the river . . . into his sleep and his dreams. All the rest but these he rejected.

CHAPTER ELEVEN

Tom turned the horse into the back lot and slapped his sweaty flanks to move him out of the path. He lifted the gate to swing it shut, and the pain which had been a dull ache in his side all day caught him again. He eased to it, and drew in his breath. He and old Buck had been dragging logs up from the lower woods lot, and he had fought a creeping nausea all afternoon. "Hit's the heat," he told himself. "Man gits my age he cain't stand as much as he oncet did. Jist take it easy," he warned himself. But the pain nagged at him constantly.

Now the day was over and there remained only the evening chores. Then he could stretch out on the bed and let the blessed relief of stillness have him. He went to the barn. Even in his pain it never occurred to him to neglect his chores. This is the way of a man on the ridge. He must take care of his animals. They must be brought in out of the weather; the barn must be kept clean and the water must be kept fresh. So Tom forked down the hay, doubling over the long handle and stopping when the pain took him sharply.

He ate little supper, the odor of the food making his stomach rise and fall uneasily.

"You ailin', Tom?" Hattie asked sharply.

"Don't feel none too good," he admitted. "They's a pain in my side been abotherin' me all day. Facts is, hit's been comin' an' goin' two or three days. Seems like it's sorta settled down in my right side, though, today."

"Likely you need a good physic. You go lie down an' I'll fix you one."

Tom eased himself down on the bed, his hand gently massaging his sore side. Hattie allus knowed what to do, he thought, comforted. Hattie was allus good with the sick. There was the tinkle of a spoon against glass, and then she was beside him, holding out the dose she had been mixing. He swallowed it and belched sickeningly.

"By gum, that stuff is shore bitter!" he complained. "Ifen its taste is any sign of its strength, hit orta work. Powerful enough to cure a sick mule, seems like."

"Well, ifen it's that powerful, it orta cure a sick man, then," Hattie retorted. "Git yerself straightened around there, an' let me git yer shoes offen you."

He twisted himself carefully around on the bed, and Hattie slid his shoes and socks off. Even when there was acid in her voice, there was gentleness in her hands.

It was a miserable night. Time and again the physic roused Tom, and each time he must pull himself out of the bed and walk, doubled over with pain, to the outhouse. The pain was sharp now, sharp and heavy, like hot hammers beating in his side.

In bed, between trips, he tossed restlessly and moaned constantly. Hattie built a fire in the kitchen stove and heated water. Then she wrung out hot cloths and laid them against his side. His skin was so hot that when she touched him she drew back involuntarily. It felt thin, and dry and papery, and it burned like a

111

stove lid heated by a slow fire.

When dawn finally came, gray and stealthy and languid, Hattie left Gramma with Tom and hurried down the road to Gault's. Smoke tailed out of their chimney and hung hazily in the still air. They were eating breakfast.

"Tom's sick, Gault," she said, her breath shallow and rapid. "You better go fer the doctor."

Without a word Gault rose from the table and reached for his hat. He had known Hattie a long time now. She was afraid. He could feel her fear, alive and swarming in her, coming over from her to him. If Hattie was afraid, there was need to be afraid, and he had best move in a hurry. "I'll make the best time I kin," he promised.

But it was noon before he was back with the doctor. Meanwhile Tom's suffering had increased until he was jackknifed in the bed, unable to straighten out, and he was delirious with fever. About the middle of the morning the fever went down unaccountably and the pain subsided. Sweating in his relief, Tom dropped off into a deep sleep, after assuring Hattie first: "Hit's better now. Likely the worst has passed." And Hattie went weak with relief herself.

When the doctor came she apologized for having troubled him. "He's a sight better now. He's asleepin'."

The doctor, however, waked Tom and examined him, probing around the sore side, and questioning him. Hattie, at first reassured, took fresh fright when she looked at the doctor's face. "Ain't it passed?" she asked.

The doctor shook his head. "Hattie . . . and Tom may as well hear this too . . . I'm afraid he's got a ruptured appendix. It may be that the attack has just passed, but the sudden easing of the pain and the drop in temperature are very suspicious. So suspicious, in fact, that we'd better get him to the hospital as soon as possible."

If the doctor had hit her suddenly, Hattie's stomach couldn't have sustained a harder blow. But she stiffened herself and laid a hand on Tom's shoulder. "What'll they do to him?" she wanted to know.

"Operate, more than likely."

"I don't hold with goin' under the knife," Gault spoke up

112

sharply. " Hit's agin nature."

The doctor waited.

" I hold with e'er thing that'll he'p Tom," Hattie said, her voice flat and level. " Ifen the doctor says this is the way it's got to be, then we'd best git busy."

The doctor smiled at her. He had seen these hillwomen face such things before, beating down their fear, stiffening themselves against an unknown danger. Hardly ever did they ask questions. When you told them what must be done they suffered it stoically and patiently. In the hospital they would sit long, long hours in the corridors. Waiting. Waiting. Never bothering nurses or doctors. Just following every move they made with their eyes. Their faces and their bodies would endure all things, but their eyes cried their fear. Tomorrow Hattie would wait in the corridor just that way. If the operation were necessary, she would sit out the long hours, neither asking nor receiving comfort. These hill people had a pride that repelled the comforting word or hand. Inside themselves they found what they needed, or else they did without.

" Make him as comfortable as you can in the back of Gault's wagon," the doctor said, " and when we get to the Gap we'll get a truck to take him on into town. I'll go ahead and make the necessary arrangements at the hospital."

When they got to the hospital, the surgeon examined Tom and confirmed the doctor's diagnosis. He told Hattie they would operate immediately. It was then, while they were preparing Tom for the operation, that she slipped out to a drugstore next door and bought paper and pencil and wrote Hod a short note. That was on Saturday.

On Monday night Miss Sadie handed him the letter as he came in from the field. When he saw it was from Hattie, he was faintly uneasy. Even at that distance he could feel Ma's iron hand. He took it up to his room and opened it. " Dear Hod," she wrote, " Tom's been took real sick and we've got him at the hospital at the county seat. The doctor says he's got to be operated on. You will have to come home and help out."

Hod looked at the words — words which snatched his hundred

113

dollars away from him — and thought numbly: I might have known! I might have known it wasn't meant for me! High and mighty notions are not for Pierces! There's no use trying to be different. There's something stronger than I am pulling at me.

He picked up the letter again, and suddenly the full import of the words struck home. Pa was sick! Hospital! Operation! What was he mooning around for! He had to get moving in a hurry! He yelled for Johnny and feverishly began throwing his clothes together.

"How's the quickest way to get home?" he asked when Johnny came running.

"Git home? Now?" Johnny said, in amazement.

"Now," said Hod. "I've just had a letter from Ma and she says Pa's bad sick and they've got him in the hospital at the county seat. I've got to get there quick!"

Miss Sadie had come panting up the stairs behind Johnny. She sat down on the edge of the bed and fanned herself with her apron while she got her breath.

"Quickest way's to take the next bus to Louisville," she said, gasping out the words. "Johnny, you run down to the store where the bus stops and find out when the next one goes through. Seems to me like there's one due pretty soon. You can change right there in the same station in Louisville," she added to Hod, "and take the bus home. What you reckon's the matter with your pa?"

"Ma didn't say. She said he was goin' to have an operation. Must be something pretty bad for him to need an operation." Hod was trying to roll his clothes into a compact bundle as he talked, but there were a few more of them now, and they made an unwieldy package which kept slipping loose.

"Here, Hod," Miss Sadie said, heaving herself up. "Let me get you a box to put them things in."

While she was gone, Hod counted his money again. Forty-three dollars, and he had eight coming to him for today's picking. He was wondering how he could get that when Johnny came back.

"Next bus comes through at seven thirty. Jist about a hour from now," he reported. "You got plenty o' time."

"Much obliged, Johnny. Say, Johnny, will you tell Carson why I've gone, and ask him to mail me the eight dollars I've got comin' for today's work?"

114

"Shore," answered Johnny, and then: "Well, wait a minnit! They ain't no sense in that. I'll give you the eight now, an' keep yore part Saturday night to pay myself back." And he peeled eight one dollar bills off the roll he carried in his pocket and handed them to Hod.

Hod took them and added them to his own small roll. "Much obliged, Johnny."

"Fergit it. I don't stand to lose nothin' by it."

Miss Sadie bustled back with a box into which she packed his clothes. Then she tied it expertly and tightly. "There," she said, "that'll hold till you get there. And here's five dollars. You're due that much back on your board this week. Better come on down to the kitchen now and eat some supper before you go."

Hod added the five dollars to the rest of his money wordlessly. He looked at Miss Sadie and there was a shine in his eyes, but there was a lump in his throat which blocked the words. She patted his arm. "Come on, now, and eat something."

Fifty-six dollars he had now. It would take three or four to get home on the bus. Say fifty dollars he had left. But Pa might be in the hospital a long time. He wished he had back the money he had spent on the new clothes, and in Louisville. He had been unthinking for certain.

Miss Sadie and Johnny went to the store with him. They said very little but Hod felt their sympathy like a warm arm laid around his shoulder. As the bus came in sight, Miss Sadie touched his arm gently. "Hod," she said, "I'm sure sorry. I'm sorry two ways. It's bad your pa is sick, but I'm thinkin' too about what you wanted to do with your money. I know how bad you wanted to go to Louisville."

Hod looked at her quietly before he spoke. "You've been awfully good to me, Miss Sadie, and I'm much obliged to you. But don't you worry about what I wanted to do with that money. When there's trouble, I reckon things like that just don't seem very important. The money, it'll come in handy right now, and I only wish it was more. I'll make me another chance someday. Maybe I'll be right back up here pickin' tomatoes next summer. I've sure liked stayin' with you, Miss Sadie, and I think maybe I'd have got fat on your cookin' in another week or two."

"It'll take more'n my cookin' to fatten you up, son," she said.

"But there's the bus, now. Try not to worry, and let us hear from you how things go along."

"I will, ma'am. Good-by. Good-by, Johnny. Next time I see you I hope you've learned more of 'Barbry Allen' than just about the young man dyin'!"

He swung himself up into the bus and was wheeled away in the night.

The trip home, with its change and two-hour wait in Louisville, was tedious. The urge for hurry was riding him hard. His mind wouldn't turn loose of Hattie's short message, and he kept seeing Tom, sick and drawn, in the hospital. What had happened inside of Tom to strike him down so quickly? He saw Tom lying still and lifeless, and the knife drawn fine down the white of his skin. He's real bad, Hattie had said. Maybe by now he was like Grampa. Nothing but the husk of a man. He shuddered away from that thought.

At the hospital, when he told them who he was, they directed him to Tom's room. Hattie was sitting stiffly in a straight chair by the window. Hod's breath sucked in when he saw her. He didn't know what he had expected, but the sight of her still, unbending figure gave him courage. Tom lay strangely quiet in the unfamiliar bed.

In whispers Hattie told him what had happened. "He was took with a pain in his stummick, Tuesday I reckon it was, an' I give him a good, big dose o' physic. But seemed like hit jist make him worse. He was jist doubled up with the hurtin', so I went for Gault. When Gault got there, Tom, he was outen his head with fever. I never seen nobody so hot an' dried out. Gault, he went as fast as he could fer the doctor, but it takened him a spell to git there an' back. Seemed like by then Tom was restin' some better. He'd quieted hisself down some, an' felt a heap cooler to tetch. But the doctor, he acted wearied like. He said it sounded to him like his appendix was busted, an' we'd have to git him in to the hospital as quick as we could. We fixed him up a bed in the back o' the wagon, an' takened him in to the Gap, an' a feller with a truck brung us on into town. They cut into him right straight, an' the doctor was right. Hit had busted wide open, an' now they say

116

they's some sort of infection. I don't rightly know what kind, but he ain't come to hisself sincet we been here."

" What's to be done now? "

" Nothin'. They done the best they could. Nothin's to do now but wait. Hit's in the Lord's hands now."

Hattie's face was still, but her hands smoothed at the blanket on Tom's bed. Like Gramma pickin' at Grampa's coverlet. Hattie was hurt through with Tom's hurt now.

So began the long vigil. Tom's body was strong and it fought valiantly, but the poison had got a mighty hold on it. For days it seemed that no power would keep the infection from having its way. In the little hospital doctors and nurses worked day and night over him, and Hattie left his side only when she was too exhausted to stay awake any longer.

Hod went on home. Someone had to take care of the stock and see to things. Irma came over and did what she could, but she couldn't leave John and her own home for long at a time. Lizzie and Becky and other neighbor women brought food almost daily, and Lizzie took the soiled clothes home with her to wash and iron. Gramma kept the house clean and cooked a little and redded up the kitchen. The menfolks came too, and put in a day in the tobacco or corn. Hod took it all into himself. The kindness. The friendliness. The brotherliness. Piney Ridge folks, he thought, are knit so close together that what is one man's suffering must needs be another's also.

The day finally came when they knew for certain that Tom would live, and it seemed to Hod that the earth turned a little truer on its axis. Not long after, he made the trip to bring Tom and Hattie home. He stopped in the office of the hospital to talk with the doctor and the superintendent. Some arrangement must be made about the tremendous bills he knew had been accumulating. The total staggered him, even though he thought he was prepared for it. A hundred and fifty dollars to the hospital, and the doctor bill was another hundred. That was the surgeon's bill. The doctor from the Gap would probably take his out in eggs and butter.

Hod knew the hospital bill had been pared down almost to the

117

costs. But it had been an expensive illness at best. He had no idea how they were ever going to pay it. The doctor and the surgeon were sitting in the office as he studied it over. All he could say, finally, was, "We'll try to pay you a little along as we go till we get it all paid."

The doctor laid a hand on his shoulder. "When Tom gets on his feet again, you'll make out. Don't fret too much about it."

Hod reached in his pocket and pulled out his small roll of bills. "Here's fifty dollars now, and I reckon we can pay a little more when the tobacco's sold."

The doctor looked a long time at the stern young face. Then, without comment, he took the money from the hands that shook only the least little bit as they offered it. He knew that this was a sacrificial offering.

CHAPTER TWELVE

Tom's recovery was slow. The poison seemed to have inched its way into every part of his system, used it ruthlessly, and left it drained of strength and vitality. For weeks he could do little more than creep around the house, breathless at the slightest effort, and complaining constantly of pain in his legs. Work of any sort was out of the question.

Hod cut the tobacco, working grimly from dark to dark, sweating to get it into the barn. If it cured rapidly enough, he could strip it and get it to the early market. The early market generally paid the best prices, and this year they had to have the best prices. Hattie's jars, on which they leaned so heavily during the winter, were half empty, because Tom's illness had come in the middle of the canning season. That meant they must buy more food from the store than usual. Tom had to have a tonic, a golden elixir of two dollars in solution, every other week. And there was always the debt to the hospital and the surgeon.

That debt walked through the days with Hod. Its harsh reality drove him brutally, dogging him and whipping him with lashing authority. It could be whittled down only a few dollars at a time, and the tremendous total laid claim to so long a stretch of time. There was nothing to do but settle the harness of debt to his back and bend himself to the aching years ahead. It never occurred to him to do anything else. It never occurred to Tom and Hattie that he should do anything else. Tom laid down the troublesome load of responsibility and Hod picked it up. It was that simple.

The economic system on the ridge was elementary. You raised tobacco and you sold it, and you made do with the money you received. What influenced the price and how it was controlled was a mystery. Some years the price was good, and you had a little more; some years the price was bad, and you pulled in your belt and made out the best you could.

But when Hod's tobacco went on the floor at the warehouse that winter, he was stunned by the price it brought. When the entire crop brought less than two hundred dollars, he stood fingering the check numbly. What was happening that good burley could sell so low?

He cashed the check and took the money home to Hattie. She would have to dole out the cash for only the absolute necessities and make it go as far as she could. One thing was certain. Nothing of that slim hoard could be spared to pay on the debt. One more year must be added to the total.

The winter was harshly interminable. Hod worked at every odd job he could get. He cut timber for the sawmill, freezing his hands and face in the bitter winds until the sawmill closed down. Then he split rails for Little Wells's lower pasture fence — split rails until he felt as if he had split his insides loose. He cut and sawed wood and carted it into town to sell. He strung a line of muskrat traps, and ran them in the frozen dawns when his body shook so hard with the cold, and his hands in the icy water turned to such rigid lumps, that he couldn't release the traps. He hunted coons at night, skinned them, and dried their pelts to be sent off along with the muskrats. He did anything and everything to make three, four, or five dollars to add to the dwindling store of cash. Everything but make moonshine, and he grimly considered that. He kept going, somehow, because his lean, gaunt tiredness was all that stood between them and hunger.

But that winter was only a beginning. A whole country was sick and the years of famine were upon the face of the earth. There were long winters of scrabbling like an animal for scraps, pride crawling before the goad of necessity. There were blistering summers of working the tomatoes, running a feverish race of energy against time. The bony spikes of Piney Ridge wore Hod's soul to a keening thinness, and hope was a thing he had forgotten.

Tom laid his hand on Hod's shoulder one day. "Boy, I ain't heared you hollerin' at that ole cliff in a time an' a time! You done fergot yer Hod Pierce?"

Hod lifted the shoulder wearily. "I've not forgotten. But there's not much use remindin' myself."

The summer he was twenty-one Hod came home from working in the tomatoes in Indiana so worn that even to himself he seemed but a shadow. His skin felt dry and drawn, and his bones were painfully sharp. Hattie was alarmed. "Hod," she said, "yer so thin you kin read a newspaper through yer ears! Didn't you have nothin' to eat up there this year?"

"Same as always," he shrugged. "I'm just tired. Don't sleep good, and I don't seem to want anything to eat much."

"Well, you jist rest up a spell, now that yer home agin."

Rest up a spell! How was he ever going to rest again! Each day that dawned prodded him on. Night brought no surcease. There was never any letup. He was racked and strung daily. The tomatoes had paid practically nothing this year, and for all his backbreaking labor he had less than forty dollars to show for the whole season. Tobacco was still to cut, although there was hardly any use cutting it, it would bring so little. Rest up a spell! What was rest?

On Friday Little Wells came by and stayed for dinner. In the summer like this they fared pretty well for food. Hattie's garden could be depended upon to dish up green beans, tomatoes, and corn throughout the season, and the table held plenty for all.

"Well, Hod, how was the tomaters this year?" asked Little Wells.

"Not much good," Hod said, shoving his chair back from the table. "Only paid four cents a bushel, an' a man can't pick enough to do much more than come out even at that price."

They went out to look over the tobacco field. "Looks purty good," said Little Wells. "Growin' tall, an' they's been enough rain, fer a wonder, this year."

120

"Much good'll come of it," said Hod bitterly. " It won't bring hardly enough to pay for loadin' it into town."

"Well, things is bound to git better sometime. I allus say, when they git so bad they cain't git no worse, they've got to take a turn fer the better. An' I'd say they cain't git no worse'n they are this year."

"I sure hope you're right!"

"Anyhow, I'm glad yer home agin. They's some folks comin' over to our place tonight fer a little practice singin', an' I thought mebbe you could come an' he'p out. We got a new songbook, an' they's some mighty good songs in it. We aim to try to learn a few 'fore meetin' tomorrer. Reckon you could come?"

"Don't know of any reason why not."

"We'll be lookin' fer you then. Any time after supper that suits."

"I'll be there."

After supper he shaved and put on a fresh shirt and walked across the pasture. It had been hot during the day, steamy and sticky hot, but, with the sun almost down, the earth was resting and cooling off. A blue haze hung over the beeches when he cut through the woods, and he loosened his shirt collar to let a wispy breeze play around his throat. The ground was springy and easy under his feet, and he wished for time to stop and sink his weary body into its darkness. He felt as if it would go on down and down, and then he could rest.

Across the clearing Little Wells's shabby frame house looked like a sodden slattern. The front porch sagged and the steps were splitting away from it. Paint peeled in scabrous patches from the siding, and there were cardboard squares in several of the windows. Hod supposed the children had broken the panes and Matildy had stuck the cardboard in to make do for the time being. But they gave the house a leering look. Matildy met him at the door and pushed the battered screen open for him.

"Here's Hod," she called to Wells, "and he's brung his gittar! I tole Wells I was hopin' you would. I ain't heared you play all summer. Some o' the others has done come, an' yer girl's asettin' over there on the davenport awaitin' fer you. Looks like you could a went by fer her."

"I didn't know she was comin'," he said, his eyes moving past Matildy into the dim room and to Lily Mae. Lily Mae had been

121

his girl for a long time now. The slow years had yoked them in the familiar pattern, and they and the ridge took the situation for granted.

As he walked across the uncarpeted floor, she made room for him beside her, but said nothing. Ferdy Jones was already there on the other side of the room, and one or two others. Gault and Becky came in soon after Hod, and Becky slipped wordlessly into a chair beside the door. She gets thinner and quieter all the time, thought Hod.

Matildy lighted the lamps and placed them around the room, and Little Wells passed out the songbooks. Lily Mae held Hod's book because he needed both hands for his guitar.

"This looks like a good 'un," said Wells, and he called out the number. When they had all found it, he cleared his throat and hummed a tone.

And they were off, feeling their way through the first line or two. You've got to live your religion every day, the song said. Not just on Sunday, but on Monday, Tuesday, Wednesday, Thursday, Friday, and Saturday. Every day. It's too fast, thought Hod, fingering the strings nimbly, trying at the same time to bring his bass in when Little Wells expected it. Lily Mae's alto beside him was strong and sure. But he never had liked a song that raced itself. To get real harmony you needed time for all the parts to blend into each other.

When they had finished, Little Wells shook his head. "Takes all the wind outen a feller, that 'un does. Let's try another'n. Ferdy, you pick one this time."

Ferdy picked one, a slower one, and they achieved a real melody this time. I'll meet you in the morning, the words promised, with a how do you do! They liked it and tried it again and again. There was a strong part for the bass in this one, and Ferdy kept motioning for Hod to bring it out.

The evening wore on through song after song. New ones, over which they stumbled awkwardly, and the old, familiar ones which brought ease from the harrying burdens of the day. "Rock of Ages." "Amazing Grace!" "Sweet Hour of Prayer." In song, they who were "weary and heavy-laden" brought their loads to "the everlasting arms," which gave them an hour of rest. Long after their voices were tired, they kept on singing, loath to put away these moments of peace, this evening of release.

But finally Gault said they must go. " Have to git up early in the mornin'," he said, " an' ifen I stay up too late at night, I'm druggy the next day." Becky nodded, and followed him out the door.

" I'll walk home with you," Hod told Lily Mae. He leaned his guitar in the corner by the davenport. " If it won't trouble you too much to bring it to meetin' tomorrow night, Wells, I'll just leave my guitar here."

" Shore, shore," Wells chuckled. " You'll likely be needin' both arms on the way home! "

Hod grinned, but made no answer. Lily Mae came through the bedroom door, with Matildy following. " Tell yer ma," Matildy was saying, " that ifen she'll sleep with a dirty sock tied around her neck, hit'll ease that sore throat o' her'n. Many's the time I've did it, an' I've never saw it fail."

" I'll tell her," promised Lily Mae. " You ready, Hod? "

They said their good nights and went out the rickety screen, down the unsteady steps, and across the trodden-down yard to the path that led to the woods. The moon was up, and until they reached the woods, it made a bright road for their feet. But in the woods it could not penetrate the heavy foliage, and all was shadow. Hod's feet knew the path so well that he needed no light to follow it, but Lily Mae stumbled when it pitched down-ward suddenly.

Hod steadied her with his hand on her arm. She laughed as she recovered her footing. " Reckon you'd ort to of brung yer lantern 'stid o' yer gittar! " she teased.

He let his arm rest lightly about her waist. She slipped her arm around him and they went on down the dim path. " There was a time," he said, " when you asked me to bring my guitar, remember? "

She leaned back against his arm to look up at him. " Hit's been a time an' a time sincet then, though," she said.

Hod brushed a dried blackberry cane from the way. " Mind the thorns," he said automatically, his thoughts going back and back to that night so long ago. So many long weary years ago. So many lifetimes ago. Back to when he was young and gentle and full of dreams. Had he ever dreamed? Had he ever hoped there might be a way? Had he ever been young and tireless?

123

Forever, it seemed to him, he had been stooped under the cruel load of necessity. He had almost forgotten there had ever been yesterday, and he had entirely given up hope there might be tomorrow! "Yes," he said, and there was a wistfulness in his voice. "Yes, that was a long time ago," and the frailty of his words on the night air sounded his renunciation. They were softly said, and, as softly, the darkness swallowed them and they were gone. And with them went the ghost of his dreams.

Arm in arm they came out of the woods, crossed the pasture, and followed the road to Lily Mae's. Hod felt no inclination to talk and he let Lily Mae's chatter fall unheeded on his ears. At the gate he took her in his arms and kissed her briefly. She pulled his head back down when he would have let her go. "Hod, why don't we git married?" she whispered.

He took her hands away, but he held them gently and swung them back and forth. "How can we?" he asked. "There's Ma and Pa and Gramma already over there dependin' on me. We couldn't set up by ourselves, and you'd not like livin' with Ma."

Lily Mae pulled her hands away. Her voice when it came was sharp. "Ifen you loved me, you'd find a way." She moved toward the house. "I'm agittin' tard o' this waitin', Hod."

He leaned against the gate and felt all his tiredness drain down to his feet. All his tiredness and his hopelessness. All right, he thought. All right. I'll try to find a way. But as he turned away into the night, he knew it was useless. He even knew that he was not too sorry it was useless.

CHAPTER THIRTEEN

THE DAYS OF THE AUTUMN PASSED. At home things were not much different. Tom was not ill, but he was never very strong. He tired easily so that he could help only with the simplest chores. His shoulders stooped now, and his neck looked stringy and thin. Sometimes, looking at him, Hod thought he looked as old as Grampa.

Hattie too was thinner and more bent. But it was as if she had only stripped herself down for a long race. She worked constantly to make the little they had go as far as it would. She patched and turned and darned their clothes as long as they held together by a shred. She raised her own seed and made her gardens each year, and she found ways to can and preserve everything that grew in them. Nothing was wasted. Nothing was thrown away. Nothing was bought that could be done without. She seemed possessed of a holy zeal to make do, to eke out, to drink the last grim drop of poverty's threatening cup.

On Saturday nights Hod bathed, put on fresh clothes, saddled old Buck if he hadn't been worked too hard that week, and rode over to see Lily Mae. He walked if the horse was too used up. Lily Mae was still his girl. She had never once referred to that dark, summer night. It was a closed chapter for them both.

One Saturday night she met him, excited, flushed, and eager. " I was hopin' you'd git here early tonight," she said. " They's to be a housewarmin' over to Mort King's place. I'd like a heap to go."

Hod warmed to the sparkling glow on her pretty, heart-shaped face. He laid a cool hand against her cheek. "We'll go if you want to," he said. Lord knows, neither one of us has much fun, he thought.

It was a mile down the Gap road to Mort King's new house, and they could hear the sounds of the party before they came in sight of it. On the night wind the singing voices were carried far:

> " ' Skip, skip, skip to m' Lou,
> Skip, skip, skip to m' Lou,
> Skip, skip, skip to m' Lou,
>   Skip to m' Lou, my darlin'. ' "

" O Hod, hurry," Lily Mae pleaded. " They're playin' ' Skip to M' Lou,' an' we'll miss out on it! "

He caught her hand and they ran the last hundred yards, joining the circle out of breath but in time to share in the game.

> " ' Lost my girl now what'll I do?
> Lost my girl now what'll I do?
> Lost my girl now what'll I do?
>   Skip to m' Lou, my darlin'.
>
> " ' I'll get anothern, prettier, too,
> I'll get anothern, prettier, too,
> I'll get anothern, prettier, too,
>   Skip to m' Lou, my darlin'. ' "

125

An old man was dragging the tune out of an ancient fiddle, and the people chanted the words and beat out the time with their hands. Skip, skip, round the circle, choose a partner. Skip, skip, round the circle, choose a partner. Skip, skip, round the circle, choose a partner. It was such a nonchalant tune; such a gay, uncaring tune. "'I'll get anothern, prettier, too.'"

> "'If ya can't get a redbird, a bluebird'll do,
> If ya can't get a redbird, a bluebird'll do,
> If ya can't get a redbird, a bluebird'll do,
> Skip to m' Lou, my darlin'.

> "'Skip, skip, skip to m' Lou,
> Skip, skip, skip to m' Lou,
> Skip, skip, skip to m' Lou,
> Skip to m' Lou, my darlin'.'"

The fiddler drained off the last notes from his strings, and the crowd stood getting their breath and fanning their hot, perspiring faces.

"All right, now," bellowed a hoarse voice from the porch, "sets in order!"

There was a scurrying as the squares formed. The fiddle whined up. The caller lifted his voice: "Salute yer lady, an' it's eight hands round!" Then the fiddle broke into the audacious tune, "Little Brown Jug."

"Oho!" someone yelled. "Bird in the cage!" Everyone laughed. The dust in the hard-packed yard shuffled up, under the prancing feet.

> "First top couple to the right

> "Circle four!

> "Bird in the cage, shut the door,

> "Bird flies out, crow flies in
> Crow flies out, bird gits a spin!

> "Swing her in the middle
> An' six hands round!"

When Hod swung Lily Mae, her long, wheat-colored hair flew out behind her, and her skirts whirled until the backs of her knees

126

gleamed white. She was a good dancer, he thought. Always sure of the figure, always ready for the next step. And she loved it! Her head was high and her foot was light, and her laugh rang out from time to time clear and sparkling above the music. He was glad she was having a good time.

> " First side couple to the right
>
> " Circle four! "

On around the square the call went until the dance was over. " Draw yer breath, now, while Clem rests his fiddle a minnit," shouted the caller, and the group dispersed to wander around the big yard. Lanterns placed on the porch and on the gateposts made light for the party. " Ain't it purty? " sighed Lily Mae. Hod squeezed her arm but made no reply. It was good to be young, to have dancing feet and a light heart. He was happier than he had been in a long time.

The sets formed and the people danced. The air grew heavy with the dust from the shuffling feet. Before the evening was over, they would all be invited in for supper and to see the inside of the house, but as long as the dancing went on, they were content outside. A barrel of sweet cider stood at one side of the yard, and the folks made frequent trips to dip out cups of the sweetish, sour liquid. Some of the men slipped away from time to time to sip furtively at a moonshine jug which was hidden out back.

During a break Hod found a bench by the fence, and he and Lily Mae gratefully sat down. " You havin' a good time? " he asked her. A lantern on a nearby post threw a feeble light over them, and made quickening shadows on her white dress. Her hair had pulled loose from its ribbons, and she was shaking the yellow mass back before retying it.

" I shore am," she said, " never no better in my life! I jist love to dance anyways! Here, you tie this here ribbon fer me, while I hold my hair back."

He took the strand of ribbon and she turned her back to him, lifting the heavy hair so he could slip the ribbon under it. Clumsily he managed to tie it in a knot and bow. The feel of the skin under his fingers prickled him and he bent, filled with a compulsion to lay his lips against that spot where the hair pulled softly away. He touched it lightly, and thought how clean and cool and sweet it was. There was a faint odor of soap. He let his hands slip down over her arms.

She twisted impatiently. "Not now, Hod," she said, "yer mussin' me." And she pulled away to straighten and pat her hair into place. "Let's go on back," she added. "I promised Ferdy Jones I'd dance this next 'un with him."

Lily Mae pressed her white dress close to her waist, and smoothed its gathers over her thighs. The movement was catlike in its grace. They walked back toward the dancers.

"Come to think of it, I've not seen Corinna here tonight," Hod said.

"She ain't here. She's gittin' too heavy to git around much now. Ferdy come with Little Wells an' Matildy."

Hod surrendered Lily Mae to Ferdy's lanky arms and went to cool off with a dipper of cider. He stretched the drink out until the end of the set and then went looking for Lily Mae. The dancers were milling around, but Lily Mae wasn't among them. Ferdy was gone too, he noticed. Hod frowned. Lily Mae oughtn't to go wandering around like that with a married man. She'd get herself talked about, first thing she knew.

He roamed restlessly about the yard while another set formed and was finished, and another after that. And then he spied Lily Mae coming out of the house, cool, unruffled, and luscious in her thin white dress. He waited for her. "Where've you been?" he asked.

"I been goin' through the house," she answered. "O Hod, it's jist the purtiest thing you ever seen! You'd orta go through an' see. Hit's jist fixed up real nice!"

"Is Ferdy in there too?"

"Ferdy? Why, I don't know. I've not saw him sincet we was dancin' together. I reckon he went off to git him a drink."

Hod didn't know why he felt such relief. He laughed foolishly. He edged Lily Mae toward the gate. "C'mon," he said, "let's go home."

She flashed a quick, bright smile at him. "All right," she said, "let's."

CHAPTER FOURTEEN

They were on their way home from meeting one night when Lily Mae said to Hod: "I'm goin' over an' he'p out Corinna fer a while. I reckon you knowed she was expectin' agin, an' Ferdy says she ain't doin' so good. He's comin' after me tomorrer, an' I'll be gone till after the baby comes an' she's up an' around agin."

Hod frowned. "I don't much like for you to go 'way over there," he said.

"I know," she answered quickly, "an' I wouldn't go, only he says they cain't git nobody, an' he'll pay me five dollars a week an' my keep."

"How long you think you'll be gone all together?"

"Well, hit's three weeks 'fore the baby's due, an' I doubt she'll be up 'fore another week or two after."

"That's a pretty long time. And I can't hardly get over that far to see you very often."

"I know. We'll just have to make out. Will you miss me?"

He bent her head back, and sought her mouth. "What do you think?"

She was gone nearly two months, for Corinna was poorly for weeks after the baby was born and kept her there much longer than had first been intended. Hod didn't know how he would ache for her. She had come to be so much a part of his life that he felt lost without her. He was restless and moody, and he took to staying home nights because there was no joy in a singing or a party without her. In the two months he wasn't able to get away a single time to make the trip over to see her. He was splitting rails for Gault, and by the time the long day's work was over he couldn't find the energy to make the five-mile trip and back.

It was early winter, and the first snow had fallen before she came home. She met him at the mailbox the next day, and he thought she looked tired.

"I am tired," she said, when he questioned her. "It's enough to wear a body plumb out, cookin' an' doin' fer a family as big as

129

that 'un. Corinna, she wasn't stout enough to do nothin' fer six weeks, an' I had the washin' an' ironin' an' all the cookin' to do. She's not learned them girls o' her'n to do e'er thing, neither. They jist set there an' play all the time. 'Course I was gittin' paid fer doin' it, so I reckon I've no call to complain. But I'm plumb wore out jist the same."

"Where'll we go to talk?"

"Matt Jasper's moved an' the house is still empty. We kin go there. You kin build a fire in the fireplace so's we won't freeze to death."

They walked down the road half a mile to the shambling, unpainted old house in which Matt Jasper had housed his brood of epileptic children. Its roof sagged and its sides leaned, and it looked as if you could push it over with one good hard shove. There were a few sticks of wood in the corner of the yard, and Hod gathered an armful while Lily Mae opened the door. She sniffed when they were inside.

"This place smells somethin' awful! I don't reckon Lutie ever cleaned it."

"When would she have time with all those sick kids?" Hod asked, as he knelt and shaved kindling from a pine board with his knife. "Of all the people on the ridge that's had a hard time I've always felt sorriest for Lutie Jasper. I wonder why she ever married Matt."

"Mebbe he was the only one ever asked her."

"Well, I'd have stayed single if I'd been in her shoes!"

The fire blazed up and its warmth began to creep into the bare room. Lily Mae took off her coat and spread it before the hearth. But without it she shivered and held her hands to the fire. "Br-r-r," she said, "this place is as cold as a wedge!"

"Here," said Hod, "come sit by me and I'll hold you and you'll get warm."

She laughed, but snuggled close in his arms.

"I sure missed you," he said, nuzzling her neck and hair. "Don't ever go away and stay that long again."

"It wasn't but two months." She pressed her finger in the dimple in his chin.

"I know, but it seemed more like two years. What's that sweet-smellin' stuff?"

"Oh, that's jist some perfume I got awhile back. Don't it smell good?"

"I'd rather just smell your hair the way it always is. Never did like the smell of perfume."

"Well, you'll smell it purty often I reckon, 'cause I aim to use it all I want to."

"Why, sure," he said, puzzled. "I didn't mean you shouldn't use it if you wanted to. I was just sayin' I like you all right without it."

He bent to stir the fire. A shower of sparks hissed up the chimney and the chestnut logs crackled sharply. When he turned back to her she was leaning against the wall, relaxed and still in the glowing heat. Her hair was thrown back and her throat looked unbearably young and vulnerable. He was shaken by a sudden yearning and he snatched at her roughly. "Did you hear me say I'd missed you?"

"I missed you too," she said, but she was strangely unresponsive — passive and dull. "I'm jist tired," she insisted.

"Well," he replied, quoting from Hattie, "you better rest up a spell."

For several weeks they met once or twice a week at the old abandoned house. Sometimes Hod reached the house first and had a fire roaring hot by the time Lily Mae came. Other times she was waiting for him. Occasionally she brought food and they swung an old coffeepot on the crane over the fire and picnicked merrily. Times like this Hod felt close to her — almost married to her. The room closed round them tightly and shut out the cold and the harshness and the dreariness. Times like this he almost wished they *were* married. He felt happy and easy inside.

And then he had to go over to the lumber camp to work for several weeks. A fellow had to make all the money he could. When he returned he found a note from Lily Mae in the mailbox saying that she wanted to see him.

He met her at the empty house again. A deep snow lay on the ground and they both had wet feet. "When I get the fire built up we'd better take off our shoes and dry 'em," Hod said.

Lily Mae bent to unlace hers. Hod set his own shoes beside

131

her and rid himself of his leather jacket.

Lily Mae played with a loose button on the front of her blouse. "Hod," she said suddenly, "we're goin' to have to git married."

She said it bluntly . . . flatly . . . inevitably. Hod looked at her, startled and questioning.

"Folks are talkin'," she said. "I had a big fight with my brother Saturday, and we've not spoke sincet. He'd been ahearin' things about us meetin' here in this old house. Come right out and point-blank accused me o' carryin' on here with you! Said ever'body on the ridge was asnickerin' behind our backs — asayin' all kinds o' things!"

A deep flush burned up Hod's neck and anger flooded him. "Who'd he say was talkin'?"

Lily Mae shrugged. "He wouldn't name e'er one person. Jist said he heared it at the mill."

Fleetingly Hod saw the familiar group of men banded around the hopper. Heard them chuckle slyly and slip their tongues over his name. Heard them roll this gossip round and round in their mouths, spitting it out like the constant stream of amber from their jaws. Saw them nudge and poke each other. That Hod, now. He's a good 'un!

His anger flamed. "I'll go down there Saturday and I'll whale the daylights out of every livin' one of 'em," he gritted between his teeth. "They'll not dare say such to me!"

"Hit wouldn't do no good," Lily Mae said, her fingers fumbling the loose button. "You've done ruint my name here on the ridge. You know as good as I do they ain't but one way to put a stop to it. Folks'll never believe e'er thing but what hit's true. But ifen we're married they'll soon hesh up!"

Hod knew this was true. Bitterly he knew it. Once a girl and a boy got married folks let bygones be bygones. But it would be the only way Lily Mae could ever hold her head up again! He felt helpless . . . trapped. He didn't want this! Everything in him protested against it. He worked his knuckles, and his eyes went back to the fire. He watched the flames lick along the logs, sending sparks shooting off onto the hearth. He shrugged. There was nothing to do but make out. He'd have to take Lily Mae home and fit her somehow into the already crowded little house. He reckoned he'd have to take her up in the loft room . . . Gramma couldn't climb those stairs. They'd have no place to be together, no way to be alone, ever. But he couldn't walk out on Hattie and Tom and Gramma. And Hattie would be frashed, and she and Lily Mae would grate on each other.

"Well," he said finally, "when do you want to do it?"

"The sooner the better."

He was silent. Lily Mae slanted her eyes at him. "They ain't no use waitin'," she said.

"I reckon you're right. I'll see if I can get someone to take us into town next week. Will that do?"

Lily Mae nodded and curled against him, comfortable now and relaxed. But the moment had gone flat for Hod. He looked down the years and saw them spinning themselves into nothingness. Already he and Lily Mae were old with the struggle, and when he looked at her again he seemed to see her bright young eyes rheumy and cast over, and her skin withered into wrinkles. He shivered. The hills had closed in and pressed him flat. The tight hills. Forever and enduring. Caught, they said harshly. Now he's caught!

On Monday he walked through the snow to Irma's, thinking to get John to drive him and Lily Mae to the county seat one day that week. Irma was happy to see him. "O Hod," she said, "I'm so glad you come! The weather's been so rough, an' we been housebound so long, yer as welcome as spring! But what in the world you doin' out in sich weather? An' jist look at yer feet! Here, set down by the fire an' take off yer shoes an' dry them feet out!"

"I came over to see John a minute," Hod answered, stretching his wet feet toward the heat. "Is he around?"

"He's jist out choppin' some firewood. He'll be in in a minnit. Is ever'body all right over home?"

"Everybody's fine, I reckon. Pa complains a lot of his back. But that's not new."

Irma shook her head and bent to put Hod's boots by the fire. "I don't believe he'll ever be no account no more. Seems like that there operation takened somethin' outen him."

John came in with an armload of wood and dropped it noisily by the fireplace. "Well, howdy, there, stranger! You ain't been over in quite a spell. Been mad at us or somethin'?"

"Just busy. John, are you aimin' to go in to town any day this week?"

"Hadn't aimed to. Why? You wantin' to go?"

"Yes." He paused before going on. The words came hardly. "Lily Mae and I are goin' to get married, and I thought maybe you'd drive us in to the county seat to get the license."

Irma's hand flew to her mouth. "Oh, no! Hod, no!"

He looked at her in surprise. "You surely knew we'd get married sometime, didn't you? As long as we've been goin' together?"

"No!" she shot back at him sharply. And then, "John, ifen you don't tell him, I will!"

John was nervously fingering his chin. "I'd think about that a long time if I was you, Hod. You'll have to stay married a purty good while."

"Well, I know that! What in the devil's the matter with you two? I've been goin' with Lily Mae off and on for over four years, and nobody's objected before!"

"You ain't talked about marryin' her before!" Irma cried.

Hod looked at his feet and wiggled one toe, up and down . . . up and down. "Well," he said, "I am now."

"Hod," John put in, "I'd make mighty shore about things 'fore I stuck my neck out."

"What do you mean?"

"He means," Irma flared, "he means that ever'body on the ridge knows she's been acarryin' on with Ferdy Jones fer ever so long! That's what he means!"

"Ferdy Jones! Why, you're crazy! He's old enough to be her pa, an' besides, he's married!"

"As if that made any difference to Lily Mae! Him bein' married wouldn't stop her none!"

"How do you know about this?"

"Hit's common talk, Hod. Hit was goin' on even before she went over to take keer o' Corinna. Reckon that's why she went. He's give her presents, an' I reckon might' nigh ever'body's seen 'em one time or another out awalkin' or atalkin' together. Corinna knows, now, too."

Hod was stunned. He remembered the perfume. "I don't understand," he said. "I never dreamed there was anyone else."

134

"There's allus been somebody else," Irma cried. "You never thought she was true to you, did you? Why, ever' summer you been up in Indianny they's been a different one she's been talkin' to! Jist about ever' man on the ridge by this time! She ain't no idee of bein' true!"

"Why didn't somebody tell me?" he said angrily.

John spoke, kindly. "Hod, I reckon a man's allus the last to hear the truth about somethin' like this. Didn't nobody have the heart to tell you."

"Irma," Hod pleaded, "you're not just tellin' me this because you don't like her, are you? I know you never did like Lily Mae much."

Irma's eyes softened and she reached a gentle hand to his arm. "Hod," she said, "hit's true I never liked her overmuch, but I'm yer sister, an' we growed up together. You he'ped me an' John git married, an' you kin believe me, no matter how much I didn't like her, that wouldn't stand in the way ifen she was the decent girl you thought she was. But ever' word I've said is true, an' John'll back me up, an' half a dozen others knows the same things we do. I'm only wantin' yer happiness, an' how fur could you go toward findin' it with a girl that never knowed the meanin' o' bein' true to nobody."

Hod laughed shortly. "I've sure been a blind fool." He rose and walked to the window, looking bleakly out at the stainless snow. It was ludicrously out of place. He scratched idly on the frosted glass and thought of Lily Mae! Remembered all the times they had laughed and sung and walked the ridge together. Remembered her wheat hair that lay so softly under his hand. Her red, red mouth that lifted so eagerly to his. Remembered, and then let the bitter ugliness shoot through him. Lily Mae! Why, she was his girl! Surely she was his girl!

He swung away from the window. "You think, then, this is Ferdy's doin'?" he asked Irma.

"I know so. Ifen you marry her you'll fall right into the trap they've set fer you. She even made her brags to Corinna that she could allus git you to marry her an' take keer of her."

"We'll see about that!" And he was on his feet, struggling into his coat.

"Where you goin'?"

"Does it make any difference?" Slamming the door fiercely he went out into the blowing snow, and Irma and John looked at each other helplessly. Irma began to cry.

"Somebody had to tell him," she sobbed. "He had to know, but I wish it hadn't been me had to hurt him."

John comforted her. "He'll take it better from you than from anybody else. Don't fret, now. His pride's hurt, but his heart ain't broke. Hod's got too much sense to grieve long. An' even if he does, it's better to grieve now than later. She'd a really broke him up sometime ifen he'd married her."

Hod went straight to Lily Mae's home. She was sewing quilt pieces when the wind blew him in, and she screamed at him, "Shut the door!"

"Get your coat on," he said bluntly, "and come outside with me."

"Have you lost yer mind?" she asked, amazed. "Hit ain't fit weather to git out in! Take yer things off an' set here by the fire."

"I said get your coat on and come outside with me! There's something we've got to talk about!"

She looked at him quickly, and a strange, furtive look hooded her face. Without further argument, she put her coat on and went out with him. They walked down the road toward the mailboxes. He stopped when they were out of sight of the house and faced her. "You've got Ferdy's perfume on again, haven't you?"

"What do you mean?"

"What's been goin' on between you and Ferdy Jones?"

She jerked her head up, startled. "Nothin', Hod. Not e'er thing! I swear it!"

"You're lyin'!" and his voice was a growl between his teeth. He took her by the shoulders and shook her until her hair flew wildly around her head.

"Stop it!" she screamed at him, clawing at his hands. "You stop it, Hod Pierce!"

"Quit lyin' to me, then! Tell me what's been goin' on between you and Ferdy Jones!"

"What's been goin' on between me an' Ferdy Jones is my business! An' don't you lay yer hands on me agin!"

"It's my business too, when you try to pull the wool over my eyes! Have you been carryin' on with Ferdy?"

She was stubbornly silent. She bent and scooped up a handful of snow, and stuck her red tongue in it, like a child being deliberately insolent.

Hod gritted his teeth. "If you don't answer me, I swear I'll shake you till every bone in your body comes apart!" He slapped the snow from her hand, and swung her roughly around toward him. "Answer me! And don't you lie to me again!"

She spat the words in his face. "Yes! Now are you satisfied?"

His hands fell limply to his sides. "That's all I wanted to know," he said. He looked at her and let the acid of her lush ripeness eat itself into him. His girl. Ferdy's girl! Anybody's girl! He could have killed her! She gave him back look for look, and even now her eyes were cold — disbelieving. Abruptly he turned and walked away, leaving dragging marks in the snow. As far as Lily Mae could see him down the road, he hunched into the wind, and his boots raised a small snowstorm behind him. He never once looked back.

Shortly after, he heard that she had gone to Louisville to stay with her sister and work. Hattie was the one who told him. "I reckon Lily Mae'll do right good in Louisville. She's a fair hand to work when she's a mind to."

Hod was oiling a stiff harness strap by the kitchen stove. He jerked the strap into an angry knot.

"Didn't you hear me, Hod?"

"Yes."

And he put the grease away, carefully, and went out to the barn where only the animals could see his tight mouth and his burnt-out eyes. He walked like an old man as he went down the path.

CHAPTER FIFTEEN

Hod never knew how he got through the rest of that winter. He only know that all the days ached with him and wept gray tears for weeks at a time. All Piney Ridge was sodden and mired in mud, and he let himself down into his own pit of despair. Spring came, and he went through the motions of planting the tobacco, and another summer soon bore down upon the leafy green. He worked now, not only to make a tobacco crop, but to forget. If he could drive his body through enough merciless hours, he could sleep at night. Otherwise he would lie awake, tormented and haunted, and, above all, empty.

After the tobacco was in the barn in the early fall, he turned to other tasks. He was plowing the field next to the road one day, thinking he would put the corn patch there next spring, when Gault came by.

"Howdy, Hod."

"Howdy, Gault. Whoa, Buck! Whoa there — whoa, I said! How's everything, Gault? Whoa, Buck! Whoa! You dad-blamed, consarned, doggoned idiot, I said whoa!"

"Purty good, I reckon. How's Tom?"

"About the same. He does most of the chores around the place and feeds and takes care of the milkin', but I doubt he'll ever be real stout again."

Gault shook his head. "I allus said I'd never go under the knife. Did the Lord aim fer me to do without some o' my innards, he wouldn't never have give 'em to me in the first place. They takened somethin' outen Tom when they cut into him, an' hit'll never come back."

Hod made no reply. He plucked a stem from a dry vine clambering over the fence and stuck it in his mouth. Tom and Hattie halfway believed the same thing, and he knew they used it to excuse Tom's failure to pick up in strength.

"I hear they're puttin' through a W.P.A. projeck to gravel the section roads," Gault went on. "Thought you might like to know."

Hod wrapped the lines around the plow handle as if he would walk out of the field at once. "Where do you see about gettin' on?" he asked.

"They got a office in the county seat. Wells was in there yesterday an' he said they was a line plumb up to the corner, folks waitin' to sign up. The talk is they're tryin' to put them that needs it worst to work first. I told Becky they wasn't nobody needed it worse'n you, an' I aimed to name it to you first off."

At eight o'clock the next morning Hod was in line. He had walked to the Gap that evening, and from there had hitched a

138

ride to the county seat and had spent the night in the bus station.

The line moved along at a snail's pace, and it was the middle of the afternoon before he was inside the door. Hunger gnawed at him and his head had begun to ache, but he didn't dare leave the line long enough to eat. He might have asked someone to bring him something, but there was only a dime in his pocket and pride forbade his asking a stranger to buy cheese and crackers to bring to him, and he knew of nothing else he could buy for ten cents.

When finally it was his turn to be interviewed, he was swaying on his feet and he sat down suddenly, letting the flood of relief stream through him. The interviewer was a tired man who spent his days behind this desk, asking questions, filling out papers, hiding himself behind the impersonality of red tape. He snapped the questions at Hod. Name. Address. Age. How many in family? Ages. How many employed? Family income last year? What type of work applying for? Qualifications. Education. References. He was impatient with Hod's hesitant replies. How could he know that to the proud hill heart this probing into personal areas was like baring a quivering nerve? Hod felt as if he was begging for alms as the cold, disinterested voice droned on. He was asking for work, not relief! That the man spent his days asking these questions of hundreds of people, and that the replies had no meaning for him except to fill in the proper places on the innumerable forms, Hod never thought. He only knew that he felt a sense of outraged self-esteem and that this man was the instrument which heckled him.

"That's all," the man said finally. "You'll be notified. Next!"

"Does that mean I get the job, mister?"

"It means you'll be notified whether or not your application is approved. If your application is approved, you'll be assigned to a public works project."

"Much obliged," and Hod was out the door, surging with the release of his pent-up emotions. That was that! How in the world a man could hold his head up if he had to go through all that every time he needed a job he didn't know! It made a man feel like poor white trash. Like nothing human. But it was over, and if he was lucky he'd have steady work before long, and a pay envelope regular. He hadn't known he could feel so light and happy! If

139

he could get a regular job, the whole world would be different. They could all have some new clothes and something to eat besides beans and fat back. He could get that plow he saw in the mail order, and, by golly, he'd have him a new guitar! He could pay on the debt regular, and sometime he'd even get it all paid off. A regular job! What a wonderful sound it had!

He saw a familiar figure down the street ahead of him. There was Irma! He lengthened his stride to catch up with her. "Hello there," he hailed her. "Where have you been?"

"Why, Hod," she said, jumping a little, "you skeered me! I should be askin' you where you been! Hit's been so long sincet I seen you! Ever' time I been over home lately you been off the place somewhere."

"It takes a lot of rustlin' these days to keep the wolf from the door," he answered.

"I know it's the truth. What you doin' in town?"

"I just put in for a job on one of those W.P.A. projects. They say they're goin' to gravel all the county roads and build new bridges, and I figured I could swing a pick and shovel as well as the next one. Don't know whether I'll get on or not. He said they'd let me know."

"I shore hope you do, Hod. You've had it hard long enough. An' don't nobody deserve to have one o' them jobs more'n you do. I dunno what Ma an' Pa'd do without you. Hod, do you ever think Pa could do more'n he lets on? Sometimes I think he's jist content not to have to weary no more."

Hod's mouth tightened. "I don't know. I used to look for him to take hold again, but I've quit expectin' it now. And it doesn't help to fret about it. He's the way he is, and there's nothin' to be done about it."

"Well, it ain't right, an' I *do* fret about it. Hit ain't fair to you." Irma shifted her packages and clutched her purse tighter. "Whyn't you come go home with us an' stay the night? They's goin' to be a pie supper at Blain's Chapel tonight an' a spellin' bee, an' we'll all go an' have us a big ole time. C'mon. You ain't been over to see us in a coon's age."

Hod pondered the question a moment. "Believe I will," he decided. "The folks can make out another night, I reckon." Somehow it was fitting that this hopeful day should hold the promise

140

of a happy night.

"Good fer you," said Irma. "The car's parked down in front of the hardware, an' I reckon John's ready to leave out by now."

They set off down the street, and Hod took most of her packages out of her arms. "You been buyin' out the town, looks like," he teased.

"John's goin' to think so too," she laughed. Then she glanced at him cornerwise. "Reckon you've heared Lily Mae's come home."

So. She was back. "No," he answered slowly. "No . . . I've not heard. When did she get back?"

"One day last week." Irma hesitated and then went on. "Oh, she's been tellin' it big about her fine boy friends she had up there. One, she said, had a big Buick car an' takened her out in it ever' night!"

"That," said Hod, "should have pleased her right well."

"You don't act like it troubles you none."

"It doesn't."

Irma smiled at him. The brief exchange of words had told her exactly what she wanted to know. He didn't mean to take things up with Lily Mae where they had left off. He was through.

John's old Model T rested its flat nose against the hitching rail in front of the hardware, and John was waiting comfortably with his feet propped up on the door. He and Hod exchanged greetings. "Hod's goin' home with us," Irma explained, "an' we're all goin' to the pie supper tonight."

"Now that's fine," said John. He moved over and let the two of them in.

Irma's home was still the little two-room tenant house in which she and John had started out. But it was a sweet home, neat as a pin, with bright, clean curtains at the windows and gay, plaited rugs on the floor. Hod loved it because it had such an air-swept, uncluttered look and he thought that Irma must be a fine wife for John. They had lost two babies, both stillborn, but while they had grieved over the tiny, lifeless forms, they had not let it embitter them. It was Irma's way to believe that all things happened for the best, and she had dried her tears after burying her babies and had taken up her life again, glad for John's love, her pretty house, and the fact that in a time of want they had enough and to spare.

Folks were already gathering when they reached the chapel that night, and the pies, disguised in gayly decorated boxes, were lined up on a long table at the back of the room.

Soon the chapel was full to crowding and seats were getting scarce. It was almost time for the spelling bee to commence when Lily Mae came in, late, with her mother and Matildy and Little Wells. Hod saw her immediately. She went down the center aisle carrying her box, her eyes searching the room as boldly as ever. She had on a new dress, he saw — a tight-fitting blue silk of some sort. When she saw Hod, she met his eyes full, and then, tilting her chin, she tossed her heavy hair back with the old familiar gesture.

Hod let the spasm of pain which started in his tightly knotted chest run thickly down into his arms and legs. How could he not hurt over this girl who had taken so much of him? Why, every move she made was as known to him as if he had made it himself, so much of him had become a part of her. He saw her clearly. Cheap. Bold. Vulgar. He didn't miss any of that, and well he knew how shameless she was too. But she was part of him and he couldn't tear her out. He turned away, while the pain still ripped through him.

The preacher was talking now, explaining about the spelling bee. And Hod tried to listen though his mind felt numb. John and Little Wells were elected to choose sides. No one was omitted from the choosing, from the oldest down to the youngest, and as they were chosen they lined up along the opposite walls of the building. The preacher, who was to give out the words, took his place behind the table, on which three spelling books were arranged.

Word after word was given out, down both lines, with very few missing on the first round. The next round the words were harder, although they were still fairly simple. A few more persons took their seats. The next round there was a perceptible tightening up and the little fellows began to fall out. They had known from the beginning they wouldn't last long, but it had been fun to try.

The lines were only half as long now. The words flew from one side of the room to the other. " Fascination." " Minimum." " Embargo." " Cynical." One by one the weeding out went on. The excitement grew and the tension mounted, and there were cheers when favorites successfully hurdled a particularly hard word, or

142

moans when they stumbled and failed. Irma went down on " ecstatic." Matildy caught the word on the rebound and took it in her stride. A moment later she was down on " dubious."

There were only four left standing now . . . John, Little Wells, Hod, and a man from Pebbly. Faster and faster the words flew. The preacher was down to the hardest words of all now. The words in a spelling bee had no reality for the people who spelled them. They could spell words of whose meaning they had not the vaguest idea, and which, in a hundred years they would not have used. Words like " heptagonal," " interdependent," " managerial," and " parsimonious." Little Wells went down on that one. Hod picked it up. Wells had used an " e," so he tried it with an " i." " Correct," said the preacher. The man from Pebbly went down on " admonition." John skimmed through it easily. Now only he and Hod stood facing each other. By golly, Hod thought, he's good! I'm goin' to lose me a spellin' bee if I don't look out. He tightened up carefully. But so did John and the match went on. Finally the preacher said: " We've still got to have the pie supper, and it's gettin' late. Suppose I admit I can't spell you men down, and suppose you all call it a draw between you. Will that suit? "

They agreed it would suit and got a big hand from the audience as they took their seats. Hod felt a moment of pride that the two best spellers on the ridge were in the family.

The preacher was talking again. " And now, friends, we're going to auction off the pies. We've got Uncle Billy Barton, from down at the Gap, to do the selling, and you all know that he's the best auctioneer outside of a tobacco warehouse. And the money from this pie supper is going to buy new songbooks for the church. So let's not let a single pie go for less than a dollar. There's some mighty good pies lined up on this table, and any one of them is worth a dollar, to say nothing of getting to eat it with the lovely young lady that made it. Uncle Billy, are you ready?"

" Ready an' rarin' to go," said the sprightly, white-haired little man. " Now, folks, we're goin' to start with this here red, white, an' blue box. This here is the dad-blamedest most patriotic box you ever seen an' it's yer bounden duty to start the biddin' high. Now, what am I offered fer this artistic creation? Twenty-five cents, I hear from the redheaded young man on the back row. Twenty-five . . . twenty-five . . . twenty-five-five-five! Who'll

143

make it thirty? Thirty cents, says the gent in the middle. Thirty cents I'm bid. Who'll make it forty? Thirty . . . thirty . . . thirty . . . Who'll make it forty? Forty cents from the redhead. Who'll make it fifty? "

The bidding went on up, ten cents at a time, until it reached a dollar and a quarter. The redheaded boy then went his blushing way up the aisle to pay for his girl's pie. The hypnotic singsong chant of the auctioneer rapidly disposed of one pie after another. Most of them sold for around a dollar. Occasionally there was a flurry of excitement when a group of fellows ganged up on a boy and ran the pie of his girl up to two or three dollars. It was a point of honor, then, for the boy to stick it out. Manfully he would stay with the bidding until his last cent and all he could borrow was gone. Lord, how young they are, Hod thought. Was I ever that young? His twenty-second birthday had passed in July.

Then Lily Mae's pie went up. Hod knew it by the little bunch of artificial roses she always tied into the knot of ribbon around the box. The hurt, which had eased in the excitement of the spelling bee, clutched him again. Used to be, he always bought that pie. He remembered the first time. He'd had two dollars saved up, and Pa had given him another. He'd been scared to death it wouldn't be enough. That must have been the winter he was eighteen. It had been enough, and he'd always managed to get that pie one way or another. Tonight the boys eyed him expectantly when the artificial roses bloomed in the auctioneer's hand. But Hod sat still.

Lily Mae's profile was carved from stone when he looked at her across the room. Feeling his eyes, she turned to look at him. He held that look steadily, and it was she who looked away first. But the pain flickered through his chest. Lily Mae! Lily Mae! And then it was that Hod learned another truth. There are some things, hurt though they may, that you cannot amputate. Instead you must take them, hurt and all, into yourself, and close them over with the dignity of your manhood. You have done these things. You have known them and felt them. They are part of you now, forever and enduring. You cannot put them away and deny them. The best you can do is let them heal, scarred and roughened, inside of you. In time the jagged edges of the gash would grow together. But the scar was there, for always.

The bidding on Lily Mae's pie was listless, and it was knocked down finally to a boy from the Gap. Irrelevantly, Hod thought the roses looked a little faded. Lily Mae had better buy a new bunch pretty soon.

CHAPTER SIXTEEN

DURING THE MONTHS THAT FOLLOWED the mailbox became very important to Hod. Daily he walked down to the crossroads and looked hopefully inside the box. He didn't know when he could logically expect the notice from the office, but each day he would tell himself, today it might come. Each day he would pull the little hinged door down, wishing some magic would make it be there. The box remained empty for so long that finally the edge wore off his eagerness, and while he continued to make his regular trip to the crossroads, the emptiness of the box became a part of the routine.

The circle of time completed the cycle of seasons and brought tobacco-planting time again, and his days were crowded and full. The impregnation of the earth in her period of fertility makes a ceaseless demand upon men who walk behind a plow. The days lengthened until Hod could feel them yawn and stretch; the sky bent a cerulean hood over the world; the soil swelled in gestation and cracked its sides with new life. The winter was past and " the time of the singing of birds" was come.

One day the white envelope was in the mailbox. It looked alien and lonely lying there, and for a moment Hod couldn't remember its significance. Realization dawned slowly, and he reached for it with a shaking hand. Let it be a job, he prayed. Please let it be a job. He opened the letter, searching quickly for the important news. " Your application has been approved . . . you have been assigned to . . . report May 10, to . . ." There it was! In black and white there it was! A job! Regular pay check! Real money! It was all there on the paper. Hod saw it through a mist, and only then did he know how much it had meant to him to have a door opened even to such a stingy release from anxiety. Now, he thought jubilantly, now we'll have it better. Now, we'll be people again. Now, things are going to be different. He felt mighty and strong, and he walked the road home with free, long strides.

145

Watt Jones was foreman of the project to which Hod was as-signed. They were putting in new culverts and bridges on the pike between the Gap and Campbellsville, filling in the wheel-eaten holes and resurfacing the whole pike. Watt looked at Hod's paper when he reported that Monday morning, grunted, and made a notation on his payroll sheet.

"Can you mix cement?" he asked.

"Never have," Hod answered, "but I can try."

"Humph! Well, that's all there is for you to do right now. Go on down the road there until you come to a bunch of men workin' this side the culvert. They orta be mixin' a batch. Tell one of 'em I said they was to let you help."

Hod did as he was told, and when he relayed the foreman's message, one of the men handed him a big shovel. Two men stood on either side of one end of the long frame that held the mixture, and Hod and the third man were at the other end. He noticed how they used their shovels to stir and mix and push the cement, and after a moment he bent over his own shovel and fell into the rhythm of pushing, heaving, and pulling. It was hard work, and before long his muscles felt the drag of the heavy shovel, but he was glad of the ache in his shoulders. It reminded him that he was being paid thirty cents an hour. Thirty cents an hour, eight hours a day, and his notice said he was entitled to fifteen days' work each month. He had added the total a hundred times. There would be thirty-six dollars each month, and thirty-six dollars was more that they had sometimes had in three months. He could af-ford to ache for that!

For several months he mixed cement, pushed a wheelbarrow, filled cuts, and smoothed gravel. Then one day the foreman called him into the shanty that served him as office. "Hod," he said, "you reckon you could handle the timekeeper's job?"

"If Masters could handle it, I can," Hod said.

"Well, Masters is quittin' this week. Got him another job over at the county seat, and if you want to, you can take a try at it. I been watchin' you. You're dependable and you've got a head on your shoulders. I've seen you more'n once figure out the best way to do a piece of work. You don't loaf on the job and you ain't just tryin' to put in eight hours a day. Timekeepin' will pay you forty cents an hour, and I reckon you can use the extra cash as well as

146

the next one."

So Hod became timekeeper. Each morning he took his lists and made the rounds of the crews scattered up and down the road, checking each man on the list. He wasn't pushed for time, so he frequently helped out the men at work.

He liked to work with his hands — to make things, to handle tools, to put things together. He liked the feel of things in his hands. Something outside came over into him through his hands. A hoe handle made him feel the warm and living earth. The pull of a plow through his hands into his shoulders made him aware of life, pulsing and growing and moving on. If he could touch a thing, and feel its texture — its smoothness or roughness, its thinness or thickness, its grain or pile — he got a knowledge of it that was surer than his mind could give him. And now when he hefted these tools the roadmen used, his hands tested their fineness and sharpness clear up into his mind.

Watt Jones watched him sometimes. That boy would make a good toolman, he thought. So he gave over to Hod the responsibility for the care of tools for the whole outfit. At first this applied only to the commoner tools, the ones the laborers used, checked in and out daily. These Hod worked over, keeping them in fine shape, loving even their coarse edges and heavy bulk. They were things to use — things for a man to put his hand to. They deserved care.

Later, some of the engineers, seeing his way with their instruments, began to let him make minor adjustments and repairs for them. They learned that if a thing had a gadget on it, Hod could set his fingers to probing its inner secrets and make it work. Screws, knobs, hinges, edges, came to life under those searching, patient fingers.

Now he made fifty cents an hour. The summer went by, and the winter, and then another summer. His job on the road project held.

Things were easier at home now too. Hattie, who was always a good manager, did wonders with the cash money. Little by little she replaced their worn clothing, added a few luxuries to their food, and even saw to it that Hod got his new guitar. It sat in the corner most of the time, for Hod was too tired to touch it often, but it was there, a symbol of their progress. The debt had been

147

paid out too. In many ways, life was better.

But as the time went by and Hod took stock, he saw the job for what it was. W.P.A. Temporary. It wasn't doing anything more than stopping the gap. He had not been able to accumulate anything for himself. He had a dollar or two in his blue jeans most of the time, but he could never get ahead. It took all he could pour into Hattie's asking hands to keep them going. Where was the end of it? He saw that he had no identity except that of Joseph, the opener of the storehouse. And a man had to be more than that. However commendable it was for him to do his duty, duty was slim fare as a daily diet.

His resentment flared at times, but not to the point of prodding him to do anything else. And now he was twenty-five.

One day in the late fall, when there was just enough frost in the air to make the beech-log fire feel good, Hod was sitting straddle of a chair by the fireplace when Hattie passed between him and the window. He straightened with a jerk. There was an unmistakable swelling to her silhouette. He flung the chair from him and plunged violently out of the house. No! Not that! Not now! It can't be! Not after all this time! That ought to be all past for them! Why, Ma must be . . . He counted up and with a start he realized that Hattie was only forty-four. He had always thought of her as old. He felt sick, suddenly tired and very discouraged. He flung himself down the road, not knowing where he was going and not caring. He had to get away. I must be blind, he thought. All these years he's been taking it easy around here! And all the sweating I've been doing while he lies around and gets another mouth for me to feed! Another back for me to keep warm! Another ten years on the W.P.A.! I will not. *I will not!* He gets his kids. He can take care of them. I will not. By heaven, I will not, I swear!

He turned off the road through the woods and came to the edge of the hollow. Where the path pitched steeply down the hill, he sat down and leaned wearily against a tree. A hundred drums beat in his head. His lips felt sore and his eyes were dry and hot. Wretchedness flowed its bitter way through his whole body, its gall lapping at the edges of his very soul.

148

Suddenly he twisted away from the tree and stretched his lean frame against the uncomforting breast of the earth. Sobs racked his body, and one clenched fist pounded the rhythm of his pain into the stony ground. The soil soaked up the blood from his cuts, and he never knew that he bled. "God," he cried, beating the prayer into the earth. "God, I've got to get away from here. I've got to get out! I've got to! Let there be a way. Please, please let there be a way!"

CHAPTER SEVENTEEN

Hattie's time came in April. She got up that morning and did the usual tasks, built the fire, made the bread and the coffee. She asked no extra help. But from the way she caught her breath from time to time and bent over to hold to something, Hod knew it was upon her. And Tom was not there for breakfast, so he knew she had sent him to get Becky or Lizzie. This was one of the days Hod was not working and he had expected to mend the pasture fence. "You want me to stay around for a while?" he asked.

She shook her head, and he saw that her mouth was set. "I'll make out," she said. "Tom'll be back in a little. I told him to git Lizzie if he could. She don't never git flustered. You could put some water on to heat in the biggest kittle, an' build up the fire good 'fore you go out."

When he returned from the spring, Hattie was in bed, and from the kitchen he could hear her smothered moans. He set his own teeth and went to the back door to look down the road. He wished they would hurry.

Restlessly he built up the fire again and put the water on in the biggest kettle he could find. Then, noticing the confusion of breakfast dishes, he set to work to redd them up. His hands felt awkward in the unfamiliar task, and he was conscious constantly of Hattie in the bedroom, but he kept his mind firmly on what he was doing. The dishes, then the milk things. Or had anyone milked yet? Yes, the pails were dirty. She must have had Pa milk before he went.

A broken cry from the bedroom brought him running to the door. "Ma? Ma, you all right?"

"Go away, Hod. Git on away. I'm all right. See if they're comin'."

He went again to the door. This time he could see the wagon far down the road. Finally they were coming! He called through the door: "They're comin'. They're at the bend in the road now." And he went out to wait at the gate for them.

"You better hurry," he said curtly, when they drove up.

"Is she bad?" asked Lizzie, heaving herself over the wheel to the ground.

"I don't know," answered Hod, "but she's been takin' on a right smart, an' she's been askin' for you."

"She's likely got a good while yit," said Lizzie, but she hurried toward the house. "They ain't none of it easy."

Tom spoke. "I'll drive around an' unhitch," he said.

"I'll do it."

"Well, I kin . . ." Tom's voice trailed off, and he looked at Hod helplessly.

"It's hard on you, isn't it?" Hod's young, thin voice said. "Powerfully hard on you to stand around and listen to what's goin' on in there? Well, you had your part in it. Now get in there and see if you can help!"

There was no effort to veil the contempt in his voice, and Tom was small and helpless before it. Tom stood a moment, as if he would say something, and then he turned and walked toward the house.

Hod jerked the horse around the house. Let him help birth it, he thought. Let him stay there and listen every time she yells. Let him pay a little too!

The day wore on. It seemed to Hod an awfully long time. When he went in that night to look at his new sister he felt no tenderness. He looked at the red, wrinkled little face with no expression on his own. "She looks like a tomato," he said, and walked away.

The birth of the baby broke the straps of the harness Hod had worn for so long. Something that had been warm and gentle in his feeling toward Hattie and Tom hardened and iced in his veins. He had accepted the frustration of his deepest wants most of his

150

life as a matter of course. He had picked up the burden of caring for the family as his duty, not expecting to escape it. He had yearned and dreamed, but he had not particularly resented the fact that his yearnings and his dreams must be put away. But this was different. This ate at him and chafed him, and he was moody and silent through the days. This they had no right to do to him.

On a Sunday in midsummer Hod went to an all-day singing over on the next ridge. He felt listless about the walk over there, but he liked to sing, and maybe he'd feel better if he went.

The singing began about ten o'clock, the leader starting with some of the familiar songs. Everyone sang. The volume of sound that rose to the rafters of the little whitewashed chapel would have amazed a city preacher, accustomed only to the halfhearted efforts of his congregation. This was a noisy, joyous, hearty, lifting up of voices.

On and on the singing went, alternating between the old and the familiar and the new and untried. When one leader grew tired, another took his place. And special numbers by duets, trios, and quartets were occasionally interspersed. The people seemed never to tire. An all-day singing on the ridge was really an all-day singing!

When they stopped for the picnic dinner and Hod followed the crowd outside, he was delighted to see Johnny Knight squatting on his haunches under a big tree.

" Hi, there, Johnny," he called. " Where've you been keepin' yourself all this time? I've not seen you for a coon's age! "

" Oh, I been around," Johnny said nonchalantly. " Been workin' first one place then another. Not doin' much good no place, though. What you been doin'? "

" I've been workin' on the road project for three years now."

" Pretty hard work, ain't it? "

" Not too hard. Don't pay much, though."

They talked of other things and finally the conversation came around to the new conscription act before Congress.

" You think it's goin' through? " Hod asked.

" Shore. Hit'll go through, an' I been thinkin' what's the use o' waitin' fer 'em to come git me. Might as well go on an' enlist an'

151

git it over. I've heared you could name yer pick o' the service ifen you enlisted ahead o' time. I've shore been studyin' on it."

Hod was startled. Why hadn't he thought of this before himself? This was the perfect escape from the ridge. He turned to Johnny suddenly. "I'll go with you. When you want to go?"

Johnny rolled a cigarette and sealed it. "Ifen you mean it, an' I reckon you do, they ain't no use awaitin'. How about tomorrer?"

"The sooner the better," Hod answered.

"Well, meet me at the Gap in the mornin', an' we'll hitch our way to Fort Knox. They'll take us in there."

"I'll be there," Hod promised, and he felt a great lift of his heart. Now he was finally going to be free. The folks could fend for themselves or do without. He was through. No man, he thought, has a right to make himself a way of life that binds another. And Tom, he was convinced, was doing just that. Hod laid down the load this time, and he didn't care whether Tom picked it up.

The next morning he put ten dollars in Hattie's blue bowl on the mantel. Then he shaved, put on fresh clothes, and walked out the door. He didn't even look back as he went down the road. He had said nothing to anyone of what he meant to do. Hattie thought he was going to work, as always on Monday. She could not know, as she watched him down the road, that it would be thirty-three months before she would see him again.

He walked to the Gap, where Johnny met him, and they hitched a ride in to Campbellsville. There they debated the possibility of taking the bus to Louisville and on out to Fort Knox. But with only five dollars in Hod's pocket, and less in Johnny's, they decided against it. So they stationed themselves on the highway at the edge of town and thumbed a ride. They managed, by short hops from town to town, to arrive at Fort Knox by the middle of the afternoon. They were lost in the big camp, but when they stated their business an M.P. directed them to the recruiting office. A young lieutenant sitting behind a desk looked up as they walked in.

"We want to enlist," said Johnny.

"Just a minute," said the lieutenant. He finished what he was

152

doing.

" Now, then. Your names? "

" Johnny Knight."

" John . . . any middle name? "

" Leslie." With a slanted look at Hod.

" John L. Knight. Your name? " to Hod.

Hod had caught on. " Thomas Hodges Pierce."

" Thomas H. Pierce. And what branch of the service do you want to enlist in? "

Johnny spoke up immediately. " Tanks."

" O.K. You'll train right here. And yours? "

Hod would have liked to be with Johnny. He hadn't thought but what they would be together. But he didn't like the idea of tanks, and besides he didn't want to stay this close to home. Guess I'll have to go on my own, he thought. He took a deep breath and plunged. " I'd rather be in the engineers," he said, " but I want to get as far away from Kentucky as possible."

The lieutenant scribbled a moment. " You can take the infantry and be sent to South Carolina, or you can take the engineers and go to California."

" I'll take the engineers and California."

" O.K.," said the lieutenant. " There's a line of men in the next room waiting to go through. Fall in and take your turn."

The line moved fast and, before Hod had time to quiet his heartbeats, it was his turn. He stripped and went through a routine but thorough physical examination. He was nervous about it, for he had some bad teeth and he was afraid he might be turned down because of them. When it was over and he was told to dress again, he asked the officer, " Did I pass? "

" You're O.K.," was the answer. " Get your serial number over there."

He drew his serial number . . . 15042375 . . . and was told to memorize it immediately. " Wait outside," the group was ordered, " and draw your blankets and bedding."

The ceremony of being sworn in the following day was not impressive. The new recruits lined up in the same long room in which they had waited yesterday, raised their right hands, and repeated the oath of allegiance after the officer. Scarcely were the last words said when a busy corporal shouted: " All right. Form outside to draw your uniforms."

Hod felt strange and uncomfortable in his uniform. It fitted him tighter, for one thing, and all the regulations about its proper wear made him uneasy. But at the same time he settled it on his body with a feeling of pride. Another man might have thought of himself as shackled and regimented in the Army. But to Hod it meant freedom, and being Pvt. Thomas H. Pierce was infinitely better than being plain Hod Pierce. Instead of regimenting him, it set him apart.

The three days passed quickly. Johnny was permanently assigned and moved to another part of the camp. But Hod was kept so busy that he had little time to think of it. He wrote Hattie a card during that time — one stabbing sentence: " I have joined the Army." He dug the point of the pen into the period at the end of the sentence. There was satisfaction in waving his banner of freedom.

When they were loading onto the bus to go to Louisville the day they left, Johnny showed up. He didn't have much to say. Just shook Hod's hand and warned him, " Keep yer nose clean."

As the bus pulled into the drive, Hod looked back and watched Johnny walk off. Suddenly he felt friendless and very much alone and there was a knot in his stomach. He liked Johnny Knight. He'd always found him a bighearted guy. That time Tom was sick, for instance. And you couldn't ask for a better guy to have fun with. He remembered the night in Louisville. He wished they could have been in the same outfit. But it was too late to think about that now. A man had to go his own way.

He didn't examine his feeling any further than that. He didn't realize that it was mostly because Johnny was his last link with Piney Ridge that he felt this sudden appreciation of him, and that even while he was fluttering his brave new wings in flight, they were circling once more around home.

CHAPTER EIGHTEEN

THE TRIP TO THE WEST COAST was an enchanted time to Hod. He had seen trains before, but he had never ridden one. And here he was riding for three days and nights in a Pullman. He marveled at the way the beds were pulled down at night and deftly made up by the porter. He stretched out between the crisp sheets and let himself be lulled to sleep by the swaying motion of the train, and felt old and wise and experienced.

He was shy in the diner, studying long over the menu until the waiter helpfully made suggestions. He didn't think the food was anything to brag about. Hattie could beat the cooks they had on the train all to pieces. But it was something just to sit down at that little table, with its snowy white cloth and baffling array of silver, and order whatever you wanted.

The thing that fascinated him most was the broadening country he saw from the car windows. Never had he dreamed of such vastness! Distances, space, the fathomless reaches of the sky shook him, and left him feeling small. He hadn't known or suspected how the land could roll out as far as the eye could see, flat, level, and endless.

When they reached the mountains he was stunned by their magnificence. Piney Ridge was left a puny, paltry little hump against the earth by the side of these sleeping giants. The other fellows poked fun at the way he kept his face glued to the pane of glass by his seat. " He's a regular Kentucky hillbilly," they said. " Never been nowheres before."

But he didn't mind. He admitted quickly he had never been anywhere before. He had to know about them — this new land and these new skies. This was what he had come for.

After two weeks at March Field, Hod was sent to the presidio of Monterey. There he began to learn how to be a soldier. Day after day of close order drill. Inspection. Guard duty. Reveille. Retreat. Gold-bricking. Week-end passes. All the official and unofficial things that make up a GI day he learned. He shook down into the routine, added several hundred new words to his vocabulary, got sucked in on the usual number of old Army games, and gradually the rawness wore off the recruit and a soldier was made. And Hod was a good soldier. Hattie had prepared him well for the discipline of the Army, which expected him to do as he was told, to question no command, and to jump when he heard the word " frog."

On his week ends he wandered through the city, going off alone so that he might seek out the things he wanted to see. He stood on street corners and watched the fast lines of traffic and the crowds of people. He listened to the gabble of voices on the sidewalks and in the stores, and he searched out queer places to eat, trying new foods and not liking most of them. He was like a sponge soaking up every new experience.

Most of all he liked to go to the beach. He would sit hour after hour watching the waves roll up on top of each other. The rhythm of their inward surging held him hynotically and he watched and listened. This was another thing he had come to see — these far waters lapping on the sand. He let a wave roll over his foot and looked at his wet foot strangely. Did these same drops wash up against another land? The ocean was too big for him. There was no comprehending such width and such depth. A man's mind wouldn't stretch that far. He wished he **could** tell someone about this now. He would say this water is **bigger** than all the words that tell of it. The waves come creeping **up** on the sand, like a cat licking cream, soft and smoothlike. He would say the sky comes down to meet it in the west, and the sun is drowned each night in the water. And it paints the water red and purple and gold. He laughed. Anyone on Piney Ridge would answer that he didn't keer for sich!

When he signed his first payroll, Hod found that after all he did care whether Tom picked up the load, and that two thousand miles between him and home did not make it any less home. He sent ten of his twenty-one dollars home every month. The rasping file of his resentment against Tom and Hattie had dulled and he was remembering, nostalgically, only the things he loved most about the ridge. Out from under the chafing yoke, he could have a more selfless understanding of their helplessness to be anything other than what they were. He remembered with shame his indifference to the new baby, and he was careful always to ask about her when he wrote. He sent her small gifts and in other ways tried to atone for his spiritual denial of her.

The months slipped by. Hod dug trenches, built barbed-wire entanglements, learned to purify water, shoveled gravel and sand on roads, and braced heavy bridge girders. He was sent over to

Fort Ord and made his first rating there. After nine months there he moved on up the coast into Washington, and from there he went to Colorado. Wherever he went, he tested the feel of the land and the people.

"This here's a soft country," he wrote home of Washington, "soft with mist like that which wraps around the trees down in the holler. The grass and the trees are a downy green, and the sky blue is like a baby's eyes. There are the prettiest creeks I ever saw. Tumbling and rushing down the hills. But it's a strange-feeling land at that."

Of the mountains in Colorado he wrote briefly: "There are some things just too big to tell about. A man feels like a little ant standing under these mountains. I would be hard put to be content with them towering over me."

The poet mind, which in the little boy had avidly absorbed Tennyson and Keats and Browning, struggled now with these new beauties, to find a way to tell of them. Something in him hurt with beauty, opened wide to it and let it in. And he wanted to let it out again, transformed, made vocal, singing a new song. His letters were full of what he saw, but they hardly scratched the surface of what he felt.

A year and a half went by. There were times when Hod felt as if he had never known any other life than the Army. But there were other times when he looked down at the strange soil his boots strode across and wondered how Hod Pierce happened to be there. Then the Army and Pvt. Thomas H. Pierce, 15042375, were dissolved, and he walked the ridge again, old Duke to heel and his gun cradled in the bend of his arm. Those were homesick moments when he wanted achingly to see the folks, and to ramble through the woods and fields again. Jeems, he thought, must have yearned for Abigail and the cabin in the holler in much the same way.

Along in November he put in for a Christmas furlough. It would be good to be at home for Christmas. Hattie would cook a goose and make a pile of dressing to go with it. They would have a little pine Christmas tree, fragrant and fresh from the woods, star-bright and spangly with ornaments. Irma and John would come over and they would all go to church on Christmas Eve and walk home through the brittle cold. Maybe it would even snow and they could crunch through its crispness, making it squeak under their heels. He would buy Sarah a big doll, and she would be as pretty as a Christmas doll herself! Ah, they would have a wonderful Christmas!

The furlough came through and he wrote saying he would start home on December 20. He was counting the days. Week ends he haunted the stores doing his Christmas shopping. He got a warm, fleecy robe for Hattie, who was up in the night so often . . . and a pair of fuzzy little slippers for Gramma's tiny feet. He held them in the palm of his hand and laughed at their size. " I reckon they'll do," he told the clerk. " She isn't any bigger than a minute."

And he found the big doll for Sarah — a beautiful, lifelike doll with blue eyes and yellow hair. He could see Sarah now, hugging it close. He couldn't wait to watch her eyes when she saw it under the tree!

But his Christmas furlough was not to be. On December 7 the stars changed their courses, and his destiny and that of millions of other men like him was shaped to fit a new world.

The night after war was officially declared, the captain called the men together. It was a solemn moment. " Men," he said, " this is it. We're at war now. Our job is plain. Nothing is important now except winning the war. We're in the Army for the duration."

The duration! Not for one year. Not for three years. For the duration. And no one could know how long the duration would be! The words echoed down the unknown years and rolled on into infinity. No one in the room that night knew where he might be sent before the year was over, or what awful thing might happen to him. The ink in which each man's lease on life was written dimmed and blurred, and the future faded into darkness.

Hod knew his own moment of panic, along with the rest. Then he wrote home: " This war changes everything. I can't come home now, and it's doubtful when I'll get to come. I am mailing you the presents I wrote about. I was going to give them to you myself. But now that can't be. I'll come when I can."

The 19th settled down to the serious business of training for specific jobs. There was a grim purpose now which had not characterized their work before. Hod was counted an old soldier, and in June he was picked to go on a cadre to a camp in Missouri. He felt fine about being chosen to go. It was no mean recognition to be selected as one of the small group of noncommissioned officers to form the skeleton of a new outfit. He had been tool corporal for nearly six months, and he took a pride in keeping the company's tools bright and shining and sharp. It was no accident that on every company problem the men maneuvered to get his tools. "They're always in first-class shape," they said. Going on the cadre was a sort of special reward.

The camp in Missouri was another arid concentration of men who had been drafted to learn the art of war. Hod's job was to teach them what he knew of it. Shortly after reporting in he had been made sergeant, and he was now out in front of a squad, drilling the feet off of them, whipping their curved spines into taut, lean thongs, stripping the fat from their soft sides, pickling, hardening, tightening them against the day when their lives might depend upon their being indurate as steel. Better to be merciless now than sorry later.

But no rookie ever sees past his swollen feet and his aching back, and a top sergeant is always Simon Legree. Hod, having been through the mill himself, knew when they hated him most, but he flogged them hardest then. And when they went into the Tennessee hills on maneuvers that fall they were tough as leather, resilient, stretchy, springy, and unbreakable. He was proud of them during those killing days. Men who had already seen action in Africa shook their heads over the Tennessee maneuvers. "War ain't no worse," they said. But that was the reason for the maneuvers — so that war wouldn't be any worse.

The Tennessee hills were enough like home to make Hod look longingly north over their rolling curves. He would have walked every mile to get there, but there wasn't time for even so much as a week-end pass. He was lucky to get twenty-four hours once, to go into Nashville.

When the 44th went to Wisconsin that October for winter training, Hod went along. There, in weather thirty below zero and in snow up to their knees, those same tough kids did four-, six-, and eight-mile marches with full field packs. The winds jelled the marrow in their bones and congealed the blood in their veins. But they didn't fall out. "They're O.K.," Hod said to the captain. "They'll do." And then, in the middle of the worst cold spell they had had all winter, the 44th were issued tropical clothing, mosquito nets, Atabrine tablets, and were shipped out to Africa!

Hod didn't go with them. The old soldiers were still needed too desperately to make new soldiers. A good top sergeant was often worth more in camp than he was on the beaches. This time he was sent to Texas.

After the misery of his northern winter he couldn't get enough of the sun, and it was paradise to be where it beat down hotly day after day. He scorched himself into brown leather and felt his blood thaw and run free again. But there was little else about Texas that he liked. The brown, wasted reaches of western Texas held no attraction for him. He snorted as he looked out over the vastness one day. Grampa would say this land ain't good enough to raise a fuss on, he thought, chuckling!

It was now that Hod had his biggest chance to become somebody, according to Army standards. And it was now that he learned exactly how much Piney Ridge he was.

After a series of intelligence tests, given soon after he reached the camp, Hod was called into the office.

"Pierce," the captain said, "your I.Q. is in the upper bracket and you've got a good record with the men. We're sending a bunch over to Belvoir next week to O.C.S. You can go along if you like."

Officer Candidate School! The gold bars of a second lieutenant . . . more pay . . . men saluting him . . . responsibility . . . prestige! He wanted it more than anything! And, wanting it, he should have said yes immediately, while he was still Sergeant Pierce standing at ease before his captain. He should never have asked for time to think it over. But some deep-rooted uneasiness took hold of him.

"May I let the captain know later, sir?" And he gave himself time. Time in which to sink back into the timid inertia of Piney Ridge. To sink back into a distrust of change . . . a fear of failure . . . a dark clinging to the slow, familiar things . . . a wrapping of the self in the womb of safety.

He tried to pull himself up to the bars on the shoulders; dreamed of himself at staff meetings . . . in an officer's uniform.

160

But something else kept saying: That course at Belvoir is tough . . . They really put you through the mill over there . . . It would be tougher for me than most . . . I'm older than the others . . . I wouldn't have a chance in a million to make it . . . I've got a good thing where I am . . . I like my job . . . why should I frash myself?

Thus he argued with himself, and was torn between the dream and the reality. Finally he pulled the blue heights of the dream down to Piney Ridge and leveled it under the thin dust of rationalization. He told the captain he preferred to stay with the outfit. He made it sound as if he thought he could best serve where he was. He could not admit even to himself that the familiar job and the family of enlisted men supplied him with confidence in himself, and shored up his frightened sense of inadequacy. He could not confess that he dared not risk this hard-won security in a new and untried world.

Perhaps a lot of his fear lay in his intuitive knowledge that to him the men in the Army paralleled Piney Ridge. The officers were over across a fence, where the language was foreign, the customs were alien, and the standards were strange. With all his heart he had wanted to climb over that fence. But something that was part of the breath of his life wouldn't turn loose; wouldn't let him frash himself. He put it behind him uneasily . . . tried never to dig it up and look at it. But it lay there, heavy, just the same.

Hod was shifted from squad leader to weapon sergeant. His sentient fingers handled guns with the same genius with which they had handled tools, and not only could he endow them with a personality of their own — he could teach other men to do so too. He turned out gun crew after gun crew who worked together with perfect precision and co-ordination, turning in consistently high scores.

But there was something different about this outfit right from the start. It was in the nightly NCO meetings, the urgency of maneuvers, the nervous energy of the officers, the razor edge of the men themselves. Hod felt it, and let it run through him like quicksilver. This battalion was being groomed for special work. There was no mistaking it. This was it.

They moved over to the Gulf coast for the summer, and the emphasis shifted from road construction and bridge-building to assault landing, removal of underwater obstacles and mines, and the clearing of beaches. They knew then that this was the real stuff. This was invasion engineering; combat engineering. This was the kind of stuff that moved in on the beaches with the infantry. And their minds were full of questions. Where will it be? When does it come off? How soon will we ship out? The rumor factory worked overtime. Men in his outfit asked Hod, " You know anything about it? " And he shook his head, " Not a thing."

But he knew as well as they that they were headed for some long stretch of sand where the far waters lapped lonesomely. Only a man wouldn't have time to stand and watch the waves come creaming up on the beach. He wouldn't want to if he could. He would be too busy trying to keep from getting shot.

CHAPTER NINETEEN

NOTHING HAS CHANGED, he thought, as he started up the ridge from the Gap. It's been a hundred years since I left, but nothing has changed. The rocks are just as sharp, the trees are just as old, and the hills are just as steep. Forever and enduring the hills are the same. The words of the ancient psalm came to his mind: " I will lift up mine eyes unto the hills, from whence cometh my help "! He dug his toes into the acid dust, scuffed it on his shoes, and sniffed the smell of it. Kentucky dust. Kentucky sky. Kentucky hills. Fly away, Kentucky babe . . . fly away . . . but come home to the hills to rest.

He paused in the quiet little woodsy place and laid his hand against cool, white birch bark. He smiled when he saw where he had cut his initials. He remembered the time. Grampa had just given him a new knife. He couldn't wait to try it out! A mocking-bird poured a liquid song over him from the treetops, and an old blue jay scolded him from a sumac bush. " Did you miss me? " Hod said softly. " Did you think I wasn't comin' back? "

The last mile of the road seemed eternally long, and when he rounded the bend and could see the low roof of the house, the supper smoke tailing out of the chimney, his heart ballooned into his throat and pumped achingly there. He wanted to reach out his arms and pull it close. He wanted never to let it go.

He hadn't let them know he was coming. Furloughs had started coming through suddenly about midsummer, and when he drew fifteen days the latter part of July, he knew that port of embarkation was just around the corner. By the time he was sure of his furlough, he had known he could beat a letter home.

The front room was empty when he walked in. He dumped his musette bag on the floor and called, " Anybody home? "

Hattie ran from the kitchen. She stared at him, unbelieving, for a long moment. Then she began to cry. " Hit's Hod," she said, and her thin brown arms reached for him hungrily and drew him close. It was perhaps the first time since he was a little boy that she had touched him in affection. But gladness broke down her wall of reserve. She rocked him gently back and forth, her wet face pressed against him. " Hit's Hod," she said, " hit's Hod." Over and over she said it, as if she could not get enough assurance it was really he. " Hit's Hod."

Finally she stepped back and wiped her eyes with the heels of her hands. " Let me git a good look at you," she laughed shakily. " Hit's been so long! Jist let me look at you! " She turned him round and round and pulled and picked at his uniform. " Hit don't seem natural," she said. " Hit jist don't seem right fer you to be wearin' sich clothes! An' yer thin, Hod! Don't you git enough to eat? "

" I get plenty," he answered reassuringly. " They feed us fine. But I walk it off and work it off. Anyway, I've never been fat, and you know it! "

" Well, I jist weary myself plumb to death! Nights I jist cain't sleep, seems like, thinkin' 'bout you, way off somewheres away from home. Nobody to do fer you. Jist seems like it's more'n I kin bear."

Hod pushed away from him the knowledge of how much heavier her nights would be before long. He didn't know how he could tell her. Best leave it lie.

" Where's Pa? " he asked. "And where's Gramma? "

But Hattie darted suddenly to the kitchen. She came back holding a small girl by the hand. " This here's the tomater! " Hattie said proudly.

Sarah was three now. And when she saw Hod, she ducked her head in unbearable shyness and hid her face in her mother's apron. But she peeked out, to blink one wide blue eye at him.

"I don't believe it," Hod said, going down on one knee and holding out his arms. She was a Botticelli angel, head covered with a fluff of silvery duck curls, and chin pressed with the same deep, probing finger as Hattie's and Hod's. She looked warily at Hod, but as he coaxed her she moved inch by inch, one step at a time, toward him. Finally he lifted her in his arms. She was so soft; so almost fluid in her roundness. As he held her, he had a sense of his own loss. If he had married, one like her might be his own. A wave of tenderness for her flooded him and he buried his nose in the feathery down of her hair. *I didn't mean you looked like a tomato! I didn't mean it at all!*

He followed Hattie into the kitchen where she was rattling pots and pans and poking up a fire. "Law me, Hod," she was saying, "I ain't got e'er thing fitten to eat tonight! I was jist aimin' to have leftovers from dinner. You ortent to come in this way an' surprise a body! I wasn't expectin' nobody but us."

"Don't fret, Ma," he assured her. "Anything you've got'll taste good to me. Just be sure and make me some hot corn bread. I've dreamed about that corn bread of yours. And many's the time I'd have walked five miles for a piece of it. Where'd you say Pa was?"

Hattie laughed. "I plumb fergot you asked! Why, him an' Gault's aworkin' in the tobaccer. They got a new patch over on a piece o' Gault's land. He'll be home directly. An' Gramma's feedin' the chickens."

Tobacco! From everlasting to everlasting tobacco! Now he knew he was at home!

It was good to sit on the porch after supper in the last cool dimness of the day. To pick at his guitar, listen to the gossip of the ridge, and talk quietly. He sat in his old place on the step, with his head against the post, and Tom loomed over him on the porch railing. Gramma squeaked her little rocker, and spat into the dark when her snuff overflowed. Hod thought she had grown even tinier, and her mind wandered these days so that she moved almost constantly in a misty dream of the past. Times, she knew him. Spoke of his boyhood and young manhood. But mostly she

164

thought he was Tom. Or again, appallingly, she thought he was the young Dow. She dimpled then, and hung her head, and chided him for staying away so long. Gramma moved in a dream. But it was a gentle dream which wrapped her from the pain and worry and loss of her life.

Hattie sat near Hod, and her eyes seldom left him. She felt whole and filled full again. She reached out a hand to him time and again, as if her entire being was still saying, "Hit's Hod."

The western sky rested on the tops of the beeches across the road, and fireflies punctured the growing dark like a thousand candles. Katydids sawed on their tuneless fiddles. The cinnamon vine and the yellow rose poured out their sweetness. Down in the holler an old bullfrog garrumphed doggedly, and under the porch Duke thumped at his fleas. Around the world guns were roaring, and tomorrow he would be deaf from their sound. But tonight, in this blessed spot, there was peace. The earth hung suspended, and tonight was all there was of time.

It was Saturday when Hod got home, and he went with the family to church the next morning. The little white church was packed. There always was a good crowd, but on this Sabbath there was a gathering of the clan to welcome Hod. Hattie stood aside while he exchanged howdies with the friends and relatives, quietly refracting the rays of his glory in the prism of her pride.

Inside, even the preacher took note of him. After the opening prayer and song he pointed out that Hod was there, calling him one of the "stanch defenders of our country." Hod was uncomfortable. He hadn't defended anything yet. But it was nice of the preacher to notice him. This was a new preacher since Hod left, and it was doubly nice of him to take note.

"Sergeant Pierce," he was saying, "we'd like to have you lead us in a song. They tell me you used to lead the singing quite a bit before you went in the Army."

Hod, who was holding Sarah, fumbled a moment as he handed her to Hattie. "Well, I never was a real expert, like Little Wells over there. But if you'll put up with me, I'll try." He started up the aisle, the back of his neck pink with embarrassment.

Sarah was struggling to follow him, and when her mother took

165

a firm grip on her and set her down solidly, she set up such a wailing for Hod that the whole church rang with it. Hattie tried desperately to quiet her, but she wouldn't be hushed. "Hod," she kept crying, "Hod," in a bereft and heartbroken little voice. Hattie rose to take her out, but Hod walked back down the aisle, stopped her, and took the little girl in his arms. She rubbed her nose against his chin and sniffed contentedly.

> "'Faith of our fathers! living still
>   In spite of dungeon, fire, and sword,
> O how our hearts beat high with joy
>   Whene'er we hear that glorious word:
> Faith of our fathers, holy faith!
> We will be true to thee till death.'"

With Sarah on one arm and the other marking the rhythm, Hod led the congregation in the stalwart old hymn of reaffirmation.

> "'And through the truth that comes from Cod
>   Mankind shall then be truly free:
> Faith of our fathers, holy faith!
> We will be true to thee till death. Amen.'"

Amen! Hod's heart echoed the solemn ratification. Amen. In this place of his fathers, from which he was going forth, it was good to sing about faith. To touch it in the reality of his people. To weld again his link in the chain that circled the ridge folks.

Irma and John and their six-month-old Johnnie went home with them for the big Sunday dinner that followed church. The table sagged with food. Fried chicken, crisp and brown, piled on platters at either end of the long board. Soft, fluffy mashed potatoes heaped in a tremendous bowl. Rich cream gravy, which made Hod lick his lips. Green beans from the garden and early roasting ears. Great, thick, red slices of tomatoes, and thin, green curls of cucumbers. And for dessert, when they were almost too full to hold another bite, there were spiced peaches and chocolate cake. When he finally pushed back his chair, Hod groaned. "Ma," he said, "the way you cook is a gift from God."

Hattie flushed with pleasure at the compliment. "Well, I orta be able to cook right good," she replied, "after doin' it fer all these years."

While the womenfolks washed up the dishes, Tom took himself to the back room for a nap and Hod and John wandered out onto the porch. They talked of crops awhile, and the weather. John told of a different kind of corn he was going to try next year. " Leastways ifen they don't call me in the Army 'fore then," he said.

" You won't have to go yet, surely."

" No. Not right away, I don't reckon. I ain't any too happy 'bout stayin' out. Sorta feel like I'm lettin' somebody else do my fightin'. But they's Irma an' the baby to think of. An' the farm. 'Pears like they need what we kin raise as bad as e'er thing else. I reckon if they git to needin' me they'll let me know."

" You've no call to feel bad," Hod assured him. " There's still plenty of single fellows that haven't been called. They're the ones to go first."

" You think it's goin' to be a long war, Hod? "

" Well, I think it's goin' to last so bitter long we'll all forget there ever was a time when it wasn't goin' on. I think it's not even good started yet. And I wouldn't care to guess when it might end."

They were silent, pondering the immensity of the octopus that was gripping the world in its tentacles. John shivered. " Think you'll go over across the waters? "

" Bound to." Hod couldn't say he was already on his way.

" Hit'll jist about kill Hattie when you have to go."

" That's what I hate most about goin'. She'll worry herself sick."

John pulled a straw of dry grass and stuck it between his teeth. " Reckon you heared Johnny Knight was killed."

" No! " Hod said, and his chair legs bumped the floor. " No. I hadn't heard. Where? "

" On one o' them little islands out there in the Pacific. Got blowed to bits in a air raid is the way I heared it."

Hod's heels bit into the chair rung. He saw the pieces of Johnny Knight, red and dripping like a butchered beef, hurled violently into the air. No! No! He swung his mind away from it. Johnny, how far is it home? About two hundred miles. It's farther than that, Johnny. It's a heck of a lot farther than that.

The women joined them on the porch, Irma carrying Hod's guitar. " Sing somethin' fer us, Hod," she said, handing him the guitar.

He hesitated. He didn't feel much like singing. Then he reached for the instrument. All right. He'd sing. Requiem for Johnny Knight, blown to bits on an island in the Pacific!

> " ' In Scarlet town where I was born
> There was a fair maid dwellin';
> Made every youth cry well aday,
> Her name was Barbry Allen.

> " ' 'Twas all in the merry month of May,
> When green buds they were swellin';
> Sweet William come from out the west,
> An' courted Barbry Allen.' "

"You goin' to do any courtin' while you're home from out the west?" teased Irma, when the last notes of the song died mournfully away.

"Not a bit," he promised lightly. "I'm savin' my love."

"What fer? A rainy day?"

"For ' the lily maid of Astolat,' " he whispered, only half joking.

The days went by all too fast, and as they slipped carelessly into the past, Hod threaded the present carefully through his fingers and knotted it into himself. He pulled down the hills and packed them into the places that would be empty inside of him. He stored the baby's gay laugh and rippling stream of words into the voiceless regions of his mind, to drink from when the sands were hot and dry. He took the slow, sleepy days and stitched a cushion against the sleeplessness to come. He wrapped Piney Ridge around him and pinned the edges down, tight.

He said good-by.

CHAPTER TWENTY

THE BUS WAS AN HOUR AND FORTY MINUTES LATE at Bowling Green, where Hod made connections going back to camp. And when it nosed its way into the dock, there was still a thirty-minute supper stop to wait out. As the passengers poured off the bus and streamed into the station, Hod watched them hurry past and restlessly lighted a cigarette. He wanted to be on his way.

Through the open door of the bus he could see a girl sitting in the first seat. The contagion of haste seemed not to have touched her, for she was fluffing a powder puff against her nose and applying fresh lipstick to her mouth. She slapped a little circle of shiny black straw, not much blacker than her hair, on the back of her head, patted it a couple of times, wriggled her dress into place, and crawled down out of the bus. He watched her walk across the station platform, noticing the free swing of her legs, the slender length of her body, the lift of her head on her throat. He got a whiff of some flowerlike smell as she went by, and he noticed that her eyes were almost as dark as her hair. His tongue probed the rough spot on his tooth. She wasn't a kid. He judged she would be about twenty-seven or -eight. Somewhere near his own age. Then he shrugged her from his mind, and took up again his boredom with the long wait. A paper boy came by and he bought a paper, glanced at the headlines, read the funnies, and folded it to throw away.

"Don't throw it away," said a voice at his elbow. "If you're through with it, let me have it." The girl had come back and was standing just back of him.

"Sure," he said, handing it to her. "You must have eaten in a hurry."

"I didn't eat," she answered. "We're due in Nashville at 8:30, and I'd rather get a good meal there than to grab a sandwich here. Thanks for the paper. They were all out inside." And she got back on the bus, seated herself, and was immersed in the paper before he could think of anything else to say. He liked her voice too. It was pitched low, with a richness that sang. Like the G string on his guitar. He had been surprised when she cut the conversation short. Experience had taught him that when girls opened the way for talk, they were usually opening the way for more. Could be she just wanted the paper, though, he concluded.

The passengers filtered back onto the bus and Hod waited until it was loaded, knowing they were entitled to their former places and he would have to take what was left. When the bus driver nodded for him to get on, he swung up the steps and paused just inside the door to look the situation over. There were two seats, one beside the girl, and one on the long seat across the

169

back. He grinned as he stopped beside the girl. "Is this seat taken?"

She grinned back at him. "Not unless you want it."

"It's taken." He racked his musette bag and hitched up his pants.

The girl had taken off her hat and she handed it to him now. "Put this up for me, please," she said, and by the time he had carefully made a place for it, and seated himself, she was deep in the paper again. Home, James, he thought, and determined to let her alone. Nuts to women who act like the queen of Sheba!

The bus was well on its way, rolling into the sun toward Nashville, when she finished with the paper. She folded it and tucked it neatly down by the arm of the seat. Now she was ready to talk, he supposed. He braced himself. They always said the same old things, and he was weary of the answers. Been in the Army long, soldier? Been home on furlough? Where are you stationed? What branch are you in? What does that shoulder patch mean? It was a game you played to be polite.

But she said nothing for a while. Instead she leaned her head back against the seat and kept her eyes fixed out the window. The bus tires were hissing on the pavement, and the sun was a golden coin dropping into the slit of the hills. She turned to him suddenly. "Did you ever see anything as beautiful as that sunset? Look, it's all red and gold and purple! And look at the way the tops of the hills stand up against it . . . like they've been drawn in with black ink!"

Hod followed her pointing finger. "It sure is pretty," he agreed. "That gold band back of the hills looks like it was sewed to the sky, doesn't it?"

"Oh, yes!" she laughed, delighted. "Yes. With nice, neat seams."

She was quiet for a time, watching. Then: "A sunset's such an extravagant thing, isn't it? Like the day had flung every color in its paintbox into the sky before going to bed at night."

"A sunrise is mighty pretty too."

"Oh, a sunrise is a pale, weak thing compared to a sunset! It's so timid!"

"Well, I've seen many a one that wasn't! The break of day's not always so timid! Especially over the sea. One minute the light is dim, and the next minute the sun has turned it to brass."

"Lovely," she said, and then, suddenly, "What is the most beautiful thing you ever saw in your life?"

"The most beautiful thing I ever saw?" Hod was surprised, but he tried earnestly to think, turning over in his mind all the forms of beauty he had ever stored there. "I don't rightly know. There are so many beautiful things in the world. There are the stars over the holler on a clear night. And mists in the valley early in the morning, rising and curling around the trees like smoke. A rainbow's a mighty pretty thing too. And a crab apple tree in bloom is just about the sweetest sight you could ever hope to see."

"Oh, yes! We had a crap apple tree in our back yard in one of the places we lived once. It has a pinky bloom!"

"That's right. And young beech leaves are soft and pretty when they first come out," Hod went on, "and a dogwood flower would be hard to beat. A field of green corn's mighty sightly too. I don't know as you could say what's the most beautiful. But I believe the hills against the sky, sort of like they are tonight, is just about the best."

"You were born in the hills, weren't you?"

"Yeah. Just a Kentucky hillbilly, and I don't reckon I'll ever get very far away from it."

"Why would you want to?"

"Well, there's better ways of livin' than the folks back in the hills where I come from know about. If you could put good livin' into the hills, I'd have no wish to leave them. But the way it is, it takes the soul out of a man just to scrabble a livin' out of the ground. Hill ground is always poor ground for raisin' crops, and hill people don't usually know enough about makin' it any better. Things sort of jog along. Nobody's got anything, nobody ever expects to have anything. It's that hopelessness that I'm afraid of and want to get away from."

"Is that true of all hill people? Do they all have that feeling of hopelessness?"

"No. No, I don't reckon you could say it's true of all hill people. If you've never had anything, and don't even know there's more to be had, you can't feel hopeless about not havin' it, can you?"

"That's just what I mean! You're afraid of hopelessness because

171

you've been waked up to what it means, isn't that it? "

" Partly. But mostly I think I was born knowin' what it means. I can't remember when I wasn't strugglin' against it . . . when I didn't wonder why my family was the way it was . . . why the Pierces settled on Piney Ridge, and why none of them ever amounted to anything, or ever wanted an education, or ever thought of livin' differently. Nobody told me those things to think about. I was just born different, someway or other. I've been pulled back and forth between bein' a Pierce on Piney Ridge and lovin' it, and wantin' something better and not knowin' what it is, ever since I can remember."

The girl was listening intently, and she was still when he finished talking. After a while she said: " What would something better be? Do you have any idea? "

" It would be . . ." he struggled for the words, " it would be makin' something out of myself. When you've not had much all your life, it sort of gets important to have things. I'd like to have a good job. And I'd like to have things nice. You know . . . pretty things, I reckon. Like a nice home . . . nice furniture . . . that sort of thing. I used to say I was goin' to be somebody! I don't rightly know how yet, but I still think I'd like my chance at it."

And then he found himself telling her the things he would have resented her asking. " I wanted more education than I had a chance to get. And there wasn't any way I could get it. I tried. Once I thought I had a good start on it. But my father got sick and I had to go home and take over. And I had to stay on makin' the livin' after that. And then a thing happened that made me feel like I had a right to leave. And I joined the Army. All I could think of was gettin' off the ridge, and I took the Army as the best way out. I enlisted for three years, and my time would have been up this summer, but the war came along. Now if I've got any future, it's got to wait awhile. But if I come through the war, I'm still goin' to try. Somewhere. Somehow. I'll find where I'm supposed to belong . . . the place where I fit best . . . and the thing I'm supposed to do."

The girl's finger was drumming on the arm of the seat, and she smiled at him. " Man looking for his home," she said. " As far back as the first man who could think, men have been trying to find their homes in this universe. Some call it security. Some call it

172

peace of mind. Some call it religion. But it's a yearning that's as old as time. 'To be somebody' — that's putting it very well."

Hod was embarrassed suddenly. "Look," he said, "I didn't mean to talk so much. I wasn't tryin' to tell you the story of my life!"

"I'm interested," she protested. "And I want to hear some more. Go on. Tell me about those hills of yours."

"Oh, they're just hills. A little steeper than most. A little rockier than most. They look just like any other hills. The only difference is that I've lived in them all my life. They're down in the southern part of Kentucky."

"And you were born and raised there?"

"Me . . . and my father . . . and my grandfather . . . and his father. That's about as far back as we know."

The girl looked at him, her dark eyes wide and full. "Imagine living all your life where your people have always lived!" She caught her lower lip between her teeth and shook her head a little. "Tell me what your home is like."

"It's a little old house my Grampa built nearly seventy-five years ago. At least he built the first of it. My father built onto it later. It's got four rooms and a loft room." He laughed. "The old cat 'n' clay chimney's still standin'."

"What's a cat 'n' clay chimney?"

"It's sticks and rocks and mud plastered together. Easiest way to build a chimney . . . out of whatever's closest to hand. When the mud dries, it's as stout as concrete almost."

"Doesn't it crumble?"

"In time, I reckon. But it takes a mighty long time."

"What else is your home like?"

"Well, there's a picket fence around the front yard, and a yellow rosebush by the chimney. My grandmother planted it. She got the cutting from Grampa Dow's mother. There's a saying that there's always a yellow rosebush in a Pierce yard. There's domi-necker chickens scratching around in the grass in the yard, and there's a couple of cows in the pasture. One has a new calf. And there's old Buck, the horse, and old Duke, my dog. And there's a beech grove across the road, and a spring down under the hill."

The girl caught her lip again and breathed deeply. "It sounds beautiful."

173

"It is beautiful. It's the most beautiful place in the world. There's times when I want to be there so bad I hurt. But when I'm there too long, it gets to be ugly. Then it hurts me to stay. I get all mixed up."

"Everyone gets all mixed up at times."

"Yes, but I've been mixed up all my life!"

"What about your people?"

"There's my mother — Hattie's her name — and my father, Tom Pierce. And Gramma lives with us since Grampa died. And there's my sister, Irma, who's married and lives about four miles from us. And then there's the baby, Sarah."

"The baby?"

"Yes. She's just three. See," he said earnestly, "Ma and Pa had eight of us, but only Irma and I lived. And we were grown and Irma was married when Sarah came along. That's what made me leave home, like I said awhile ago. I hated the whole business. I felt sorry for myself, I reckon. Seemed like I'd been chained there makin' the livin' for so long, and another mouth to feed was just the last straw." He fumbled with his hands and eased his eyes away. "I'm sort of ashamed of it now."

"The way you felt was pretty natural, don't you think? Most people would have felt that way, I'm certain."

Hod sighed and stretched his long legs out in front of him. "Now, that's enough about me," he said. "It's your turn, now. What about you?"

The girl spread her hands and laughed. "There's not much to tell about me. I teach school in Louisville, and I live in a tiny little apartment there. There's no picket fence, and no yellow rosebush, and no dominecker hens there! Just three little rooms."

"Haven't you got any folks?"

"My father and mother are dead. My aunt lives in El Paso. I have a sister and two brothers, but they're all married and live in the west."

"Were you raised out west?"

"In Texas. My father and my mother were both schoolteachers. My aunt is a teacher too, and when both my parents died, I went to live with her until I finished college."

"How did you happen to come to Kentucky?"

"Maybe I had to find something better for myself too."

174

"You mean you had to get away from something?"

"No. Not that exactly. But I had to make my own way. I had to find out what would make me myself . . . just like you're looking for yourself."

"Did you find it?"

"Not entirely. Yet."

"Look," Hod was eager. "Look. This is the funniest talkin' I've ever done with a girl. I don't even know your name and I've told you things about myself I've never told anyone before. I feel like I've known you all my life!"

"That's because you don't know me at all, isn't it? You can tell a sympathetic stranger things you wouldn't dream of telling someone you knew well. Just because you don't know the stranger, and he won't be critical of you and judge you."

"Yes, but I do know you . . . now. I know that you know all about me, because I've told you all about me. And I know you feel like I do about the things that are most important to me. I could stand by your side and look at the sunset, and I wouldn't need to say a word. I'd know what you were feeling and thinking. And I know that you know what I mean when I say I have to be somebody . . . have to find myself. Because you've been looking for yourself. How can that happen in an hour?"

"I don't know."

"I don't know, either. Who are you?"

"Mary . . . Mary Hogan."

"Mary Hogan," he repeated the name. "Mary Hogan." He reached over and took her ringless left hand and spread the fingers gently apart. "You didn't say Mrs. Mary Hogan, did you?"

"No," she laughed, freeing her hand. "It's just Mary Hogan."

"Is Mary Hogan promised to someone? Please, I'm not just bein' curious. At least I don't mean to be. It's awfully important."

"No," she answered, "she's not promised to anyone, either."

Hod sighed with relief. "Good," he said. "Where are you goin'?"

"To El Paso. I'm on my vacation, and I usually spend part of it with Miss Willie."

"Miss Willie?"

"My aunt."

"Oh. Hey, you'll be goin' through Dallas, won't you?"

"Yes. I have to change there."

Hod did some figuring. "You know this is wonderful. I'm goin' to Texas too. I'm stationed at Camp Swift, just outside Austin. I hadn't planned to go any farther than Nashville by bus. I usually save a little by hitchhikin'. But I can go as far as Dallas with you."

Mary wasn't so sure. "Maybe you'd better not change your plans," she said. "You might be disappointed in the rest of the trip."

"I'll take a chance on that. I wouldn't miss ridin' as far as I can with you for anything in the world! I've dreamed about someone like you! Almost as long as I've dreamed about that something better. Used to call her 'the lily maid of Astolat'!"

"Now, look!"

Hod laughed, quickly and joyously. "Don't quarrel with fate, lady! I think it's wonderful!"

The bus driver, directly in front of them, joined in the conversation then. He had settled down to the run and wanted company. He took over the talk and began telling long stories about the peculiarities of the people who lived in these hills. He was a rambling, loquacious sort of person, talking with a slow, drawling voice which pointed up a story to a fine, dry humor. They laughed partly at him and partly with him, and Hod felt himself slipping deeper into the most relaxed feeling he had known in several months.

The girl bubbled over when she laughed, somewhat like a child, and she laughed readily. There was a gayness about her which transferred itself to him and he caught it eagerly. And her face, when she talked, lighted up with a look of shining intensity. Her eyes took fire then and grew brilliant. She was interested in everything, with an eager, compelling interest, and yet when she was impressed by something she was still, all over still, as if she were taking it into herself. She's different, Hod thought. She's the most different person I ever saw. She's friendly and gay and happy, and yet she thinks about things — 'way down deep inside of her she thinks about everything.

Almost before they knew it, the lights of Nashville were ahead. They would change busses there, and there was a wait of several hours. How best to spend it, thought Hod. How make it memorable.

176

"You know what I think would be fun?" he asked, when he had thought it over.

"What do you think would be fun?"

"When we get to Nashville, let's find some nice place to eat, and let's have the best bang-up chicken dinner in town!" A table was such a quiet place to sit and talk.

"I think that's a wonderful idea! Give me fifteen minutes to freshen up when we get in, and then we'll hunt for the best bang-up chicken dinner in Nashville!"

While she primped, Hod found the men's room, shaved, retied his tie, brushed off, and felt ready to go. There was one thing you could say for a uniform. You were always dressed up — ready to go — as long as you were clean and had a crease in your pants, that is.

They left the bus station and walked up the hill, looking for a place that would serve their chicken dinner. But it was too late, and they finally settled for steaks at a steak house. They found a table over next to the wall, snug in its own lamplight and out of the path of other people. Mary had put on a bright little jacket and had added white gloves to her outfit. She looked quite fine to Hod.

With enormous appetites they ate, enjoying the big, hot steaks; the crisp curls of French fries; the round, red slices of cold tomatoes. And then over coffee they dragged out the full two hours they had allowed themselves, talking and talking, as if they had only these minutes left. When finally the clock on the wall warned them they must go, Hod paid the checks, glad it had been an expensive dinner, and they walked back down the hill to the station.

He queued up to buy his ticket and Mary went to get her bags. The busses were loading by the time he had got his ticket and joined her at the dock. His heart sank when he saw the milling crowd. Three or four sections were running, but if they ever got on one they would have to stand.

"This is goin' to be pretty tough," he said to her.

"Where did all these people come from?" she wondered. It was eleven o'clock at night, and there were young mothers with sleepy, crying babies, struggling to manage the babies and their luggage; there were girls with heavy, tired eyes, worn out from a sleepless week end visiting their soldiers; there were old women with aching lines of fatigue in their faces; and always and everywhere there were the soldiers.

"Oh, I shouldn't have come," said Mary. "I'm just taking up room these people need. My trip's not necessary at all. It's purely selfish!"

"Don't say that," Hod begged. "It's *very* necessary to me!"

"I had no idea it would be like this! Will it be this way the rest of the trip?"

"I'm afraid so. From here on we get deeper and deeper into the section of the country where most of the camps are located. People have got to go see their men, and the men have got to go see their people. And that makes a lot of travel."

Just then the loud-speaker behind them blared out: "Two sections for servicemen loading at Docks 7 and 8! Servicemen only! Two sections, now loading at Docks 7 and 8!"

Hod thought quickly. "Mary," he said, "we'll never get on one of these busses. Come with me and I'll get you on the servicemen's bus."

He picked up her bags as he spoke and began shouldering a way for her through the crowd. She grabbed the back of his shirt and hung on, laughing, as he made a wedge of the bags and shoved their way through the jam. He reached the end of one of the lines waiting by the special busses, set the bags down and turned to her. "Give me your ticket," he said.

"My ticket? What for?"

"Don't ask questions! Just give me your ticket. I'll explain later."

Without further argument, she dug down in her purse and brought out the envelope containing her ticket. He took it and placed it with his own. They inched along with the line, and when they reached the driver, Hod handed him both tickets.

"My wife goes to El Paso. I go to Dallas."

"O.K."

Mary's eyes flew wide open, but she said nothing. On the bus they found a seat and settled themselves. Mary nudged him and whispered, "Why did you tell him I was your wife?"

"Because only a serviceman's wife, mother, sister, or some sort of special relative can travel with him on special transportation."

"Couldn't you have told him I was your sister?"

"I preferred the other relationship," and he grinned wickedly.

A journey is a strange suspension of time in space. You have left one place and have not yet arrived at another. In between is a small pendulum of time which is unidentified, unowned, unmoored. In the arc of that swing of the pendulum Hod and Mary talked the night away . . . softly, because the other passengers were sleeping. They found so much to say . . . so much to laugh about. They were the only two people in the world.

When, just before dawn, Mary slept for an hour, Hod turned so that he could watch her face. In the last shining brightness of the moon it was washed with silver. There was a purity in its unguarded stillness which made him long to touch it. Gently he reached one finger to the corner of her mouth, and felt its soft immobility. This is my girl, he thought. Out of all the world, this is my girl! I wish . . . and he flung it bitterly away. A man can't ask a woman to start out on a journey with him when he doesn't know where it ends. Or can he? Can a man find his destination truer with a woman taking one step at a time with him? Mary! Mary! Love me, Mary, and heal me!

"You're wonderful," he whispered, when she awoke.

"At five o'clock in the morning?"

"At any time!"

"That's because we're riding a bus from Nashville to Memphis."

"That's because you're Mary!"

At Memphis they worked out a system. As soon as the bus unloaded, Hod found a porter. "Where does the Dallas bus load?" he asked.

"Dock 6," was the answer. They took their bags to Dock 6 and set them down on the curb.

"Now, I'll stay here with the bags while you go eat your breakfast. Then when you come back, I'll go eat," Hod said.

"We're the first in line this time," Mary observed.

"We'll be the first on that bus," he promised.

A long day and another night went by. There were no more changes until Dallas, and they made a home for themselves of the familiar seat on the bus. They had never lived anywhere else. They slept in snatches and talked interminably. There was so little time . . . only now . . . today, tonight. And beyond that

179

the spread of a sea between them, and the dark night of war. He must know what she thought, what she did, who she was. What kind of little girl were you, Mary? Whom have you loved, and who has hurt you? Do you like squirrel an' dumplin's? Do you like to fish? Do you know the sweetest sound in the world is the G string on my guitar, and do you know your voice is like it? And he must tell her about Hod Pierce. Make her remember Hod Pierce! Make her love Hod Pierce!

All too soon they came to Dallas, in the early morning hours of the third day. The light was strained and thin, and they were lost in it. Their home was gone. Hod drained the cup of the last drop of her presence. There were two hours before her bus left and he drew her to an island around the corner of the station, where they could grab at forgotten words.

" Will you write to me? "

" Of course."

" Mary, don't forget me."

" I won't."

" Even if it's a long time? "

" Even if it's a long time."

" Will you write soon? "

" Just as soon as I get there."

" Mary . . ."

" Hush, now. Be still."

At last he had to take her to the door of the bus. " This is my wife," he told the driver, dedicating himself. " I have to leave her here. I'd appreciate it if you'd look after her the rest of the way."

" I'll do that, soldier," promised the driver, and he placed Mary's small bag and her coat in the seat directly behind him. " You'll ride there better than anywhere else in the bus," he said.

They clung to their last moments as long as they could, but the time came when the driver touched Mary's shoulder apologetically. " You'd better get on now, ma'am."

She turned to Hod and went homing into his arms. She knows, he thought, she knows I have to hold her in my arms, so they can remember. So they won't be empty ever again. He held her hungrily and closed his eyes against the parting. Then he found her mouth and was pulled down and drowned in its sweetness. Suddenly he released her and walked away . . . out of sight . . . without looking back. He didn't want to hear the bus leave. He didn't want to watch her go.

He had sixteen cents left in his pocket. He breakfasted on doughnuts and coffee and then shook the dust of Dallas from his feet. He hitched a ride to Austin, and all the way he remembered Mary . . . Mary.

CHAPTER TWENTY–ONE

Back in camp, Hod counted the days. If she gets to El Paso tonight and writes tomorrow, then I should hear from her on Friday. He sweated out the days. Suppose she doesn't write. But she said she would. She's not like other girls. She wouldn't promise and then not write.

He was due to go back to the Gulf coast on Monday, and he was desperately afraid he would have to leave before her letter came. Mail call, which had not been overly important to him before, suddenly became the center of his days. Even before Friday he was hanging around, waiting. And on Friday he was panicky. All at once he wished the mail would never come, so he wouldn't have to know she didn't write. He was a fool for thinking it had meant anything to her. There wouldn't be a letter, of course. It was just a pickup on a bus.

But he made himself go over and stand around as nonchalantly as possible. He watched each letter, wondering what it would look like if it did come. Pierce! There it was! Just a little, square envelope, with his name in a free, flowing hand across the front. He was shaking when he took it. He set his teeth and swallowed hard, and the sweat ran down his chin. He slipped the letter into his shirt pocket and walked back to his tent to read it. He wanted to be alone when he opened it. He flung himself on his cot and studied her writing for a time, deliberately postponing the joy of reading what she had written, savoring a little longer the sweetness of suspense.

181

Then he ripped it open. "Dear Hod: We arrived on time and Miss Willie met me . . . The bus driver took excellent care of me . . . a pleasant trip . . . lots of fun . . . We are going over into old Mexico for two or three days . . ." Three pages of gay, friendly news. She wrote like she talked, giving the details of the rest of her trip in a laughing fashion that made him smile. He read it through again, searching between the lines for something personal and meaningful. But it wasn't there. He could make no more of it than was written.

He didn't know what he had expected, and he felt, suddenly, a little let down. Don't be a fool, he told himself. Did you think she would write she loved you, just like that . . . out of a clear blue sky! His spirits lifted again. At least she had written. That was something. Surely, if he wrote carefully, he could keep her letters coming. That was the main thing right now. He dashed over to the PX for stationery, and although he would have no time to write before night, he was composing his letter as he went.

When Hod's letters began to arrive regularly in El Paso, Miss Willie raised a sandy eyebrow at her niece. "New heart interest, Mary?" she teased. "Army too, I see."

Mary had not told Miss Willie about Hod yet. Now she stood, tapping the letter against her chin, weighing the need to talk about Hod against the need to keep him alone inside her. She felt that her reluctance must have come from her feeling that he was different. She didn't know whether she could do justice to him. And he deserved that.

Suddenly she was telling the whole story, beginning at the beginning, with the delay of her start which had made her have to cancel her train reservation. Her decision when she was free, finally, to attempt the trip by bus. The meeting with Hod. The long hours together. Even the parting at Dallas. She told that too.

Miss Willie was silent when Mary's voice stopped. Her face reflected her conflicting emotions. And then she raised her hand to push her glasses up on her nose, a gesture which was as much a part of Miss Willie as her eyes or her hair or her thin, angular body.

"I know all you're going to say," Mary put in quickly. "I *can't* be in love with this man so suddenly. I've only known him . . . well, I've only been with him once. But remember that *once* was forty-two hours long. And I don't know anything about him except what he told me. And he's a farmer . . . a poor, hillbilly farmer at that . . . uneducated, uncultured. Except that he's *not!* Miss Willie, he's not! He has an educated heart, and a good, quick mind. He may not be cultured in our sophisticated sense of the word. But I can't tell you how weary I am of that anyhow. Hod is naturally a cultured person. He loves beauty and he has a questing spirit. He is gentle and good, honorable and idealistic, and unbelievably sweet. He's warm and big and wholesome. It's been so long since I knew anyone . . . anyone at all like that. Anyone more than half alive! Don't you see? "

Miss Willie sighed. " I see. I see he's very important to you, Mary."

" I'm afraid he is."

There was a silence and then Miss Willie leaned forward and touched Mary's hand. " Mary," she said, " forgive me for saying this . . . but if he continues to be important to you . . . important enough, say, for you to marry him . . . are you going to spend your life defending him so fiercely? "

Mary's breath drew in sharply, and her head jerked as if Miss Willie had slapped her. Her teeth caught her lower lip and her eyes filled. " I needed that, didn't I? How rude I was to him! How unjust! No! No! No, Miss Willie. He needs no defense. Thank you for reminding me! "

It was two weeks before Hod heard again, because the letters had to follow him to the coast. Then there were two on the same day, and in the second one she wrote that she was going home and she wished he could be riding back with her. She didn't think she would enjoy the trip home as much as she had the one coming out! Hope soared high on this meager strand she held out. She had fun with me! She's been thinking about me! He built a high castle with the bricks of his hopes.

The engineers spent another month on the coast and then hurricanes and squalls sent them back to camp. He dreaded any shift in his movements now, because they meant a delay in her letters.

Fellows in the outfit had quickly caught on to his concern about the mail, and his nightly absorption in his own letters. They kidded him unmercifully.

"What was it Sergeant Pierce said to you about six months ago, Hough?"

"I remember it like yesterday. He said there wasn't no woman livin' that could interest him enough to make him write a letter ever' night!"

"Yeah? And what would you call what he's doin' right now?"

"Well, it ain't washin' dishes!"

But when they returned to camp, he was in such good luck he could hardly believe it. One of the men in his company went AWOL, to see his girl in Cincinnati, and Hod was detailed to go after him. He could have cut a buck and wing right there! The way to Cincinnati was straight through Louisville, and Mary was in Louisville!

"Brother, I *love* you," he said to the first sergeant, who brought him the news.

"We love you too, dearie," said Jenkins, the sergeant, sweetly. "That's why we pulled strings so you could go. And give our love to Mary," he added wickedly.

He sent her a wire asking her to meet his train, and she was waiting by the steps when he walked through the gate. He saw her first. She's so alive, he thought. She's so terribly alive! She looks like Duke on a fresh coon scent! Even her nose is alive!

And then she was in his arms. She kept nothing back of her gladness to see him. There was no false note of coyness. She seemed to know he had come to her with all of himself, and she didn't betray him with shyness.

They found a corner table in the restaurant in the station where they could eat and talk. He had three hours, and in that time he must tell her all he had to say. He thought he knew what he wanted to say, but the briefness of the time, her disturbing nearness, and the urgency which was pressing him made him say it badly. How does a man find the way to tell a girl she has become his whole life? When he is all but on his way to battle, how does he find the courage to ask her to love him? He stumbled and halted. Mary reached across the table for his hand.

"Are you trying to tell me you love me?"

184

"Yes."

"Then just say it. There isn't need for any more."

"I love you, Mary."

"I love you, Hod."

The shoddy station restaurant became a green pasture, and Mary's words led him beside still waters. He lifted his head and drank deeply.

"I've nothing to bring you but myself, Mary."

"Can a man bring anything more?"

"Oughtn't he to have something to offer? Some money in the bank? A job? Something real?"

"Hod . . . in the hours we were together on our trip you told me all about yourself. You told me about a little boy who wanted to learn everything he could. You told me about a young man who had to step into his father's shoes. You told me about a man, who made of himself a good soldier, and a better man. More than that, in every word you spoke you told me also of a gentle, tender spirit . . . loving beauty, in the hills, in music, in people, in life. You are offering me the only things that count. You've got a mind that is eager, a sense of honor and duty, and gentleness, goodness, sweetness. Those things are real. Nothing else in the world is real, beside them. If you had a million dollars and lacked them, you would have only a barren plain to offer. A man can't fill an empty soul with money and call it riches. And no man whose soul is overflowing is ever really poor."

His eyes misted. "You're wonderful!"

"No. I just love you and I know what you are."

Hod took a deep breath, and Mary laughed gently. "Let yourself down, Hod. Don't look so hard at Tomorrow. We'll handle that together when it comes."

They turned to the food which had grown cold on their plates. It was tasteless straw, but they picked at it.

"I don't even have the money to buy you a ring. A girl should at least have an engagement ring."

"Why?"

"Well, just because . . . well, everybody does, don't they?"

"We're not everybody."

"Don't you want a ring?"

"Yes. A wedding ring, someday."

" But I want you to have something now! "

" Give me something of your own then."

He thought for a moment, then he took his engineers' insigne from his lapel and handed it across the table.

She cupped it in her hand and looked at it. " I'll wear this on a chain," she said finally. " It will be my engagement ring, darling."

The thread was spinning short. The war filled stations all over the country with such partings as theirs, and each was fraught with its own grief. But to Hod this leave-taking was unbearable. To leave her so soon! And he couldn't tell her that he wouldn't see her again. That before he could hold her close like this again he would have fought a war. That maybe he would never hold her close like this again. He could only let the bitter-sweetness of her touch flood him with a silent despair, and tear himself apart to leave it.

" I'll write every day," she promised, " and you'll come home the first time you can. The time will pass."

" The very first time I can," he repeated. " The very first time I can! "

Within two months he was at Port of Embarkation. The time there was packed with lectures, instructions, indoctrination. There were changes to make in his allotment, in his insurance, in his whole outlook. The grim preparations for actual conflict were full of implications of life cut short.

With each promotion Hod had increased the amount of money he sent home. When he made sergeant, he felt he could send enough so that the simplest way to handle it would be through an allotment which would regularly and directly be sent to the folks. He had pushed the amount up from ten dollars with which he started to forty dollars a month. Now he must think of saving for himself and Mary.

So he wrote Hattie that he was in love, that he was engaged, and that he was planning to be married just as soon as he returned from overseas, and that he felt he should put aside as much as he could spare for himself. He told her that, with times so much better, maybe they could make out with a little less. So he was cutting the allotment to them to twenty-five dollars per month; he hoped they would understand.

A sergeant's pay, plus the twenty per cent overseas increase, would be ninety-seven dollars per month. He knew he would need very little of it, so he tried then, to make a fifty dollar allotment to Mary. He wanted so much to give all his material wealth into her hands along with himself. He wanted to lay everything that was his before her and say, "I thee endow."

But he ran into the rules against making allotments to persons not related by blood, and had to write her: "I tried, but they say no. So I am making a separate allotment to Ma, and I'm asking her to save it for us."

He felt so good about saving the money. He felt as if already Mary had placed her hand in his and started down the road with him.

CHAPTER TWENTY–TWO

Early one Sunday morning in October, the 291st marched aboard a transport and was slipped quietly out to sea. No man aboard was entirely insensitive to the widening distance between him and his native land. In various ways, according to their temperamental differences, they expressed their emotions, ignored them, or controlled them.

Hod stood at the rail and let his eyes hold the dear earth as long as there was the faintest line of it on the horizon. He was leaving so much! Then he went below and sought to re-establish his identity with the familiar things of his own possessions.

Two things served to ease the tension of that first day at sea. The first was a moment of grim laughter furnished by a replacement who had come aboard at the last minute. He had been jerked out of a chair in front of a sewing machine in a quartermaster outfit, being told only that he was going out as a replacement. He uneasily eyed the men as they unpacked their bags and put things away. Finally he timidly approached an officer. "Sir," he said, "this doesn't look much like a quartermaster outfit."

"Quartermaster!" the officer roared. "This is the 291st Combat Engineers!"

"Combat engineers!" echoed the boy, and he keeled over in a

dead faint.

Because they themselves were so shaky and tense, the men roared with laughter at this. The poor guy, scared stiff of being with a combat outfit! They were tough and hard. They couldn't tremble. But when a man fainted in fear of their job, the shadow of their own fear was somewhat lifted. Someone else had trembled for them. So they laughed.

The other event was mail call. The last until the voyage ended. And there were four good letters from Mary. She wrote with no foreshadowing of grief. With no portent of loss. She accepted his going as quietly as if he had simply gone around the corner to the grocery store. In the entire two years Hod was away, never once did he receive a letter that placed the burden of her anxiety and fear on him. She carried it alone, as he must carry his. When, later, he saw other men torn and drawn by letters from home, he thought of Mary proudly. He was never afraid to open a letter from her. He knew, always, that they would share home with him in all its small details, and would offer him sanctuary in her outpouring love.

They set foot on English soil at Liverpool, and thirty-six hours later had once more settled themselves into their routine. This much of home they brought with them. The American Army on foreign soil was never entirely in an alien land. It moved into England, Africa, Europe, and the islands, but it made of every place it touched an American colony.

Along about the middle of December the first of Mary's Christmas packages reached Hod. It was packed thoughtfully, so as to get the most into the small space. And each package inside was gaily wrapped with bright paper and scarlet ribbons. She sent him a little piece of cedar, just for the Christmas smell, she said. And there was a small fruit cake, a fountain pen (he'd lost his old one), a carton of cigarettes, and, wrapped between two pairs of soft woolen socks, a small, black disk. He looked at it for a moment, puzzled. What in the world! And then he knew. She had made a record for him. She had written a letter he could hear instead of read. He waved it at the other guys in the tent. " Hey, look! Mary's sent me a record! She's written me a letter on a phonograph record! "

" Let's see! "

" Well, whaddya know! "

" How you gonna play it? " his bunkmate asked.

" On a phonograph, of course! "

" Yeah, but where you gonna get a phonograph? "

" I'll find one," he swore. " I'll find one! And you guys keep your eyes open too."

And they did. Every man in the company heard of Hod's record, and every one of them kept his eyes open for a phonograph. It came to be a matter of first importance to all of them. And one evening, Jenkins the first sergeant burst into Hod's tent. " Hey! Hey, Pierce! We've found it! Pierce! Where's your record? We've found a phonograph! "

Hod ran to his bag and dug frantically. " Where? " he said, excited, flinging shirts, shorts, and socks heedlessly into the air. " Where'd you find it? "

" Hough found it in a little pub over on the east side. It's an old beat-up victrola, but it'll still play, and they've got some needles too."

The news spread and about ten men went with Hod to the pub. " C'mon," they yelled, " Pierce's gonna play his record! "

Hod knew Mary wouldn't mind. No man's love was entirely private in such a fraternity, and she had become very real to these men who saw her picture daily, who heard excerpts from her letters, and who chaffed Hod over his own nightly letters. They were now entitled to hear her voice.

At the pub Hod was so excited he could hardly set the needle. " Here, let me do it," said Jenkins. But he too was excited, and it took several false starts before the record began to move. At last it took hold, and faintly and dimly the voice came through the wheezy old machine. The men bent closer to hear.

" Hello, darling . . ." And with the first words Hod was lost in memories. He heard her voice saying a hundred things. Did you ever see a more beautiful sunset in your life? The first words she ever said to him were words of beauty, and she had never failed to make it real to him since. Is there anything more a man can offer? The substance of faith. I love you, Hod. The green pasture and the still waters. " I love you, Hod."

The record ended, and he'd lost everything between. "Play it again," he said to Jenkins. And then, "Play it again."

"Who is it?" asked a kid who had come along just because a crowd was gathered.

Jenkins turned on him indignantly. "That's Mary!" he said.

The months turned the pages of the calendar through the long, black winter, and the 291st moved through them bleakly. Their day came on June 20, 1944. Rumor had it that they had escaped Omaha Beach by the flip of a coin. The guys liked to tell that another outfit of corps engineers was ready to go too, and it was a tossup which should go. And the other outfit lost.

On his trip home from Europe a year and a half later, a member of that battalion told Hod about Omaha Beach that day. They had gone in at H hour plus two minutes, and they had been massacred. The battalion was decimated in the carnage of a wave-washed slaughterhouse. The man who told the story to Hod said he was one of ten men out of his company who came through alive. Hod could not say why one should be chosen to go and one to stay. But for the flip of a coin, according to rumor, he might have lain on the riddled ledges of Omaha Beach.

On June 24, Hod's outfit landed on the now quiet beach. The story of its racking pain was everywhere evident in the burned-out trucks, tanks, and jeeps, and in the great litter of ruined materials and supplies which had been discarded. But the torture had moved on and the sands drifted slowly over the scars.

They moved inland fast after landing, and were under fire within twenty-four hours. They were bivouacked in an open field, unloading trucks, settling in for the night. Hod heard a whistling sound and then a dull detonation. A burst of dirt and debris flew up in the air about a hundred yards away. Hod threw himself down, hard. The high whine of another shell could be heard, and then another and another, until they were dropping all around. The noise of the explosions was deafening, and the air was full of flying dirt, pieces of trucks, lumber and metal. Hod dug himself into a little ditch and hunched himself down as low as he could. Fear gripped him and he panted and sweated against it. Nobody could live through this, he thought. We'll all be wiped out! This is the end of the road!

But the barrage lifted as suddenly as it had begun, and Hod stood up and looked around him. It had wrought a terrible carnage. Trucks, tanks, tents were blasted into heaps of burning chaos. But the worst was the wounded who lay where they had been hit. And the dead who were strewn in pieces over the wide field. He shuddered. Artillery fire! He had a new respect for it.

He felt of himself and wiped his face with his shirttail. And he watched other men crawling from their ditches and foxholes. He lost his feeling of shame for having been afraid. They had all been afraid. They crawled out, dirty, torn, and white-faced, some of them with their sickness still staining their shirts. It had been a whole community of fear, and Hod felt close to each one of them. They looked at each other strangely, as if a miracle had happened and they were a part of it. Hod felt his knees trembling and he sat down. "Next time," he said, "next time I'm goin' to dig me a deeper hole."

They swung across France that summer, sleeping lightly in foxholes and slit trenches, alert always for air raids, keeping company day and night with heavy artillery. They grew bleary-eyed, bearded, and dirty. They bathed and washed their clothes only when they hit a river or stream. They forgot what a bed felt like. They celebrated when they could forage eggs or chickens or a bottle of Calvados to add to their monotonous rations. They thinned down, whetted and honed into a tight compact outfit, snarling, cursing, griping, hating, killing, building, and loving.

Gone was all Hod's objectiveness, now. This tight little group of men was the only reality in the world. Mary's letters came as regularly as mail call. He read them avidly, and occasionally he had the feeling she was near. But mostly they were like pages of fiction. She was in the dream of peace and home. But here there wasn't time to dream.

Hod looked around him sometimes at the men and wondered at what was happening to them. There were times when he hated them and felt their coarseness and toughness rub him like a saddle on a sore back. But most times he loved them. Every day he saw an act of heroism. But heroism had become so common that it had

191

ceased to be heroic. These men sacrificed for each other as a matter of course. They cursed at each other, stole cigarettes and writing paper, articles of clothing and bedding, and then crawled out on the skeletons of bridges under the fury of machine-gun fire to drag one another back to safety. Hod won his own bronze star that way. It never occurred to him that he had done a brave thing. He had done what any other man in the outfit would have done for him. Sometimes he thought how war took men and wrapped them round with brotherhood, and, even with the sound of guns in their ears, made them think of one another.

They moved on, always eastward. They bridged the Ruhr that spring, under an incessant and withering stream of fire. It took them three days, and they lost men, but when they had finished, they had built one of the longest single-span bridges ever built by Army engineers. When Hod looked at the casualty list for his own company there was alum in his mouth. Jenkins' name was on the list this time. Every bridge they built took its toll, but the Ruhr was deadly costly.

War's end found them at a little village on the far side of the Danube. War's end! It left a flat taste in their mouths. They were too tired, too beat up, too stretched out. Hod tried to feel elated, but all he wanted to do was to go home and sleep a hundred years on a soft bed. He didn't think he would ever get the tiredness out of his bones!

And there was still a war going on in the Pacific. There was a lot of agitation in most of the outfits about whether they would be sent to the Pacific or not. But the 291st was pretty unconcerned. O.K., they said; O.K. If they need us to help finish it up. But they sure better send us by home first!

And then the outfit began breaking up. The point system started picking them off, sorting them, crating them, and shipping them home. Hod was a high-point man, with his long service, and he wrote Mary in July: "Get your wedding dress ready! I'll be home before Christmas!"

Two years to a day from the Sunday he had steamed out of Boston harbor he stepped off the gangplank in New York. Two long years of such experiences as men can never forget, no matter how deep they may bury them. Hod had not been the sort of man to agonize over the reasons for the war. Finding himself

192

drawn into it, he had gone along, wasting neither time nor tears over something that could not be helped. He had done his share of work, sweated and toiled and been horribly afraid at times. The two years had left their imprint forever. But there had been no worms in his brain — no maggots of hate either for the enemy or for his own Government. A thing had had to be done. And he had done his part. He had come through remarkably sane, remarkably balanced. He was just tired.

The first thing he did upon landing was to drink three pints, one right after the other, of fresh, cold milk, which the ladies of the Red Cross proffered each returning soldier. Hod wondered how even in two years a man could get so thirsty for the sweet, chilled taste of milk. He let it slide down his throat slowly, savoring every drop of it, making it last, not yet realizing he was back where he could have all he wanted.

At Camp Shanks, the first stage of his separation, Hod sent Mary a wire: " Just landed. Will call tonight if possible. See you soon. Love, Hod."

In the phone booth that night he listened while the operator put through his call. Heard the Louisville operator repeat the number, heard the ringing signal, and tried to imagine the small apartment where the telephone was now clamoring out the good news. The palms of his hands were wet, and a drop of sweat under his left arm trickled down his ribs, making him squirm. Soon, now. Soon. Then the receiver clicked.

" Hello. Hod? " There it was . . . the rich, singing voice. He closed his eyes and let the sound of it wash over him, pour into him, fill him and run over! Dear God, how good it was to hear it again! It made everything real. The war, the separation, the land of home. He could say nothing for a long moment, and then he forced his voice past the tightness in his throat.

" Mary . . . Mary, I'm home! "

He reached Louisville on Thursday at two o'clock in the morning. Mary's sleepy voice was startled into full awakening when he called her, and she told him to take a cab; she would dress and be waiting.

Her flying feet reached the door before his finger lifted from

193

the bell. Everything about her was flying . . . her hair, the banners in her eyes, her hands, lifted to his face, and her body fitting itself to his. She flew straight to his weary heart and cradled it in her gentleness; she rocked it to rest with her cool cheek pressed to his; she took the yoke of his bruises upon her warm mouth lifted so eagerly to his. He sighed. Now he could rest.

They were married as soon as it was possible. When they stood before the minister in the little chapel, Hod felt his stomach go shaky, and his knees trembled. He had forgotten how lovely Mary was. In all the months he had kept a sure remembrance of her before him, not forgetting the dark of her hair or the depth of her eyes. But today, in a dress of some soft, white material, she was like a tall, white candle, alight with pure fire. There was a shining look on her face, and her eyes, resting on Hod in tender possession, were still and loving. She was more beautiful than he had thought possible. The faint scent of the small bouquet she carried came to him, and he closed his eyes for a second. I shall never forget this moment, he thought. Not time nor life is going to dull it. For in this hour I am made whole.

They went to Spring Mill in the southern Indiana hills for their honeymoon. The beautiful lodge was set in the midst of the great park like a château Hod had seen on the Aisne. It had the same solid dignity and the builders had captured something of an ancient grace. The drive curved before it in a crescent of white gravel and swooped to a widened stop in front of the entrance. Hod liked it immediately.

They had a wonderful week, sleeping late in the morning, having their breakfast sent up to the room, wandering over the hill trails during the day, visiting the old mill in the rehabilitated village. They had long, dawdling dinners in the evening, and then more often than not they walked out again under a huge harvest moon. They told themselves over and over again that October was undoubtedly the most perfect month of the year for a honeymoon. The countryside was aflame with color, extravagant and riotous and gay. And the air was clear and golden and sparkling.

When they came back to their room at night, they built a small fire in the fireplace and sat before it, watching the flames lick over the logs, setting them to snapping and crackling and to shooting sparks out on the hearth. Mary would sit on a low stool and hold out her hands to the warmth, a soft, yellow robe wrapped close about her. When Hod pulled the big chair up near the fire he made room for her, and she snuggled down beside him. Holding her thus, her hair dark and fragrant on his face and her slender body warm against him, he knew a deep content. This was the way of a man and a woman, then. This oneness of spirit as well as of flesh. This taking in of each other so that never again were they clearly able to distinguish which was which. This merging and blending of self and self. This hidden pearl which a man found only in his wife.

And they talked. Hour after hour they talked. There was so much lost time to make up. And then when they had said it all, they came back ever and again to the miracle of love. To the miracle of being together after the long months of struggling toward each other through the deep fears of the war. To the miracle of holding now, for all time, only love and peace.

They would have liked to stay on at the mill, drawing out the days of their first joy in each other, but the ridge was waiting, and the folks. They left, finally, with a feeling of sadness . . . a putting an end to something they would never have again. Mary looked back as they drove down the curving drive. Nothing will ever be quite like this again, she thought. The first week . . . the first days and nights can never be repeated. And then she turned around and looked resolutely ahead. What lay there, she determined, would be infinitely better!

CHAPTER TWENTY–THREE

THEY BOUGHT AN OLD RATTLETRAP CAR and made the trip to the ridge in it. They wondered if it would get them there, but even the uncertainty was fun. When they came to Campbellsville, Hod began to get excited. "It's only sixteen miles now," he said. "It won't be long."

A few miles out of Campbellsville they left the pavement to follow a graveled road. It had been washed by rain and eaten out by traffic until it resembled a piece of corrugated tin, and it was full of holes which heavy wheels had gouged out. Hod sent the car skimming over it carelessly and casually, and the corduroy ridges made a constant, jarring vibration that shook every bone in Mary's body. Occasionally, when the wheels hit a very deep hole, she was thrown violently upward, and when she came back down, her body was slammed against the cushion with such force that she felt certain the springs would flatten uselessly and permanently.

" Did you ever herd cattle? " she asked finally.

Hod looked at her wonderingly. " No," he said. " Never did. Why? "

" You drive this car like you were an old hand at it! "

Hod laughed. " This road's better for horses and mules at that, isn't it? "

" Next time I think I'll walk," Mary threatened, grabbing at the door as they hit another hole.

" This is the county pike," Hod said. " I helped build this road back before the war. And it was a good road when we built it. Needs to be scraped, though, now."

Just then the road dipped down and to Mary's amazement she saw that a shallow creek wandered across in front of them. Hod shifted gears and nosed the car gently into the water. It was about hub deep. When they had climbed the slight rise on the other side, he didn't bother to change gears. They ground along for a few hundred feet and then dipped down again. There was the creek once more. They forded it and climbed another rise, and then dipped again.

" Don't tell me," said Mary, " let me guess. That's Wandering Creek! "

" That's Wandering Creek! " Hod affirmed.

" It lives up to its name, doesn't it? "

" Why, yes, I reckon it does. Reckon that's how it got its name in the first place. It's a humdinger when it's in flood, too. Spreads out all over these bottoms."

" When it gets up, how do you cross it? "

" You don't."

Mary thought about this for a moment. " When it gets up, then, there's no way to get to town."

"Nope."

"Suppose somebody got sick, or was dying, and you had to get a doctor."

"Well, if you had to have a doctor from Campbellsville, you'd just have to wait. But there's a pretty good doctor over at the Gap, and you can always get through that way by the old road. This creek doesn't stay up long, though. It gets up like a flash, but it goes down in a few hours."

"Why don't they bridge it?"

"It would take a bridge a mile long to make the highway safe. The county hasn't got that much money. A bridge like that would cost a small fortune to build."

The country was pretty here. They had been following the rounded edges of the hills for some time, hills that rose to the left in undulating folds. They were broken up by small ravines and hollows, and back up in each hollow Mary could see houses and barns and small, cleared fields. The houses were little unpainted shacks . . . one or two rooms slanting crazily against the hill, the yards always full of cluttered trash and swarming with children. Some of them were built on the hillsides themselves, and hugged close to the rocky slopes to keep from tumbling down. Some were built down in the hollow, perched up on stilts for safety from high water. Some ventured down near the pike, but these were few. It was as if they guarded their depressing poverty from the knowledge of the world, hiding it in the cracks and crannies of the hills.

To the right the valley stretched fertile and green for several miles to the row of trees which marked the course of the river. The fields were richer here, and the farmhouses were larger and neater, although Mary wondered if all the farmers down here kept their cultivators drawn up by the side of the front porch. They passed no large farms . . . great land holdings such as those in the bluegrass. There were no fine homes. At best there were a few rich acres, and a neat, four-room house. At worst there were the shacks on the hillsides, and a stony corn patch.

"Is this Pierce land around here?" Mary asked.

"No. We've never come this far down in the bottoms. Pierce land lies on the ridge and in the hollers on both sides. Lem, my uncle, is the only one that lives near the pike. His place is right at the foot of the main ridge, where we turn off. When Grampa Dow gave his three boys their choice of land, Lem liked the piece down here on the pike. Gault took the piece on the ridge down the road from the home place. Pa was the youngest, and he took the home place."

They traveled another mile or two, and then Hod said, " That's Lem's place right there," and nodded to the left.

Mary saw a trim white house reminiscent of a Connecticut salt-box, set well back from the road, with a stretch of green yard widening down to the road and with huge barns framing it in the back.

" That place looks right prosperous." Already Mary was developing a comparative sense of values.

" Lem's done right well down here. I reckon he's the best fixed of any of the Pierces now. Reckon he was pretty smart to pick this piece. But it's too close to the pike to suit me." Mary looked at him thoughtfully.

" Here's where we turn up the ridge." Hod was turning off the pike to the left.

Mary looked at the trail he was following. It resembled a road only because there were faint wheel tracks among the rocks and because it cut through the woods in a narrow path. Hod shifted into low, and they inched into the climb. Almost at once they were on a narrow ledge, the hill falling away to the right and rising abruptly to the left. Slowly Hod eased the car up over the gullied tracks and around the sharp bends.

About halfway up, the road became a mere thread lying close to the hillside, and the car brushed the branches of trees and the overhanging bushes as it crept along. The roadbed was solid rock, now, and the tires slipped and bit for traction. To the right Mary could see down into the tops of the trees in the ravines. She shuddered and closed her eyes.

" Would it help any to hold my breath? " she whispered.

" Oh, we're almost up now. That wasn't so bad," and she felt the car ease into a more gradual incline.

" Thank goodness," she breathed. " If it had been any worse I'd have died! " She turned to look back. " Do the folks have to go up and down this hill every time they go anywhere? "

" Just when they go to the pike, or the county seat, or Campbellsville. But that's not everywhere by a long shot. You can go all over the ridge and up and down the hollers without comin' this way at all. Fact is, they don't go in town more than three or four times a year. Do most of their tradin' at the Gap. It's at the other end of the ridge, in a gap in the hills. The road along the ridge is rough, like I said, but the hills ease off down that way more gradually. Pa and Gault and Little Wells and the others that live up here on the ridge have to haul their tobacco and corn to market down this hill, though. Nearest market's at Springfield or Greensburg. But they make out, one way or another."

"Is this Piney Ridge we're on now?"

"This is Piney Ridge. We're in Pierce country now. This ridge, the hollers on either side, and the next two ridges are all what we call Piney Ridge."

The car had nosed up over the brow of the hill and was following a narrow, rutted pattern. It wound a meandering way down the top of the ridge, humping itself aimlessly along. On either side fields stretched to the very rim of the ridge and disappeared in a final cresting wave over the edge. Here and there a wooded section stood out, scarlet and gold against the cloud-locked sky.

They passed a little two-room shack, gray with age, and sagging at the corners. The front porch had fallen in and the screen door hung in tatters from its hinges. The windows had no screens. A decrepit bedstead leaned against an apple tree in the corner of the yard, which was bare of grass, and half a dozen dirty, un-kempt children lolled on the splitting mattress.

"Who lives here, Hod?"

"Old Man Clark. This is Gault's tenant house. He lets the old man live there for nothing. None of us have got enough land to need a tenant any more, but the house was there and the Clarks didn't have any other place to go. He's gettin' too old to farm much. He makes out helpin' everybody a little."

"Whose children are those?"

"I don't know. I've been gone a long time, remember. Must be his daughter's, though. Seems to me Ma wrote something about Julie's husband leavin' her."

"Do you suppose they all live crowded up in that little house?"

Hod wrenched the car out of the ruts. "You'll see a lot of that up here on the ridge, Mary. People depend on their folks when trouble comes. And their folks always take them in and help out. Crowding doesn't mean much here. Just a few more plates on the table, and another pallet or two on the floor."

They were coming to a place on the left of the road. The house was built of peeled logs, and looked as if it had two or three rooms. Smoke was curling out the chimney.

"That's a pretty little place," Mary observed.

"That's Gault's place." He smiled and waved as they went by.

"I didn't see anyone," Mary said.

"No, you wouldn't. Becky's startin' supper, but right now she's standin' there behind the window watchin' us go by. Old Man Clark and Mamie were watchin' from somewhere on their place too. Any time you go down this road you can know everybody'll see you. You may not see them, for they'll be behind a door or the window curtain, but they won't miss seein' you."

"You mean they watch for anyone passing?"

"Well, they don't exactly watch. But there's not enough passin' up and down this road but what each one goin' by is a special event. If they know you well, they'll call out as you go by. But today they're all keepin' out of sight because they don't know you. But they wouldn't miss the sight of you for anything in the world. Tomorrow they'll all be talkin' to each other about seein' you go by. They'll know what you look like, what kind of a hat you had on, the color of your dress, and about what you weigh."

Mary straightened up and gave her hat a settling pat. "I don't know that I like that," she protested.

"Oh, you get used to it. That's the way it is here. You can't make a move without everybody on the ridge knowin' it, and you might as well tell all your business straight out. They'll find it out sooner or later."

"But suppose I don't want to tell my business!"

"Then they'll think you're stuck-up and too good for them. They don't mean to be nosy. And they don't interfere. But it's a little, close-knit world here. Every family depends on every other family. In a way it's like one big family, and you can't keep secrets or have much privacy. Comin' from the city, you wouldn't understand that. You're used to havin' people mind their own business and leave you alone. But you don't have neighbors in the city, and you don't depend on each other. Here, everyone is your neighbor. And they stand by you when you need help, and you stand by them."

Mary took a deep breath. She felt suddenly as if she had been picked up and set down in some foreign land. All of this was unreal, alien . . . even incongruous. You read about places like this in books. You saw them from train windows, or from the side of a car speeding across the country. But a road like that one up the hogback of the ridge, and shanties like those down in the hollows, and people like the Clarks . . . they didn't exist in your own world. They were out there somewhere on the fringe. But they were right here in front of her . . . and, furthermore, she had married into them. The hogback and the shanties and the Clarks. This was Hod's land and these were his people. " Thy people shall be my people . . . whither thou goest."

She swallowed . . . hard.

" There it is," Hod said, as they came around the curve. " There it is. That's home! "

Mary saw the low house, weathered to a soft, rainy gray, framed by the picket fence stitched neatly around the tidy yard. She saw the low chimney, with smoke tailing out and skirling lazily upward. She saw it set against a sunset sky and thought, It's like a picture. A pastel in rain-washed gray and blue. Ancient, peaceful, and beautiful.

Hod laid his hand on the horn and kept it there, sending a raucous, glad trumpeting into the air. And onto the porch, railed across the front of the house, swarmed a group of figures who spilled into the yard and onto the pickets of the fence.

Suddenly Mary was frightened. " Hod, I'm scared," she said. She began ineffectually to push her hair under her hat, to straighten her dress and to dab at her face with her handkerchief. " I feel so dirty and mussed. What if they don't like me! "

" They'll like you all right," Hod answered, but he was too excited to comfort her beyond that. This was home, and there were the folks. Mary's words made little impression on him, and what she might be feeling was not conveyed to him at all. In this moment of home-coming he was insulated by his own feelings of joy, becoming for this space of time the boy of the ridge, the returned son, who transcended the husband . . . the lover. He did not consciously remove from his oneness with Mary. He simply returned spiritually to a familiar world, so personally, so intimately, so obviously his own that he went back into himself, where Mary could not yet follow.

They stopped in front of the gate, and the woman hanging to the gate ran out. Hod was out of the car instantly and in her arms, and she was crying over him. A tall, stooped man joined them and laid his arm across Hod's shoulders. Mary sat still in the car and watched, feeling small and alone . . . forgotten. What they said to each other was murmured so low and so brokenly that she could not hear. Don't be an idiot, she warned herself. They haven't seen him for two years either. And he's their son. Can't you be big enough to share him for a few minutes? But the newness of her own possession was still upon her, and she was bereft by this sudden need for generosity.

She studied them as they stood near Hod. Hattie was stooped and thin, and she had run out clumsily in big, heavy shoes. But her cotton print dress was freshly washed, and the bright apron tied around her waist was stiff with starch. Mary watched her face. How finely sculptured it was! Not even age could ruin those high, molded cheekbones, nor the firm, squared chin. The skin was remarkably unwrinkled. It must once have been as creamy as a magnolia petal, Mary thought. Hattie kept tight hold of Hod's hand, and her mouth worked pitifully.

The man, Tom, was taller than Hod, but, like Hattie, he was stooped and thin. When he turned so that Mary could see his face, she was struck by the benign calmness of it. The gentle, patient kindness of it. She thought she had never seen a face on which enduring goodness was stamped so indelibly. Fine lines were etched around the mouth, and deep furrows in the forehead. But there was dignity and nobility written across that countenance, and Mary saw another thing. How much Hod looked like him! Someday his face will look just like that, she thought. Someday. Because he is the same kind of man his father is.

And then Hattie was coming to the car. "Now you're Mary, ain't you?" she said warmly, wiping at her eyes with her apron. "Git out! Git out! I didn't aim to be so unmannerly, but hit's sich a joy to see Hod agin." She searched Mary's face. " Oh, I'd have knowed you anywheres! Hod sent us yer picture, an' he's writ about you a heap. You look jist like I thought you would, only I believe yer purtier. Git out. The menfolks'll bring yer things in. Supper's jist ready, an' I'll bound yer hungry."

They walked up the path, and Mary saw that Hod was surrounded by the group on the porch.

" That there's Irma, an' her man," Hattie explained, " an' their two young'uns. They was all bound to see Hod too."

And then there was Sarah. Mary watched Hod try to make friends with her. At six she was delicately blond, with ash-silver curls. Hod held her in the curve of his arm, squatting to her height. But she kept her finger in her mouth, her eyes on the floor, speechless and timid.

" She ain't talked about nothin' fer a month but Hod," Hattie explained. " Git up in the mornin' awantin' to know if today he was comin'. Go to bed at night askin' if tomorrer was the day. An' look at her now! Cain't you say nothin', Sary? "

" Leave her alone," said Hod. " She'll get used to me."

Mary's heart went out to the little figure. She had seen those agonies of embarrassment in the schoolroom, and she knew the painful tumult that was throbbing through the child. In her own time and in her own way she would break through it. But Mary was glad Hod didn't press her now.

Irma came forward, struggling with her own kind of awkwardness, the timidity of any ridge person meeting a stranger. But there was warmth in her awkwardness . . . a warmth that expressed pride in Hod's choice. Hod had married a city girl. He had done something no other Pierce had ever done. So Irma's greeting, while brief, held that undercurrent of pride, and her eyes were friendly.

For that matter, Mary noticed that except for Hattie no one had much to say. It was only in the quick, fleeting touch of a hand, and in the glad glow of the eyes that she could tell how deeply they were touched . . . by Hod's home-coming . . . by the strangeness of her city presence.

When they went in the house, Hod stopped just inside the door. It was just the same. Forever and enduring the same. Home, embracing and enveloping him. A quietness stole over him. He took in the details. No. It wasn't quite the same. There was new paper on the walls . . . rich red roses climbing up a green lattice, with fat cherubs fluttering from bouquet to bouquet. The seams were not quite true, and Hod could see Ma and Irma struggling to match the pattern. There were new curtains at the windows too. And a new linoleum on the floor. He knew these things had been done in Mary's honor. Hattie and Irma must have worked for weeks to bring the house to this shining state of readiness. But no notice must be taken. That would shame Hattie before Mary.

Mary followed Hod through the house, and where his eyes fondly rested on the familiar things that had surrounded him always, hers took in the bare skeleton of furnishings. Everything was clean, spotlessly clean. But the wide cracks between the scrubbed boards of the floor could not be hidden, nor could the sag toward the middle from each end of the house. The new cushions on the old hickory chairs could not disguise them or make them into comfortable, easy chairs. There was one rocking chair in the house. It had been Gramma's. Mary remembered that Gramma had died while Hod was overseas.

To Mary there was something pathetic in the poverty of the house. Just now she could not see past it. She took in the oil lamps, their chimneys speckless and gleaming. The wash shelf, with the old wooden bucket, and the new white granite basin. The huge kitchen stove with the wood stacked behind it. The long pine table with the fresh oilcloth cover. And from the back door she saw the path that led to the outhouse hidden in a clump of young cedar trees.

She wandered helplessly along behind Hod, trying to sense what he was feeling . . . trying to get over into him long enough to feel a little bit at home. But there was nothing here for her to lay hold of. She had the queer feeling that she had stepped inside a history book and the pages had been rapidly leafed back a hundred years. Time stopped right there on the ridge, she thought. There was no link between her tiny efficiency apartment, with its gleaming porcelain plumbing, its instant hot water, its soft wall-to-wall carpeting and subdued silk-shaded lamps, its vacuum sweeper, electric toaster, and coffee maker . . . there was no link between that and this. There was a yawning gap which she could not leap instantly. She would have to find a hard way . . . she would have to burn oil lamps, draw water from a well, and make trips out back. Try them and experience them, before she could accept them.

But for now Hod was the reality. And she clung desperately to the only familiar thing in this whole, new, strange world — Hod, her husband.

The days flew by. Mild, mellow days which hung ripe in the October air. Hod and Mary went fishing on the river, and he showed her the hole where Little Wells had pitched him in and he had learned to swim. Mary could see the little towheaded boy, years behind the achievements of his cousins, tagging along when he could slip away, finally triumphing, dog-paddling desperately to his own personal victory. Trotting home later, tousling his wet head with his shirttail to dry it so Hattie wouldn't notice. She felt a tender affection for that little boy.

They took long walks through the red-gold beech woods, and Hod told her the habits of birds and squirrels, of coons and foxes and rabbits. He dug back into his boyhood and brought up his store of memories for her, and in doing so he shed the years that had intervened. The tenseness that had first been in him let down, and he laughed and went young and gentle before her eyes.

These days she loved. The country was beautiful. The high pile of trees along the rim of the ridge. The sweeping openings of the valleys. The soft, grayed dawns and the cool, scarlet sunsets, purpling almost instantly into night. The winy haze that sifted over the woods. She filled herself with all this, and called it good. The ridge was truly beautiful.

Sometimes Hod went off with Tom to hunt, and Mary stayed in the kitchen with Hattie. On one of these days, when they had been there nearly two weeks, Hattie was called out front. When she came back, she was laughing. "That was Little Wells," she said. "He stopped by to tell that him an' a bunch is comin' over tonight after supper to see Hod, an' mebbe to sing a spell. He's allus been one to sing, Wells has. An' him an' Hod has allus loved to sing together. Now that'll pleasure Hod a heap. I'll bound he ain't sung e'er note sincet the last time he was home."

"How many will come?" Mary asked, her mind immediately busy with details.

" He never said. Jist said a bunch of 'em. Like as not they'll be eighteen or twenty, though."

Mentally Mary counted the chairs. Six . . . seven, counting the rocker. And the bench back of the table would seat three or four. There was a stool or two, but counting everything she couldn't see how they could take care of that many people. She gave it up. If Hattie wasn't worried, why need she be?

Hod was pleased. Mary could see his pleasure spreading all over him. " Well, now, that's nice of Wells, isn't it," he said, " to get up a shindig like this for us. Yessir, that's plumb nice of him! " His voice took on the drawl of the ridge talk. Mary smiled. The soft, honeyed speech was one of the nicest things about the ridge.

Hattie bustled them through supper and quickly redded up the house afterward, and while Mary and Hod were dressing, she tied a fresh apron around herself, dampened her hair and brushed it down, and was ready to greet the first comers, who followed on the setting of the sun by no more than a good ten minutes.

" This here's Hod's woman." Mary heard it over and over that evening. Two, four, six, ten, a dozen times. Each time her hand was shaken gravely and a shy, " Pleased to meet you," accompanied the handshake.

They kept coming until the chairs and the bench were full, and then they overflowed onto the bed and the floor. When the edge of the bed was full, those in front scooted back and leaned against the wall, leaving the edge for the late-comers. The wall by the fireplace was soon lined, and a row of feet stuck out into the room like tenpins waiting to be knocked over. Hod brought in a cot and pushed the dresser down the wall to make room for it. He and Little Wells and several other men crowded onto it.

And in between, scrambling over and around and under the chairs and the beds, were the children. Mary counted twenty, and that did not take in the babies that were asleep on the bed in the next room. There were six or eight of them, she knew. She began to understand that no family left its children at home on the ridge. A party for the parents was a party for the children too. It would not have occurred to fathers and mothers to leave their children at home in the first place, and in the second place there was no one to leave them with.

But, even with all the children, there was not the usual noise of a party as Mary knew it. There was only a small hum of talk, and that came mostly from the men's corner. Some of this Mary knew was because of her. She felt as conspicuous as a sore thumb, sitting straight in her chair next to Hattie. She had put on a simple dress, but it was much too fine for this gathering. It would have been better, she decided, to have left on her house dress. She caught the women's corner glances and felt them taking her in. Hod Pierce had married a city girl and they had all come to see. She tried to be pleasant, easy, comfortable. But she had so little in common with these women. Children! She had that in common with them! She taught children. Brightly she mentioned it and talked hurriedly about it for a few flat moments. When there was no response, she let it die a-borning. She looked desperately at Hattie. But Hattie sat, complacent and silent, her hands folded across her stomach. Well. She retired into her own silence. Maybe that was etiquette on the ridge!

" How about a little music? " she heard Hod say, and she sighed with relief.

Little Wells went out on the porch and came in with a stack of paper-backed songbooks. " Jist got these in, Hod. Been awaitin' fer you to come home to try 'em. Hit's the latest Stamps-Baxter book. Orta be some good 'uns in here too."

Two or three of the men unslung guitars and Hod got his from the chimney corner. He laughed as he picked it up. " Been a long time since I chorded a tune on this old thing. The strings are probably rotten."

Briskly Hattie spoke up. " No, they ain't. Tom, he restrung it jist 'fore you all come."

" Ferdy, how 'bout you leadin'? " Wells said.

Mary watched the gangling, overalled man swallow his Adam's apple painfully. " Well, now, I ain't sung in quite a spell."

The others insisted, however, and he took his place in front of them, towering over them. He set the key in a nasal hum, and suddenly his long right arm shot out in front of him. He lifted and swung it, like he was scything hay, and a tumult of sound filled the room. They sang as if they were in an auditorium seating five thousand people, and the room rocked with their voices. The roof fairly lifted.

Mary sat very still. Nothing could have prepared her for this,

207

braced her for it. She looked quickly around, when she had sufficiently recovered, to see if the others had noticed anything amiss. But the placid faces and the folded hands told her this was usual. This was fine singing! Her eyes flicked over to Hod. His bass was growling along happily. His face was red with the effort he was putting into the volume he must attain, but he was attaining it along with the rest, she had to admit. There were no fine attempts at feeling and phrasing. The words and the notes apparently were only the instruments for the voice. The main thing was to lift up your head and shout!

When they had sung half a dozen songs perhaps, changing leaders approximately that often, there was a sudden commotion at the door. Looking up, Mary saw a man and woman coming in, with two children tagging behind them and a third in the woman's arms.

"Why, hit's Matt an' Lutie Jasper," Hattie said, rising. "Come in, come in. Come in an' set, iten you kin find e'er place."

The man was thin, almost to the point of emaciation, gaunt and shambling. He had a week's growth of beard on his face and tobacco spittle drooled down his chin. His overalls were slick with sweat and dirt, and a foul, sour odor emanated from him. His hair hung down on all sides, lank and greasy-looking. His face had a vacant, staring look, and his skin was pasty and moist like fallen dough.

The woman was almost as thin, the skin taut over her cheekbones. Her dress hitched up in front several inches and left her skinny knees bare and exposed. It was black with grease, and a rent in the skirt had been pinned together. Below the dress her legs were little more than bone and muscle. Her mouth was slack, and a twig toothbrush hung from one corner. Her hair, which had once been fuzzy with a permanent, was now matted and dried like straw.

But the most horrible thing about both of them was the flat, empty look of their eyes. They were as devoid of expression as ovals of glass. Their empty stare made Mary feel as if her look had run into something solid and glanced off. Nothing could penetrate that marbled surface. They were as opaque as if they were turned inward. Mary felt a deep shudder start within her, and her effort to control it raised goose bumps on her flesh. There was

208

something slimy and loathsome about these people.

"This here's Hod's woman," Hattie was saying.

Neither the man nor the woman spoke. They simply stared at her, the woman's eyes roving over her, taking in every detail of her hair, her face, her dress, even her hands and feet. There was no change of expression on her face. Neither interest nor lack of it. The face was blank and the eyelids drooped over the cold, empty eyes. Mary was suddenly reminded of the hooded eyes of a snake. She shivered. I am looking at the substance of evil, she thought. This is the irreconcilable distillation of sin, extracted and poured into the form of humanity. This is the prideless travesty of man. She felt her own dignity assailed, and loathed herself for the horror that filled her. Wildly she looked for Hod. But he was miles away, over there in the corner with the men of his own kind, laughing and joking and picking a nameless tune on his guitar.

He went strange and unknown to her, changing before her eyes into someone new and unfamiliar — as new and unfamiliar as this room, and the people who were packed into it, bulging its sides with their leathered bodies and fetid odors. What was she, Mary Hogan, doing here? How did she reach this place? What did she have to do with these people? And who was Hod Pierce?

A lamp smoked suddenly and a woman's hand reached out to turn down the wick. The dim, sputtering light and the crude smell of oil added the final nightmarish touch of unreality to the scene, and Mary stumbled across the room, through the door, out onto the porch. She clung, nauseated, to the railing and gulped in the good air. I will not go back into that room, she thought. Nothing can make me go back in there!

The door slammed behind her, and at once Hod was beside her. "Mary," he said, and his voice was full of fear, "Mary, what's the matter?"

His arms went round her and pulled her close. She leaned her head against him and shook with deep, shuddering sobs. Oh, blessed relief! This was Hod. This was her husband. Here, holding her. Now, touching her and comforting her.

"What is it, Mary?" he urged. "Are you sick?"

"No," she shook her head against his shirt, her voice muffled and choked by tears. "No. I want to go home, Hod. Please, I want to go home!"

209

CHAPTER TWENTY–FOUR

Gently Hod got from her what had caused her panic and her flight. He held her while she let it spin out of her, interrupted from time to time by shuddering gasps. She was cold now, and limp. Spent with the terror of her betrayal by the ridge. She loved it, she assured Hod. It was such beautiful country. But the people. Hod, the people are so unbeautiful!

"Why, that's just poor old Matt Jasper and Lutie," he reasoned with her. "There's not a bit of harm in the world in him. He's simple-minded, sort of, and he has epilepsy, but he's not mean. And Lutie. There's no harm in her either. She's about as feeble-minded as he is, but she's goodhearted when you know her."

Mary wiped her eyes and sniffed. "But you've grown up with them! You're used to them!"

Hod was still, smoothing her hair with a soft hand. He stood cradling her thus for a long time. "Sure," he said then, "sure, I know. I should have known how they would look to you. I didn't know they were coming, or I might have warned you. We can't be unkind to them, Mary. They're ridge folks too. They're neighbors. They're part of things here. Ugly, pathetic, maybe. But they belong here too."

He soothed her, his voice low and gentle, holding her, making her feel close to him again. Until finally he said: "Now, let's go back in. They'll all be wonderin' what's happened. They won't be stayin' much longer. Ma's makin' coffee now, an' gettin' the cake ready. You go on out in the kitchen and help her. And we'll go home tomorrow."

She felt better, now. Weak, craven she might be. But she felt much better. At least Hod had come back to her. And they did go home the next day.

Home was Mary's small apartment. One of those one-big-room-kitchenette-bath affairs. And it was full of Mary's things. There was her piano, her desk, her books, her clothes, and all her personal belongings. It was a gay little apartment, bright with colorful curtains and warm rugs, but it was a tiny, fussy, feminine little place. Hod set his bags down in the middle of the big room and looked helplessly around.

"Where's the rest of it?" he asked, laughing.

"This is all of it," Mary answered, and motioned vaguely with one hand. "We'd better unpack you first."

When they had finished, his things filled every available nook and cranny and overflowed into places never meant for a man's things. Mary found him standing unhappily in front of the wall cabinet in the bathroom looking hopelessly at the bottle-filled shelves. He was trying to find a place for his razor and shaving brush. She swept one shelf clear of bottles. "There, darling. You can have that shelf."

Thus, pigeonholing, they managed to clean out his bags, and stored them away in the basement.

The apartment was so small that they were constantly tangling, bumping into each other, getting in each other's way. Hod was a big man, and he spilled all over the place. He was not a neat man, strowing his belongings carelessly. The apartment more often than not took on a wind-swept, storm-torn look. Mary was careful not to nag, but her orderly teacher's mind could not restrain her from tidying behind him when it got too bad.

They put up with the crowding several days before they admitted the truth. It just wouldn't do. That was all.

Hod let himself down into his chair at breakfast that morning, rubbing his back. "That sofa of yours is about the doggonedest bed I ever tried to sleep on. I get up with a crick in my back every morning."

Mary poured his coffee and defended the couch. "It's always been a good bed for me! It just resents having to sleep two now."

"Well, whatever it is, we'd better get a new bed." He buttered his toast and looked at the lovely breakfast table. It was spread with a fresh white cloth, against which Mary's pink plates, sparkling glasses, and shining silver gleamed brightly. Two pale rosebuds lifted themselves above a slender silver holder in the center of the table. Glasses of fruit juice were nested in cups of ice, and crisped bacon curled around a beautiful omelet with a spot of clear red jelly in its heart.

Mary took her place opposite him and flipped her napkin open.

She was one of those fortunate women who need no make-up except a deepening of the red of her mouth, and she was still young enough to waken fresh, rested, and full of energy. This morning she had tied a yellow ribbon around her hair, and her cheeks were flushed from cooking the breakfast. She was very lovely.

Hod was conscious of the picture . . . the table, the plates, the silver, Mary across the table from him. This all went together, and he felt a full sense of achievement. Somehow this was meant to be. This was just the way it had looked in his dreams.

If, when he buttered his toast and bit into its thin crispness, if then he remembered Hattie's fluffy biscuits, it was only for a second. If, when he helped himself to several slivers of the crisp, broiled bacon and the airy omelet, if he thought then of the old ironstone bowl full of cream gravy, and the rich taste of home-cured side meat sliced into thick, man-sized pieces, it passed immediately. He didn't need to tell himself that he would become accustomed to such breakfasts. He needed no reassurance of any kind. This was what he wanted . . . Mary, and the white table-cloth and the shiny silver.

Mary picked up the conversation again. " We not only need another bed," she said, " we've got to find a larger apartment, Hod. This was fine for me, but it's just too crowded for two. We'll be in each other's hair all the time."

"You know I was thinking the same thing," Hod said, " and wonderin' if you'd mind."

He glanced around. Why, the whole apartment could be set down in Ma's big front room, with space left over in all four corners!

"Oh, no, I don't mind. This just won't do. But it's going to be hard to find a place." Mary's forehead crinkled into a frown. " The town is so full that apartments are awfully hard to find. And high. But," and she rose briskly and set about cleaning off the dishes, " we'll see what we can find. There's nothing like trying, I always say." She brushed the top of Hod's head with her mouth as she went by. " You've got lipstick on your forehead, Mr. Pierce! Tsk! Tsk! "

" That just goes to show," Hod drawled, hitching himself up out of the chair, " what a woman can do to a man. Such a fine, upstandin' young man too. Just gettin' a start in the city! "

" You mean I'm a bad influence on you! "

" Why, you're plumb leadin' me to ruin! "

In that mood they washed the dishes, folded the bed back into the sofa, and, armed with the morning paper, which had a scant dozen ads in the " For Rent " column, started out to look at apartments. Hod was full of confidence. With Mary by his side the world was all his. He strode belligerently along, chin up, plunging his long body over the sidewalks as if they had been new-plowed furrows. And Mary reached out her own long legs to keep pace.

They were more fortunate than most couples. One of Mary's teacher friends called her one night and told her there was to be a vacancy in her building. But they'd better come right over and look at it. The landlord would hold it only twenty-four hours.

They hurried over, and immediately they knew it would do. It was an old-fashioned apartment building with large five-room units. The rooms were spacious, with high ceilings and tall, narrow windows. There was a fireplace in the living room, and Mary exclaimed over the fine woodwork and floors. She poked her nose into the big, deep closets and yearned over their ample storage space. The whole apartment was roomy, light, and airy. It was just what they had been looking for. But she trembled when she asked the rent. Eighty-five dollars. Well, that was reasonable enough. It was the ceiling price, the man explained.

Hod tortured his tongue against the rough spot on his tooth. It sounded like quite a lot to him. This business of paying money for a place to live was one thing the Pierces had never worried about. There always had been a Pierce roof over Pierce heads . . . somebody else had paid for that roof generations ago, and it had come down through the years, tight and secure. There it was . . . home. And all you ever paid was the taxes once a year. And they were so small that even Pierces could pay them and hardly miss the money.

But if Mary thought it was reasonable, he supposed it must be. They took the apartment that night, signed the lease, and Hod pulled out his billfold and counted off eighty-five dollars. As he handed the man the money, he thought that he must do this the first of every month. Not just once . . . done and over . . . but every month, come hell or high water, or else he and Mary wouldn't have a roof over their heads. For the first time he felt the responsibility of being married settling down on him. And for the first time he felt a little bit scared.

He looked at the greenbacks as he stuffed the remainder of them back into his wallet. You sold your skill, your time, and your labor to get this kind of money. Well, that's what he had wanted to do. And he was just the man who could do it. He squared his shoulders.

"Now we've got us a place to live," he said as they walked home under the street lamps, "what next?"

"Furniture," Mary answered. "Lots of furniture. That's a big place!"

"Isn't that your furniture over at your place?" he asked, startled.

"Just the piano and desk and odds and ends. A place like that has everything furnished."

"Why hasn't this one?"

"Because it's an unfurnished apartment, silly!"

"Oh."

"Didn't you notice there wasn't any furniture?"

"Sure. But I thought maybe they'd moved it out to clean or something."

Mary laughed and ran her hand through his arm. "We'll not try to furnish it all at once. We'll start with the essentials and work up to it gradually."

The first winter cold had settled over the city, raw and damp and biting. Fog crept in from the river and mixing with the smoke became a dirty blanket of what people in Louisville called "smog." It had an acrid, penetrating odor, sharp and unpleasant in the nose and throat. Soot sifted through it and settled in greasy flakes on the skin. Hod brushed at it impatiently. The street lamps were dull-amber bowls of light, spotting the unfriendly haze spasmodically and inadequately. There was a moon shining somewhere, Hod knew. It had been almost a month since they had spent those first nights at Spring Mill, and walked the tunneled trails where, full, it had shown through in silver shafts of light. Down home . . . down home it was shining. Over the dried fields and the stripped woods. Over the hollers and the tree-locked ridges. Over the road winding ribbonlike down the saddle of Piney. Light enough, likely, to go huntin'. Old Duke would be restless tonight. He would thump the porch floor and wander out to the gate, and maybe rear back on his haunches and bay mournfully. The ground would be crisp with frost, and would ring to your heels . . . but it would give underneath. He stabbed his heel into the pavement. Cement was sure hard to walk on now.

They sat up late that night over their furniture list. The kitchen first. Stove, refrigerator, table and chairs. There were plenty of cabinets, thank goodness. The bedroom next. Bed, springs, mattress. Hod thought of his old straw tick . . . fresh-filled each winter. Nothing lay better. But of course you couldn't use a straw tick in the city. Chest of drawers, dresser, bedside table, lamps, rug, curtains. We'll leave the other bedroom bare for a while. Store things in there. Now the living room. We've got the piano, desk, and bookcases. All right. Sofa, rug, coffee table, one big, comfortable chair, lamps, curtains. That will do for now.

" How much? " Hod asked when the list was complete.

Mary hesitated. " About a thousand dollars."

Hod whistled. They bent over the bankbook. Mary had been saving too, and between them there was nearly two thousand in the bank. She looked at him questioningly. " I can cut a few corners," she suggested.

" No, you don't," Hod said. " We don't start by cuttin' corners. Get what you want. I'll be workin' pretty soon. And that back bedroom's not goin' to stay bare very long, either."

When they had moved, Hod took another two weeks to help Mary clean windows and woodwork, lay rugs, hang curtains, and get settled in, before he started out to look for a job. Mary had taken a two months' leave of absence and the time was running out. She wanted to get the home to running smoothly before she went back to teaching.

At first Hod had protested. " I don't like the idea of my wife workin'," he said. The ridge concept of a woman's place was very strong in him.

But Mary had been firm. " Listen, Hod," she pointed out, reasonably and patiently, " it will just be for a little while. Until we get on our feet and know where we're going. When you've found what you want to do, and have made a good start, then we'll buy a little place and I'll quit teaching and stay home and raise a family. But for a while, another year or two anyhow, it just makes sense for me to earn too."

" You sure you'll be satisfied to quit when the time comes? "

" I'm sure. I want a home and children, but it would be silly for me to quit now and give all my time to keeping this apartment. What I make will help out, and as long as we can't yet afford the home and family, I'll be a lot better satisfied to work."

When she put it that way, Hod had no objection. After all, Mary knew best, he supposed. He would rather she didn't work, but if she would be happier, then that was what really mattered. Mary was good at figuring things out. He swelled a little with pride when he thought of all the ways she was so smart.

The day Mary went back to the schoolroom Hod began looking for his job. As they dressed that morning, she timidly offered to advise him. " How're you going about this? " she wanted to know.

Hod was knotting his tie and he pulled it into place before answering. " Oh, I thought I'd just look around a little. Get the lay of the land . . . I know about what I want to do."

" I'd be glad to call a few people I know, if you think it would do any good."

" We'll see," he said, shrugging into his coat. " You ready? "

" Ready. Got your key? "

He held it up for her to see, and shook his head. Locking a door! He didn't suppose there ever had been a lock on a door down home. But Mary had warned him. " Always keep the door on lock," she said, " and always be sure you've got your key. Even if you just empty the garbage downstairs."

Hod browsed around the city for several days. He had learned since the days he and Johnny Knight came to town all those years ago that there was more to Louisville than Market and Jefferson Streets. He laughed when he remembered that night. Deliberately he went down in that end of town and loafed around. It sure was drab. Thousand wonders two kids like that hadn't got knocked in the head.

216

Hod took his time. He talked with men at several employment places. He had a sense of leisure and of wanting to choose carefully. And at one place he heard first of the plant that interested him immediately. Kentuckiana, Inc. They made furniture, mostly, but they made a little bit of everything that was made out of wood.

Hod asked for details and then went out to look the plant over. It was a huge industrial concern, one of the largest in the state, spread out over acres of ground. A guard stopped him at the gate, and when he said he wanted to visit the plant, he was routed to the main office. He explained once more and was told to wait. A party of visitors were going through in about thirty minutes.

On the tour he walked along silently with the group. He didn't need to ask many questions. He took in the huge machines, the presses, the small precision instruments, the saws and the lathes. And he knew that he would like to work here. Machines . . . instruments . . . tools. He liked the feel of them in his hands. Yes, this was the place.

At the end of the tour he sought out the employment office and filed his application. But he figured it would be buried in such a large place. That night at dinner he asked Mary, " You know anybody out at Kentuckiana? "

Mary thought for a moment. " No. No, I don't. But I know someone who does. One of the teachers has a friend whose husband is in Personnel out there. Why? "

" I'd like to work there. I put in my application today, but I don't think a guy'd have a chance to get on, cold like that. I thought maybe you knew someone out there who could help out a little. But a friend of a friend of a friend of yours is the long way round I reckon."

" Well, I don't know about that," Mary bristled. " She's a pretty good friend. And if her friend's husband is in Personnel, all he'd have to do is O.K. your application."

" I don't want him to do that. What I want is to get an interview, so he'll have something to go on when the application comes up."

Mary leaned her elbow on the table and pocketed her chin in her palm. " You wouldn't care if I said a word to Esther, would you? "

Hod was lighting his cigarette. He blew a cloud of smoke across the table at her. " Nope. I doubt it'll do any good, but it wouldn't hurt to try."

Mary started to ask him why he had picked Kentuckiana. But she bit the question back. Already she was learning to let him alone. He traveled by himself on certain roads.

About a week later Hod was asked to call at the employment office. The card was signed by W. A. Fleming. Mary waved it gleefully in front of his nose. " See! See, what did I tell you! That's Bill Fleming. Nora Fleming's husband. And Nora Fleming is Esther's friend. It *did* do some good after all! "

" Let me see it! " Hod growled, and grabbed at the card. He examined it thoughtfully. " Hmmm. O.K."

He put the card down and walked over to the window and stared out at the courtyard down below. A flight of pigeons whirred past the window and wheeled gently to the ground. Their jeweled wings fanned briefly in the sun and then pleated primly into a pouted, rounded symmetry. Hod stood so still that only his back moved with his breathing. Mary watched him for a moment or two, and then she slipped over to stand beside him. She ran her hand through his arm and nuzzled his shoulder with her nose. " Thinking? " she asked, when he remained silent.

" Yeah." He straightened and patted her hand. " Yeah. I was thinkin' how many years it's been." And then almost absently he pulled in his belt another notch.

CHAPTER TWENTY–FIVE

THE NEW WORK WENT WELL. The first three months Hod was on the job he advanced rapidly. This was partly due to his own initiative and energy, but mostly it was because industry was hitting its stride in postwar production. Men were being hired by the thousands, trained rapidly and briefly, and if they were efficient at all they were pushed ahead.

Another man might have found that work tedious, monotonous, and dull. But to Hod each precisely calculated operation satisfied some tidy, mathematical instinct in him. He liked the feel of metal and wood in his hands, and he liked, when he had finished an operation, to look at the piece and see it in relation to the whole. It wasn't just a panel of wood or a bar of steel; it was a chair, a sofa, a bed, something useful and beautiful.

Part of his liking for his work was due too to the fact that it was new to him. But most of it was because he had imagination with which to enliven it. In the handling of materials, in the precision operations, in the part he played in the whole, he saw an over-all plan, and it had a certain beauty of its own. Like the child who could lose himself in the story of King Arthur's Court, like the boy who felt poetry in hoeing the corn and milking the cows, like the young man who cried out against the unawareness of his people, Hod now saw something of the rhythm and surge of American industrialism, its inevitable forward sweep, its giant strides across the world, taking millions of little people along with it. He was glad to be a part of it. He took a great deal of pride in his job.

He also took a great deal of pride in the contents of his pay envelope. At first it had been fifty, fifty-five, sixty dollars a week. To one to whom ninety dollars a month, overseas pay for a sergeant, had been top pay in his life, this was a magnificent sum. He brought it home and turned it over to Mary each week, with a grand gesture. True, this sense of proportion was only temporary. He stepped up too rapidly, and each time he stepped up he looked back down the ladder, and eventually looked with contempt upon that first fifty dollars. It wasn't until then that he knew how naïve he had been. But it was a thoroughly enjoyable naïveté while it lasted.

He experienced a small return of it the first time he drew a check for a hundred dollars. He looked at the figures, and they were unreal. He remembered hoeing corn for Little Wells . . . ten long hours a day for fifty cents. He remembered the tomato money that first summer with Johnny Knight. He remembered the thirty-two dollars a month on the road project. Those amounts were real. This hundred which Hod Pierce had made in five short days had no tangible value to him. It was fantastic.

But he took tremendous pride in it just the same. Just as he took great pride in the way the apartment shaped up under Mary's capable hands. *Things* became very important to him.

219

The new, hand-blocked drapes at the windows. The cherry drop-leaf table for the hall. The mahogany beds in the guest room. The exact shade of the rug for the dining room. Even the new automatic toaster and electric mixer and pressure cooker . . . each new piece Mary added was a symbol to Hod. A symbol of success . . . of achievement . . . of being somebody.

And he smoothed off the rough edges from himself too. Clothes had never had any meaning to Hod. He never did have enough of them to give them a second thought beyond whether they were clean or not. Hattie had taken care of them, and up to the time he left the ridge, she had even bought most of them for him. And then the Army uniform had relieved him of all responsibility for nearly six years.

When he and Mary married, he was still in uniform, but shortly afterward they had outfitted him in civilian clothes. He had asked Mary to select these for him. He hadn't particularly liked her selections . . . he thought they were rather drab and colorless. But he had accepted them because he trusted her judgment.

When they went to their first party and he studied the other men in relation to himself, he was glad. Mary had been right, of course. The plainness and darkness of the blue suit, the brilliance of the white shirt, the soft casualness of the hand-knit tie . . . these were right. With only slight variations the other men were dressed the same.

Mary had been a little nervous about that party. It was Hod's introduction to her friends. She told herself she wanted Hod to like her friends. She told herself she hoped he wouldn't find them dull or trivial. But she fussed a lot over Hod as he dressed.

" Not *that* shirt, darling! You wear a *white* shirt tonight."

" Why? I like this blue one."

" Because, darling, men don't wear colored shirts on some occasions! Parties, church, things like that. And your blue suit, dear, not your brown one."

Hod obediently got into the things she laid out. " Tell me about these folks who'll be there," Hod asked, buttoning his shirt.

" Well," Mary slipped one foot carefully down the leg of a fragile stocking, " you've met Esther. She thinks of herself as an intellectual . . . dabbles in art, poetry, music, and stuff. She's a good teacher, though. And Ed travels. Salesman for some hardware firm here in town. And there'll be Joe and Daisy Prentiss. Joe is a salesman too. Daisy has a dress shop of her own, is very beautiful, and very, very sophisticated. Then there'll be Minna and Sid Bowden. Sid is another salesman. And Minna is a sort of frustrated little person. She goes in for civic work and great causes. She's a little picked-chicken sort of person and I don't think she's very happy, but she's dreadfully in earnest about her work. And then there'll be Nora and Bill Fleming. I don't know them. And with us, that's all. They're just people, dear. People like you meet every day in the week."

She preened nervously before the mirror, twisting and turning to see if her seams were straight, to see if any tiny fraction of slip was showing. She turned to the dressing table to dab perfume behind her ears, and leaned forward to redden her mouth. " Oh, I *do* hope you like them, Hod. They're really pretty nice."

Hod caught her waist and swung her around. " That's about the tenth time you've said that! What you really mean is, you hope they like me, isn't it? That's why you're so jittery. You mean you hope I remember to use the right silver at the table, and to keep my elbows off, like I usually don't. And you mean you hope I don't make any slip in my grammar. And you mean you hope I won't get started talking about the ridge, telling jokes about Old Man Clark and his third wife, and so on. That's what you really mean! "

Mary stood still with his big hands warm on her waist and looked helplessly at him. An iron hand in her chest squeezed the blood right out of her heart and sent it, weakening and dribbling, down to her feet. She caught a deep sob as it came up past the lump in her throat. What have I done, she thought. What have I done to you, my darling! In the clear, clean light of his sensitive apperception she went down and down inside herself, and came back up with her own true sense of worth and dignity restored. She lifted her hands, took Hod's face gently between them. Tears blurred her vision. She shook them impatiently away. " No," she said softly, " no, Hod, that's *not* what I really mean. I truly mean I hope you will like them. You are so much finer, so much nobler, so heads and shoulders above them, that I truly, truly hope they may be worth your respect and liking. Truly. Truly! "

Hod pulled her close and wrapped his arms around her. How

loyal she was! How terribly, terribly honest and loyal! But he'd be careful. He knew about pride. They had it on the ridge too. He'd sit back and listen mostly tonight, and he'd be careful.

Esther and Ed were giving the party in honor of Mary and Hod. Esther met them at the door. She was a tall, rawboned woman with iron-gray hair, and a high, strident voice. She drew them inside, chattering incessantly, and led them into the living room. Her husband detached himself from a group around the radio and came across the room to greet them. He was a rotund, sleek little man, balding and paunching at forty.

Hod shook hands with him and allowed himself to be led over to the group of men bunched around the radio. "Want you to meet the rest of these boys," Ed said. Hod listened to the names around the circle. Joe Prentiss. Dark, slight, nervous, his long upper lip covered with a small moustache. "Joe's over at Belknap's. My rival. Lucky he doesn't work the same territory."

Sid Bowden. Another round, sleek little man. "Sid's with Brown-Williamson."

"And I guess you already know Bill Fleming. Esther told me you were out at Kentuckiana. Bill's in Personnel out there."

"How are you, sir?" Hod hadn't seen Bill Fleming since the day he had interviewed him for the job. He reached out a firm hand and shook the older man's. The old Army " sir " had slipped out automatically. "I expect I owe my job at Kentuckiana to Mr. Fleming," he added to Ed.

Fleming, who was a big, hearty, heavy man, laughed. "That's what friends are for, Pierce. How're you getting along? They treating you all right out there?"

"Couldn't be better, sir."

Fleming nodded. "I've checked on you once or twice. You're doing all right. This may be a little out of order, and keep it under your hat, but I heard they had their eye on you for section foreman."

Hod flushed, and for the first time he felt awkward. Praise always made him feel that way. "I've done the best I could," he said. Hattie, at home, had always phrased it, " I like to do what I kin."

At dinner Hod sat at Esther's right, with Nora Fleming on the other side. She was a plain, plump little person, almost wrenlike. Immediately she began to talk to him about the country. "I hear you were raised down in Adair County," she said. "That's not far from where Esther and I grew up."

Hod laid his soup spoon down. "Where was that?" he asked.

"In Marion County, near Lebanon."

Esther leaned across. "Nora, you always bring that up!"

"I do, don't I?" Nora said cheerfully. "Well, I was raised in the country, and I like to remember it. And I wish our children were being raised in the country right now. Then I wouldn't worry about them like I do."

"Being raised in the country isn't necessarily the panacea for all ills, dear," Esther remarked.

"Maybe not," and Nora began telling Hod about Bill, Jr., and Anne, who were in high school. "They just go, go, go, all the time!" she said. "They're never at home. I don't even know where they are most of the time. And Bill is always at the office, or off on a business trip. Sometimes I feel like I don't have any family at all!"

Esther's strident voice broke in again. "Are you going to the Ice Follies Monday night, Nora?"

Nora nodded. "I suppose so. We have tickets."

Minna broke in. Minna, Hod thought. Minnow! And that was just what she reminded him of! A darting little sliver of fish. She was quick, thin, and colorless, with a small mouth that puckered when she talked. "Did you get your tickets from my girls, Daisy? You know, the Civic Duty League . . . we got a percentage."

Daisy shrugged her velvet-hugged shoulders. "I really don't know, Minna. I can't keep up with all your causes. We got them at the box office."

Minna looked disappointed. "Oh. Then you didn't. The girls were on the street in booths." She smiled across the table at Hod. "It's true I *do* work for a good many civic causes, Mr. Pierce. But I feel it's my duty. And besides, I think *people* are so important, don't you?"

Mary twinkled a finger at Hod down the table and he winked back to show he was getting along all right.

The dinner went on and the talk frothed around the table.

223

Finally it settled on Hod's and Mary's apartment.

"Esther tells me you have a beautiful place in that lovely court over by the park. Weren't you fortunate, though, to find something so nice!" Nora said.

Mary launched into an enthusiastic description of the apartment, Esther breaking in occasionally. "It's an enchanting little court," her high, cracked voice cried, "hidden away right in the heart of town. Almost Old World looking. And the apartment is lovely. The only thing," and she laughed brittlely, "the absolutely only thing wrong with it is that awful Van Gogh print Mary insisted on hanging over the fireplace! Darling, no one has Van Gogh any more! Peter Hunt would be better than Van Gogh. But, no! She hangs onto that sweet orchard in bloom as if it were an original!"

Mary's chin came up. "I like that picture! There's something very still and splendid about it. It has repose. None of us can afford originals, so what's wrong with prints? And if you like Van Gogh, what's wrong with him?"

What was a Van Gogh, Hod wondered. And who was Peter Hunt? They must be talking about the picture hanging over the mantel. He liked it too. And Mary was right. There was a feeling of repose in it. And it looked real. He could vouch for that. He should know orchards in bloom!

The talk went on. One of the men asked, "Did you get a pretty good deal on your furniture?"

"I don't know," Hod answered. "I left that up to Mary."

"Where'd you buy?" Ed asked.

"Oh, here . . . and there," Mary said. "I bought wherever I found what I wanted."

"Mary, you fool!" screamed Esther. "Don't you know everything costs you three times as much that way!"

Hod spoke up. "What's wrong with buying where you want to?"

Ed leaned back in his chair and swabbed his mouth with his napkin. "Look, Hod," he began. "I'm a salesman, see? I've got some good connections. I could have got you a good price on everything you bought. The next time you buy anything, let one of us know. That's what friends are for."

Hod smiled down the table at Mary. It's all right, he meant to say to her. We got what we wanted. That was more important than anything else. But he was disturbed a little, nevertheless. He felt as if they had been taken in.

After dinner there was bridge. Hod didn't play and Esther sat out with him. Her agile tongue slipped from one subject to another, dwelling lightly on all, leaving no burden on Hod for reply, and relieving him of the necessity of listening with more than one ear. He sat quietly relaxed in his corner, absorbing the whole scene, letting the people and the room and the hum and flow of talk eddy around him, swishing its edges near him, but not sweeping him away.

The room was expensively beautiful, and temptingly comfortable. From Mary he was learning how rugs, drapes, wall colors, lamps, pictures, and furniture blend to make a pleasing picture, and this one pleased him. Their own apartment was lovely now, but this home said so plainly, I am the result of money as well as good taste. He liked that. But he liked the way it was expressed too. With restraint and with quality rather than with ostentation.

He studied the group around the card tables. The women, even Minna, so well-dressed, so groomed and finished. He felt a swell of pride when his eyes rested on Mary. Daisy was more beautiful in a polished, smooth way. But Mary was prettier in a natural, pleasing way. These were the kind of people she belonged with, though. These gracious, pleasant, cultured people. No wonder she had run away from Lutie and Matt Jasper!

He turned his thoughts to the men, and took in their gloss and finish and easy way of talking and laughing. They were so assured. They had that easy kind of nonchalance which comes from possessing good things — good jobs, good salaries, good living.

Snatches of conversation came across the room. Sid Bowden was talking. Telling Ed about his new car. " You don't have to wait to get a new car if you know how to work it," he was saying. " It's a racket. And you've got to know where to go. It'll cost you a little extra, but what's a coupla hundred in the pocket of the right man. Presto, you've got a new car! "

Ed nodded. He fanned his cards and squinted at them. " Two spades," and he snapped the fan of cards neatly. " I've got to get a new one this year."

" Let me know when you're ready."

" O.K."

Hod thought of the old Chevrolet parked outside. Junk heap! He sucked in his cheeks and let his tongue find the familiar rough spot on the edge of his tooth. Before I'm through I'll drive a bigger car than any of 'em, he thought. Mary'll have the biggest and finest home of 'em all. And she'll wear diamonds and furs with the best of 'em! Nothing's too good for the Pierces. And nothing's going to stop them!

CHAPTER TWENTY–SIX

WITHIN THREE MONTHS the promotion came through, and Hod was made a section foreman. " This is it, Mary," he laughed that night, " this is the first step! "

He was too excited and happy to sit still. He paced back and forth across the room, rumpling his hair. Every nerve in his body was electric, and deep, rippling thrills ran clear down to his toes. Golly, he thought, it means so much more than a guy ever thought it could! Even if he has starved for it!

It was beginning to be in his grasp now. He flung himself down on the couch and slipped his feet out of his shoes, stretching back and curling his toes. He felt like that. Like his toes, freed and unloosed. The certainty that he had started on his way up was an unloosening thing. A freeing feeling. A sparkling, winy thing shooting through him, racing in bubbles down to his finger tips. He was on his feet again in a moment, pacing in his socks. He needed to feel something solid under him. " Jeff Martin says . . ." he said.

" Who is Jeff Martin, dear? "

" He's the division superintendent, the big shot. You see, there are about six sections in each division," he told them off on his fingers, " and each section has three foremen, one for each shift. And then there's a division foreman, with about six assistants. But the division superintendent is really brass. He's stuff! And Jeff Martin says I'll be a division foreman in another year. Says he's been watching me. Says if I do all right on this job, he'll see that I get the breaks. It's not being section foreman that means anything. It's where it's leading. And we're going places with it! We're going places, Mary! And nothing's going to stop us!"

But Hod didn't tell Mary about the first foremen's meeting. They were all there — the little shots and the big shots. Reminded Hod of an NCO meeting. Hod sat tight, back in a corner. Like he had in NCO meetings. He remembered the brass had watched him there too, and had picked him for the other side of the fence. He hadn't had the nerve to take it on then. And he knew a moment of writhing shame as he thought of it. Well, he had one leg over the fence again, and he was going all the way this time.

When the big shots left and they broke up into division meetings, the talk came down to local problems. For Hod's special benefit the division foreman, a big, hulking fellow by the name of Conway, outlined the setup. "This is the way it works," he said. "The rest of you guys know all this, but Pierce is new and if he doesn't know what it's all about he'll screw the works for everybody. Now look, Pierce. The division's run on a budget — an expense budget. The company have figured out what they think each division in the plant can operate on. We take that figure and break it down by sections. You section men take it and break it down into shifts. Any questions so far?"

Hod shook his head. It was like analyzing a problem back in the prewar Army.

"Well, then," Conway went on, shifting on his thick, stout legs, "here's where you'll make a good foreman, or not. It's sort of like a war. The men on the machines are out to make as much money as they can. Practically every machine in the plant is on piecework, now. You know that, and you know what the average piecework rate is, and how much it means to a man. How hard he works to get a good one, and how much he likes to draw time on it. Now, I ain't saying we're against the men. If your men don't respect you and work for you, you ain't got a chance. But all the same, you got to make that expense margin. If you don't watch out, first thing you know you'll be running in the hole. And when you go in the hole, the division begins to lose ground, and when a division begins to lose ground, a lotta foremen begin to lose their jobs. That's the way it goes."

Hod was puzzled. The strategy was clear enough, but the tactics were fuddled. "How do you stay within that margin?" he asked. "If you're expected to get out so much work, run so many pieces, you've got to do it, haven't you? And you can't get out work without its costing something!"

"Oh, there's ways," Conway continued. "Get the feel of the job, and try to keep from running behind. Keep it running through smooth and even, so you don't have to use no overtime. Overtime mounts up. The guys like it . . . time and a half, who wouldn't? But too much overtime eats up your margin. And you can always stop a man on a job. If he's running it up into pretty big pay, you can pull him and put him on something else. Pick a machine that don't pay as much. Tell him there's a hurry call for something." Conway laughed suggestively.

The other foremen settled into their chairs and laughed with him, comfortable, deep laughs, rumbling around their cigarettes. Hod tightened his mouth. Yeah. That had been pulled on him too. He had never resented it, believing honestly there must be a sudden run on a certain stock. Hillman always bustled up so importantly. "Gotta hurry this one, Pierce. Hate to take you off the machine right now. But I gotta slip on number 1088's. Need 'em in assembly by four this afternoon."

Hod looked across the room at Hillman, and Hillman winked at him slyly. Hod's tongue probed the rough tooth. He'd quit the job! He wouldn't pull stuff like that on the guys!

But Conway was still talking. "At the end of the year there's a nice fat check waiting for you. A bonus. And the size of it depends on you. If you don't make it, you can close your desk and look for another job."

Yeah. Yeah, he had a leg over the fence all right. And he was the one who wasn't going to let anything stop him. But you couldn't pull that kind of stuff on a guy like, say Demarest, for instance. Demarest had six kids. He needed every cent he could make!

He was a long time getting to sleep that night. The air was close and muggy, and the first spring warmness pressed in. The flicker from the street lamp on the corner made a fretting pattern on the blinds at the window, and streaked bars of light across the bed. The bars became real and solid and took on weight, until at last he threw them off angrily and rose and dressed and went downstairs to the court. He stretched out in the grass, then, and let himself sink into its green softness. Overhead a thin moon cut a silver crescent in the sky. Here the rumble of traffic was dulled to a faint throb, and he could almost imagine he was in the back pasture on the ridge. He listened for the night sounds . . . the lonely, lovely cry of a whippoorwill . . . the sad, sweet mourning of a dove . . . the heart-stopping trill of a wood thrush. His eyes drooped. Maybe, he thought, maybe I won't have to do it that way. Maybe I can manage without it. Maybe. And he slept.

Mary was happy for him, and proud of him. They had a new car now. It was a small car — not the low-slung, powerful convertible Hod really wanted — but it would do for the time being. That would come. In time. The small car was better than the jalopy, anyhow. Sid Bowden helped him get it. And it only cost him a couple of hundred extra.

They went down to the ridge frequently. Hod was like a small boy wanting to show off the car, wanting to give lavish gifts to the folks, wanting to spread around over the ridge and let folks see how well he was doing. He never said so. But there was a swagger in his walk and in his talk that was transparent. Mary smiled over it. She thought he had earned the right to swagger a little.

Each time they started out he piled the back of the car full of things. Clothes for Ma, clothes for Pa, and especially clothes for Sarah. New tools for Pa, a new kerosene stove for Ma, new dolls and dishes and toys for Sarah. He even included Irma and John and their young'uns in his giving. They all protested, but Mary could see they loved it just the same. And their pride in him showed out of their eyes when they spoke of him, or when they welcomed him home. Hod Pierce was really getting to be somebody!

The ridge was becoming familiar to Mary. No longer did the road frighten or shock her. When Hod swung off the pike onto the trail up the ridge, it was just the last lap of the trip to her. The hill was just the familiar old hill up which the new car sped, scorning the rocky ledges and the slipping stones. And the old weathered house no longer seemed bare and poverty-stricken to her. It too was glossed over with familiarity. It had even come to take on a feeling of home. When she closed the door behind her now, the four walls snugged in and held her with possession. She went out from this place and she came back to it, and it never changed. It's enduring sameness was like the rising and the setting of the sun. It stood here, whole and secure. It framed life gently and timelessly. And when they rounded the last curve and came in sight of it, she knew a perfect moment of stilled life within her. Everything was slowed, rested, and blessed.

She came to love the sameness. Frequently when she handled the old ironstone dishes in Hattie's kitchen she had a sentient feeling, as if old, now-dead fingers were quickening, and in her youthful finger tips they were given back their life. To feel again, to wash and scour and dry these same dishes of their own youth. Their life tingled through hers.

They had come to Hattie from Gramma. And they had come to Gramma from Abigail Pierce, Jeems's wife. Mary thought of the scenes these ironstone plates had witnessed. Abigail's tears when Jeems went away to war. She would have bent over the soapy water and let her tears drop unseen into the froth of suds. And her ironstone plates would have been gripped hard in hands that were aching to hold tight to a man they could not hold.

Or, she thought, how the plates would have bounced and clattered when Jeems came home! Oh, Abigail would have tripped so lightly around the table, flinging down the plates to their places! Setting, now, once again, that beloved place at the head of the table.

And then there was Gramma, coming at sixteen to the ridge as Dow Pierce's woman. Inheriting from Abigail the Pierce traditions and the Pierce belongings. And the ironstone plates. Again they would have seen a woman's sorrows and joys. And in her time, Hattie. Hattie too would have gripped them tight, grieving for the little lost babies, grieving for Hod during the long war years, and, Mary's mind probed on, grieving even now for him because he was not following in Pierce ways.

It was then that Mary felt a sense of loss. It was an uneasy, fretful thing, which disturbed her only now and then. Times like this, when she stood with an ironstone plate in her hand. Or when she cut a yellow rose from the bush in the chimney corner. Or sometimes when she walked by the split rail fence down to the pasture. Her feet then felt the pull of the land . . . the ease of it, and the yield of it to the foot. She stood sometimes and leaned on the fence, and smelled the earth, drawing it deep down inside her, feeling the earthy air fill her. Then she had this faintly nostalgic yearning. Out of nowhere it came, like an ache sobbing through her, a feeling in her hand, or in her feet, or a smell in the air. But it said to her: "You are not keeping faith! You and Hod are not keeping faith!"

She began too to know the people. Ridge people have a way of closing out strangers. They hood their eyes and shutter their faces and present an inscrutable countenance to outlanders. Friendship comes first from ridge folks, and when they are ready to open the door. Nothing you can do will force it.

Not that Hod's family weren't friendly. They were. Hattie and Tom, Irma and John, and all the others. There was a gentle courtesy, an inherent graciousness in their manner, but at the same time they withheld themselves. She felt that their conversations were guarded and shielded, deliberately directed and channeled around her, so that she might not come too suddenly and too clearly into a knowledge of their most intimate feelings and thoughts.

A less sensitive person might have forever antagonized these people of Hod's. But Mary, having been in her own time a shy, withdrawn person, having known the meaning of intrusion, did not intrude. She met their courtesy with her own courtesy, their friendliness with her own friendliness. And when, hospitably, they offered their home to the guest she graciously returned the gift. She never pressed against the barrier.

It was late summer, a full nine months after Hod and Mary were married, before the door finally opened to her. And it happened as simply as the sun coming up over the rim of the ridge. Hattie overslept. And she was hurrying and bustling in the kitchen, grumbling: "Hit's been a time an' a time sincet I've did sich a thing! Never even opened my eyes till broad daylight! I'll be behind with my work all day! Mary, run upstairs an' git me a jar o' them plum preserves. They're in the little chest under the

231

window."

Mary scurried for the narrow little stairs with a glad feeling in her heart. Never before had she been permitted to go up those stairs into the back room of their life. The barrier was down, and the guest in the house now became the daughter of the house . . . one to share the depths and the heights of family feeling. One to slip a sly look to across the room and share a family joke with. One to call on to help with the work, and to talk long hours to around the quilting frame. One to tell in soft whispers about Irma's two dead babies, and her long labor with the two living ones. One to laugh with over Hod's frailties, knowing it was loving laughter. One, finally, of the Pierces.

And as the family let down the bars, so too did the rest of the folks on the ridge. Little by little they forgot her city strangeness. It's true, she was quare. Allus wantin' to do the most uncommon things. But more and more she became Hod Pierce's woman, a plumb nice girl when you got to know her. And they began to let her see them as they really were.

She watched Tom and Gault, John and Lem and Little Wells, come together and walk through the tobacco or the corn, feeling it, savoring it, hovering over it. They wore dirt-grimed overalls and they smelled of the barnyard and of sweat. Their hands were horny, and their shoulders had bent from the pull of the plow. But they walked their land, free and unbeholding to any man. There was a dignity in that freedom, and it was reflected in their relationships one with the other. No man hurried them, or harried them. And they, in turn, neither hurried nor harried another. Because they were free, they could leave others to their freedom.

There was the day Little Wells bought a new tractor. The family was at supper. " I doubt that little tractor Wells has got is goin' to do the work," Tom said, pouring his coffee into the saucer and blowing upon it. " Hit looks powerful little to me. My opinion, hit won't pull worth a team o' mules."

" Hit looked so to me too," said Hattie.

Hod also shook his head. " It won't. Those little machines are no good for heavy work like Wells has to do. He'd ought to have got a bigger one."

" Did you tell him that? " Mary asked, surprised.

Tom bent a twinkling eye on her over the rim of the saucer.

"Hit would be unseemly to give a man advice he weren't askin' fer," he said gently.

"But if he needed it . . . to keep him from wasting his money!"

"He would ask fer it, ifen he felt e'er need. An' hit's his money to waste or not as he sees fit."

The silence grew and the sounds of the supper table took on new volume. Mary pondered. "Suppose he didn't have enough money to buy a big tractor with?"

"That would be fer him to say, daughter. Wells'd know that if e'er person on this ridge had it, he could borry what he needed to git what he wanted. Hit'd be fer Wells to think on."

The inviolate right of the individual! To pursue his own way . . . to make his own choice . . . to make a fool of himself if he so minded . . . to waste his money if he so wanted . . . to call on his neighbors if he so needed. But forever and enduring his right to decide for himself . . . to go his own way . . . to be himself! The obligation of the neighbor? To stand by if needed . . . to come to the rescue if asked . . . to make up the lack caused by foolishness and waste. But never to interfere. This was a fundamental conception of liberty!

Mary looked down the table at Hod. He had come out of all this. He had this gentleness, this quietness, this silent awareness of the inviolability of personality, this tall, upstanding conception of freedom, born and bred in him. They had made him . . . set him apart from all other men she had ever known. She hugged this knowledge of him close. But even as it warmed her it was shot through with a trickle of fear. Would he keep those qualities in the city? Would he lose something of himself? And if he did, would he find anything better?

Don't be silly, she told herself. Hod is Hod, wherever he is. And don't romanticize the ridge. For all this fine conception there is still poverty, and ignorance, and superstition. Don't overlook that! Her mind slewed around the edges of that thought. But it isn't poverty like the slums, she thought, honest with herself. It isn't the vicious ignorance of the city. It isn't the deliberate evil of the tenements.

What about Matt and Lutie Jasper? Even they, she thought, even they have something here they wouldn't have anywhere else.

They have a place . . . they have neighbors . . . they are treated with kindness. And to the limit of their capacity to enjoy it, they have a fullness of life. That would not be possible to them if they were swarmed into a crowded slum room.

It is ironical, she thought, that as I am drawing closer to the ridge, Hod is pulling away from it. And the thought made her feel alone . . . small, and helpless, between the sky and the earth.

CHAPTER TWENTY–SEVEN

For a few months Hod was happy in the new work. He was full of a surging power, like a man who has climbed a tall hill, and stands, winded but victorious, surveying all he has left behind him. He stood like that, straddled and tall, feeling the keen wind in his face, the sharp, exhilarating thrill of being lifted up, over, and above the flat and level land.

The symbols of his new job were important to him. The little cubbyhole of an office; the paraphernalia on the desk; his signature a hundred times a day on workers' slips; the references to him: "Ask Hod." "Ask Pierce." He liked all this.

He watched his margin carefully and managed to end each month safely. He was pleased when he did that and he tucked away into a back cranny of his mind the bleak possibility of having to cut corners. He wouldn't have to. He had the feel of things now. He had it going.

But there came a month when a sudden rush of work narrowed his margin dangerously, and the necessity became a living possibility again. When the rush carried over into the next month, he doggedly refused to look at the operating sheets and let things take their own course. At the end of the month, when the three shift foremen balanced their sheets, it was obvious that Hod's shift was out of balance. The other two men said nothing. They merely tightened their mouths and stalked out of his office.

He sat for a long time after they left, feet on his desk, a pencil turning idly in his hand. He listened to the hum of machinery out in the plant. Listened to the unspoken accusations of the two foremen. Listened to his own conscience. I'll quit the job! And he threw the pencil on the desk. But even as his feet lowered to the floor, he wavered. There was the money in the bank, rapidly mounting up to the day when they could buy that home they were always talking about. There were the nice things Mary was accustomed to. The little car. The feeling of being somebody. The smooth, easy, glossy way of life. There was the office, the desk, the walk through the plant checking things, his shoulders a little wider than the men's, his head a little taller. He shrugged, and twisted through the door. The men would get it in the neck whether he was here or not!

So Hod's shift never ran anywhere near the low margin mark again. And at Christmas when he got his bonus check, he bought Mary a fur coat. Not mink or sable — it was like the small car . . . a substitute for the thing he really wanted. But into its soft, brown pelt went something Hod had lost. His young, naïve sweetness was gone. The fur coat was the final gesture . . . the last unrelenting demand of honor. He wanted nothing that check could buy for himself.

Once he tried to talk about things to Bill Fleming. " I don't like it, Bill," he said. " It's a dirty trick to pull on the men."

Bill Fleming laughed. He slung an arm across Hod's shoulders and patted his back. " You'll get over that. You've got to look out for yourself, man! If you don't, nobody else is going to do it for you! "

Then Hod became another man. Hard, driving, ruthless. He could be ruthless. He had been when he judged Hattie and Tom so harshly and walked off without so much as a backward glance. Youthfully harsh, then — hurt, and wanting to hurt back. But now there was no desire to hurt. He hadn't that excuse, and he didn't need it. He was looking out for himself. He was getting ahead.

Gone now was the fine beauty of the plant. He no longer thought of it as something big, and grand, and splendid. He saw it now as a great maw, cruel and conscienceless, swallowing people down into its dark depths and belching them up again, crushed and broken. He no longer thought of parts as chairs and sofas and beds. He thought of them as numbers, endless spokes and rounds and surfaces, forever conveyed from here to there, to be pitted against the increasing costs of operation.

With nice, precise calculations he weighed and measured, and cut corners anywhere and everywhere, keeping within the mar-

235

gin. He did it carefully and exactingly, lacing his feelings tightly inside himself. He had only one motive now. To keep getting ahead.

At the end of the year Jeff Martin called him into his office. He sat behind his desk and built his fingers into a temple. " Hod," he began, " you've done mighty well. Your record is absolutely clean this year."

Hod lighted a cigarette and rolled it into the corner of his mouth. He squinted his eye against the smoke and said nothing. Get to the point, he was thinking.

Martin got to the point. " Conway's being transferred to the Detroit plant. How would you like his job? "

Hod tongued his cigarette and spoke around it. " I'd like it," he said shortly. He met Martin's eyes and held them.

" It's yours."

" Thanks."

He unfolded his long legs and pushed his cap back on his head. " Thanks," he said again briefly, and went back to his own cubbyhole.

Martin watched him and his eyes slitted. He collapsed the temple of his fingers. That young man, he mused. That young man. He drummed slowly on his desk. But he let the order stand.

Now Hod was division foreman. And he stood up in front of the men at division meetings. In clear, unminced words he told the new men how to cut corners. He didn't laugh about it as Conway had and there were no innuendos in his speech. He made it deliberately rough. They could take it or leave it. " If any of you have got any idea you can do it any other way, get it out of your minds. Take it or leave it, but this is the way it is."

If their eyes betrayed their contempt, he met it coldly, unwaveringly. This is the way it is. Take it or leave it. And most of them took it. They wanted to get ahead too.

At home he was much the same, except that he was often tired, and he had begun to be troubled with indigestion frequently. There were nights too when he didn't sleep well. " You're working too hard, Hod," Mary accused him. " Let up a little. The plant'll be there in the morning! You're getting a case of city

236

nerves and jitters! "

"Yeah," Hod answered. And he shrugged off her worry.

They seldom went to the ridge any more, either. Mary suggested it occasionally. "Let's go down and spend the week end with the folks, Hod."

"I promised Bill I'd play golf with him Saturday."

"You could call him."

"What do you want to go down there for? "

"Well, we haven't been in quite a while. The folks like to see you. And I thought maybe . . ."

"It's too far to drive down and back in a day. I come back more tired than when I started."

He played golf a lot now . . . with Bill Fleming and Ed and Sid Bowden. And he and Mary frequently went to parties with the crowd on Saturday nights. When he dressed for a party now, there were five or six suits to choose from — suits tailored for him out of fine, rich materials. He no longer needed Mary's guidance. He had developed an impeccable taste, patterned after the men with whom he associated. And when they parked their car in front of Ed's or Sid's or Bill's it was no longer the small new car. Now it was the long, low-slung convertible. This year's bonus check had helped pay for it. And they had taken the balance from their home fund. Mary had protested that. "We don't really need a new car, Hod," she said. "And we have enough saved now for a down payment on a home. We could get a small place out in the edge of town."

"I want the car," Hod answered. "There's time enough for the home."

He knew what he wanted. The car now, and the home later. The home, out in the edge of town, yes. But not a tiny place like Mary had in mind. He had seen those new bricks building up on the long, outreaching roads and lanes, nesting snugly in their broad, sweeping lawns. One of those now. Why not? Division superintendent paid seventy-two hundred. But Martin was division superintendent! Yeah. Still . . . time enough, later.

Mary watched him with mixed feelings. So conflicting were her emotions that she could not find the point at which she was apprehensive. When he sat across the bridge table from her, his steady, smooth game balancing her own rather erratic one; when

237

they dined out and danced together; when he took his place naturally with the other men in a corner of the room; when he handed her into the long, low car, she was extremely proud of him. He had come so much farther in these two years than she had ever thought possible. Even her faith in him, and her love for him, had not envisioned this sure, steady climb on his part. Nor had she foreseen his adaptability . . . to the city, to their friends, to the gracious, easy life of which they were a part.

Well, she asked herself, isn't that what you wanted him to do? What's the matter with you, then? And she couldn't say. It was vague, elusive, a feeling of loss — real only in that it was constant. A troubled feeling that they were missing something. She reassured herself by looking around, telling herself they had everything . . . youth, security, friends, a satisfactory social life, Hod's good job. What was missing? The feeling was too persistent to shake off. And sometimes she looked at Hod and wished he weren't so often tired. Weren't so often engrossed in something he brought home from the office. Weren't so often unhungry and unsleepy.

Not that he wasn't always gentle and good to her. Not that he wasn't still a dear lover. When he had time. When he wasn't too tired. When they weren't going somewhere. There were yet those high moments of the recurring miracle. But they were dimmed by the race of time, the demands of living, the jaded body and spirit used up by the day's work.

She remembered the warm gaiety of the first months. Hod had had a merry, roguish wit which had sparkled for her when they were alone. An earthy, pungent speech, so different, so peculiarly his, that she mixed him and his way of talking all up together. But this too had disappeared. It was as if the inspiration and source of himself had run dry. He could bring forth nothing except clichés. Nothing particularly Hoddish. Apparently his mind was as cubbyholed as his body. Mary mourned for the loss, but didn't despair of it. He's too busy, she told herself. When he's settled down into this job and doesn't feel so burdened, he'll be himself again.

She felt restless. She wanted the settled feeling of home and children. Time was fleeting, and they were both past thirty now. She didn't talk about this to Hod. She was afraid it would

238

trouble him, and in these days she was seeking in every way she knew to spare him additional burdens.

And so the time went by. Went by so tightly and so tensely for so long without surcease that Hod felt an unutterable weariness overtaking him. He thinned down to a flat leanness, and developed a tremor in his right hand. He was never rested. Sleepiness came over him early at night, overtaking him at the table, or even at parties. Overpowering sleepiness, wilting him and making him ill. And yet when he slept, later, it was a sodden, loggy sleep that left him unrested and nauseated with weariness. He felt a compulsion to swallow constantly, and when he tried to eat, he felt sick.

Now he was compelled to look at himself, at his life. His body which had endured the strain for so long now compelled him to think of it. And he could not think of his body without thinking also of the conditions that surrounded it. Not for a long time had he done any objective thinking. He had walked so surely, stepping so firmly from one stone to another, that he had never noticed the stream which he was crossing. Now he had to look down. But so stubbornly dedicated was he to the steppingstones that even as he looked down he denied the necessity. Why, things were going too well. He was on top. Just one more stride and he'd be sitting in Martin's office. All he needed was to take it a little easier. Get a little more sleep. Get out in the open more often. Quit going to so many parties.

The parties bored him anyhow. He sat, now, on the fringe, and looked on with sated eyes. Ed, Sid, Joe, and Bill . . . he saw them in their shiny, bursting skins . . . he knew the line of their talk by memory. Deals, and more deals. So I told him. So I said to him. So I made him an offer. And the complacent laughter that always accompanied the telling. Hod sat in his corner and let his anger and his nausea beat against him. He rarely entered into their conversations any more. And he tried not to listen.

The women were just as bad. Esther, veiling herself in the smoke from her long amber holder, shrieking her eternal cry of culture down the room . . . pseudo art . . . pseudo music . . . pseudo living! Nora, insulated in her country memories, inept

239

with her offspring, escaping her impotence by constant nibbling at the past. Daisy, lean and lithe, satin-cased and slick, eating away at Joe, wearing him down with her hatred and nagging. And finally Minna Bowden. Minna, on her everlasting search for reality. Running like a rat in a maze after this good cause and that, shutting her eyes to life and raising them skyward with pious mouthings.

And what was it any of them wanted? What drove them to this insane life? What was it they still kept running after? For they were all in a race — a mad, rat race, chasing their tails, clawing the barriers, frothing after something else. What would it take to release them? A little more money in the bank? A little better job? A little bigger house? A little more powerful car?

What? What? What? He slitted his eyes and let the room whirl around him until the figures of the people were on a treadmill before him. Circling like little squirrels running, stepping on each other's tails, biting and snarling, circling, circling . . . and getting nowhere. The treadmill only went faster. Mary was in the circle, her black head thrown back and her breath laughing out of her mouth. And then as the room whirled faster, he joined the circle, and his long legs hurried to catch up.

In his bone weariness Hod took to walking at night. Maybe, he thought — maybe if I get tired enough physically, I can sleep. Sometimes Mary went with him. She was genuinely worried about him now. And she felt better if she was with him. At first they walked at random, seeking no special place, thinking no special thoughts, not noticing the people they jostled or were jostled by. They rarely talked. But one night Hod spoke suddenly. " Did you ever notice the faces of people? "

" The faces of people? "

" I mean just people in general. Like these we meet on the street. Ever look at them good? "

Mary was startled. She thought for a moment. " Not very often," she finally admitted.

" Take a good look at them," Hod said. " Try it for a block. Look carefully at the face of every person we meet."

At the end of the block she looked at him. " Well? "

" Did you see anybody who looked happy? "

" I wasn't looking for that."

" Look for it in this block."

Mary shook her head at the end of the next block. " There aren't many, are there? "

" Did you see *one* face that looked happy? "

" I thought maybe that old woman looked happy. Not bubbling over with it . . . but sort of serene and calm."

" Yeah, I counted her too. But nobody else. The faces look tight, screwed up. They look like they're hurting. Even the young ones look stretched out thin. And nobody's got time for anybody else. Everybody's in a hurry, got to get somewhere, fast. Now watch this."

They were walking down Fourth Street, and as he touched her elbow, they stopped to watch a bus load passengers at the curb. The bus was already crowded to standing room, and about thirty people on the sidewalk swarmed around the door as it drew up to a stop.

" Let 'em off," the driver yelled. " Let 'em off, first."

But the packed mob at the curb wouldn't give an inch, and the people coming out had to fight their way through the pack, clothes being pulled, hats knocked awry, bundles dropped. Muttering, they made their way through, only to be caught in the surge of the pack toward the door when the last person cleared it.

" All the way to the back, now," the driver called hopefully, screwing his head around to see if there was room. Outside, the crowd shoved until the starter called: " That's all. Close the doors."

" You'd think that was the last bus tonight," Hod said, and he pointed up the street. Another bus was nosing into the curb there.

" Funny what being jammed and crowded together in a city does to people, isn't it? Seems like they turn themselves wrong side out, and you can only see their worst sides. They've got to get so much for themselves so fast that they haven't got time to think of anybody else. Everybody's out to take care of himself, and the devil take the hindmost."

They walked on up the street and crossed to avoid the starlings that circled the hotel. Since the old post office had been torn down on the square, the homeless starlings roosted there. Each evening at dusk they circled and swarmed, their shrill cries filling

241

the air. Mary and Hod stopped to watch them.

"A starling is such a hideous bird," Mary said. "And it has such a pretty name. A bird with a name like that should be beautiful, with a song like a thrush's. But listen to that hoarse cry of theirs! It's worse than a crow's."

Hod watched silently. Finally he pulled at Mary's arm. There was a bitter taste in everything tonight. "Yeah," he said, "we're like those birds. Those of us who live in a big city. Crowded and quarreling for room and life . . . pecking at one another . . . ruffling our feathers and screaming at each other. We've got no more dignity than the birds. Just a little more modesty."

Mary's mouth fell open. It was the first time she had heard one of Hod's pithy, wry remarks in months and months. She kept still, hoping he would go on. But his ire was spent and he felt the futility of sermonizing. Who am I to talk, he thought. I'm just as unlovely as the rest. And I won't do any more about it than they will.

But he had a sudden vision of a place where time stood still . . . a green and sweet place, where life flowed slowly. Where a man could prop his foot up on a fence rail and spit a puddle of brown tobacco in the dust, and talk about the weather, the crops, the state of the world, with all of time and space to spare. Where people were busy with purpose, but never too busy to stop and be kind and neighborly. Where you were never alone in sorrow, grief, or sadness. Where a man could stop in the middle of a corn row on a bright June morning, if he was of a mind to, and grab his fishing pole. Where, on a moony night, he could whistle up his coon hound and take to the woods. Oh, life is never so sweet as when it is distilled slowly, one drop at a time . . . lived fully, one hour at a time!

Hod was filled with a nostalgic longing for the ridge. But he turned on the pavement and set his heel down hard, denying it.

CHAPTER TWENTY–EIGHT

THE SECOND SUMMER CAME ON. The sun blasted the city day after day and it stewed in its own juice. The streets softened to an oozy, viscous dough, kneaded by traffic until a muggy, smothering wave of steam rose from it, like a solid column, from which there was no escape. The brick buildings absorbed the sun, and gave it off again, blowing a furnace breath into the air. The lowering pall of heat did not cool until late at night. Never completely cooled, really, for morning came too soon.

Hod's office, which had been Conway's, was a box which held the heat like an oven. The big plant sprawled in the sun, taking it in and spreading it through the low, flat-topped buildings. Hod never used to mind the heat, but it wilted him these days. By the end of the day he felt like a starched shirt that a hot shower had spattered.

He was feeling like that late on Friday afternoon just before the five o'clock whistle when Bill Fleming sent for him.

" Sit down, Hod," Bill said when he went in, offering him a cigar. Hod shook his head. He wasn't smoking as much these days.

" What's on your mind? " he asked, tipping the big electric fan so that its current played over him. " I need this more than you do," he laughed.

" Sure," Bill agreed. Bill cut the end of his cigar and rolled it around in his mouth before lighting it. Hod knew Bill would take his time. When he had something he considered important to say, ho always played with a cigar that way.

" Hod," when the cigar suited him and was lighted Bill spoke, " how'd you like Martin's job? "

The legs of Hod's chair came down suddenly. " Martin's? "

" That's what I said."

Hod felt a gushing thrill pour through him, like an emptying and draining of all the fluid of his body! Division superintendent! Six sections under him! This was what he'd been waiting for! He grinned at Bill, and Bill's mouth widened in an answering grin.

" Sounds pretty good, huh? "

" Sounds mighty good! " He kicked the chair back and walked over to the window. " Can you swing it? "

" I think so."

Hod drummed his fingers on the windowpane. " What about Martin? "

Bill leaned back in his chair and swiveled around. " Martin? " he said, as if it were a new problem. " Oh. Why, Martin's been

243

slipping pretty badly lately. I guess you'd say Martin's just going to be a casualty."

Hod cracked the knuckles on his right hand. Martin had been pretty good to him. Martin had seen that Conway gave him his first break, and he'd come through with division foreman when Conway was transferred. He hated to see him get it this way. Still. "If I don't take it, who gets it?" he asked.

Bill looked at him a long moment, a bleak look and a final look. He shook his head and when he spoke his voice had a dead, level sound. "Nobody. This job is strictly for you. Take it or leave it, Hod."

Hod knew then. There was nothing wrong with Martin's work. He hadn't played ball with Bill somewhere along the line . . . or he'd got fed up with playing ball, and Bill was putting the skids under him. And Bill was putting a friend of his in Martin's place. Another one of Bill's deals.

"O.K., Bill." What else was there to say?

Mary had learned that the little courtyard was cooler than the apartment in the afternoons when the building next door shaded the tiny grassy plot from the sun. It was far from cool, but it was more bearable than their third-floor rooms. Late each afternoon she moved there with her reading or sewing, taking along a tray of cold drinks, and tried to make herself comfortable. She wished Hod could take his vacation soon, and they could get away from the city. She thought longingly of the mountains, or the sea, or even of the ridge. Any place where they could escape the pavements and the hot buildings.

That Friday afternoon she had been especially fretful. She was trying to decide whether or not to sign her contract for another year. Hod had been urging her to quit teaching. They no longer needed the money, and that had been her principal reason for teaching at first. But she wondered what she would do with herself if she gave it up. As long as they lived in an apartment and had no children, she would find life pretty sterile and empty. If they would only buy a place and get settled!

Hod found her there when he came home. He swept his hat onto the ground and stretched out with a moan, letting his body

244

sink into the cushion of the grass.

"Pretty bad today?" Mary asked.

"Oh, the same old thing! But it's so hot I feel like I've been fried!"

"I know. Something cold to drink before dinner?"

"Yes, ma'am, please! And you can just keep on serving me something cold to drink! I don't care if we never have dinner." He turned over and buried his face in the grass, letting it tickle against his cheek. He bit down on a blade, remembering the pungent taste of crab grass when he was a boy. But this tasted dusty, oily, flat. He spat, wrinkling his mouth.

When Mary nudged him with the toe of her shoe, he sat up to take the drink from her. He sipped, and then drank gustily. "More," and he held out the glass.

"You'll ruin your dinner, Hod!"

"Dinner can wait. What is this?"

"Tea, with pineapple juice and ginger ale."

"Wonderful!"

He leaned back against the chair in which she was sitting, rubbing his head against her knee. "Got some good news."

"A house!"

"No. But we can get the house soon. I'm the new division superintendent."

"Hod! Hod!" Mary's hands flew to his shoulders and shook them delightedly. "How wonderful! Darling, I'm so glad! When did you find out?"

"Today. Just before quitting time. Bill called me in and told me." That was all he'd tell her of that, though.

"O Hod, I know you've been hoping you'd get that job someday. But I thought you'd be lucky if it came five or ten years from now. When Mr. Martin retired. Oh, what about Mr. Martin?"

"He's quitting."

"Quitting? Is he sick? Is he going with another company?"

"I don't know. All I know is that Bill called me in today and said Martin was leaving, and did I want the job."

"Are they firing him, Hod?"

"How should I know?"

"Well, don't you think you *should* know? After all, Mr. Martin's

245

been pretty nice to you."

Hod threw the handful of dirt he had been sifting through his fingers to the ground. He squared around and faced her. His jaw jutted stubbornly and his mouth was tight. "All right, you asked for it! They're firing him."

"Why?"

"I don't know. But I strongly suspect he got tired of playing ball with Bill. I don't know, and I don't want to know the straight of it. But my guess is Bill's got to have a friend in that division job. I'll pat your back and you pat mine. So Martin gets fired, and Pierce gets the job. Pierce is Fleming's friend. I don't know any more than that. I don't need to know any more."

Mary sat there, stupidly trying to take it in. This wasn't Hod talking. She brushed her hair back from her hot forehead.

"Well, say something!" Hod shouted at her.

"You mean —" she said finally — "you mean you'll go along with Bill? You'll let Bill fire Martin, and you'll take his job?"

"Sure I'll do it. It's not much worse than what I've been doing all along. I've been stealing time from the men for two years. Been stealing money from their pay envelopes so I could pad my operating sheets. Oh, not literally," he said when he saw her face. "I haven't really gone into their pockets. But I might as well have. I've kept their wages down and cut 'em out of time. It's the same thing."

"Hod, what's happening to you? Jeff Martin was your friend. You could keep Bill from doing this to him!" Mary's voice was trembling, and it hung broken in the air between them.

Hod was on his feet now, shouting at her. "What's happening to me! Nothing. Nothing at all, except that I'm learning how to get along in the world! I'm learning that you can't be soft. You can't think about other people. You've got to take care of yourself. And when it comes to cutting throats, I'm learning not to let mine get cut, that's all!"

"Even if you cut Jeff Martin's?"

"Even if I cut Jeff Martin's! If it's his or mine, it'll be his! Mary, you live in an ivory tower! If you get ahead, if you ever amount to anything, you can't be careful how you do it. If you have to step all over the other fellow, it's just his tough luck for being in the way! He'd step on you if the cards ran the other way!"

246

Mary felt sick and dull. This was Hod shouting these terrible things at her. Hod, who was so tender and gentle with her. She hadn't known he could talk like this . . . do things like this! She felt as if he had struck her down and trampled on her. "Then everything I've ever believed in is false," she said. "Everything I've ever tried to teach children to believe in is false."

"You're darned right it's false! You don't get ahead by honesty and integrity. You get ahead by making friends in the right places. And by pulling wires. And by forgetting your conscience. You learn right away that deals are more important than ideals! They're no good to you when you come up against the world. And only a few people like you still believe in them — and you don't practice what you preach!"

Mary's hands cupped her face and she shook all over with the ague of her horror. Let him stop, she prayed. Let him stop talking! But the silence was dead and white, and she dropped her hands limply. "Hod, if you take that job, we're through. You know that, don't you?" There was a trembling down her legs and her chest felt caved in.

Hod's head flung up at her words. "Well, what makes you think your skirts are clean? You cry crocodile tears, you don't soil your lily white hands, but, brother, how you do gobble up all the good things that come your way from somebody else's soiled hands! You wanted solid mahogany furniture, didn't you? You wanted an electric kitchen, didn't you? You wanted a Chinese imported rug, didn't you? And you didn't complain over your new fur coat, did you? Oh, but gee, how shocked you are when I tell you that the way I made the money to pay for 'em was by stepping on people like Jeff Martin! Do you want to examine every dollar I make to be sure it's clean? Well, precious few of them are, I can tell you that!"

Mary's face came clear before him in the haze of his anger. He saw it naked and white and crumpled. A blaze of sunlight through the interstices of the buildings cut across it and marbled the pure white of her skin. He lifted an arm, and then let it fall heavily to his side. He whirled toward the house.

"Where are you going?" Mary cried, running after him.

"Out! Out! I'm going out! I don't know where, and I don't care where! I'm going to see if I can drive far enough to get a breath

247

of clean air! I'm sick of this town. I'm darned near sick of everything!"

"Let me go too!"

Hod stopped and looked at her, and everything inside of him melted and ran down. "Mary," he whispered. "O Mary, forgive me! It wasn't true. It wasn't true!"

She came into his arms and wound her own arms tight around him, hugging him closely as if she couldn't get near enough. Oh, he had been so far away! And then the tears came — wet, freeing tears that drowned his shirt collar and trickled down his neck. He let her cry: "It's such a mess, Mary. It's such a mess."

She smeared her nose on the front of his shirt and lifted a shaky smile. "Let me get a scarf for my hair. I won't be a minute."

Hod drove and drove, not thinking where he was going. He sought the outer edges of town and turned the car loose on uncrowded roads. The wind in his face felt clean, and the dark, sparsely lighted roads were good. Mary sat close, saying nothing. Only her hand on his knee never lifted. From time to time he reached down and took it, held it for a short time, and then laid it back on his knee.

Far into the night they drove, circling and circling, out one road, in another. And then, just as dawn grayed the sky, Mary bent her head against his arm. He thought she had gone to sleep. Looking down, he saw she was crying again. He pulled the car up to the side of the road and drew her gently against him, cradling her and rocking her. She flung her head back then, and sobbed: "Hod. Hod, let's go down home!"

Home! Neither of them thought it strange that she should use that word. Neither of them remembered the other time when she had cried, "I want to go home."

Hod started the car and turned it into the road, and, straight as an arrow released from a taut string, it sped into the rising sun.

Three hours later they were climbing the ridge, and then they were nosing the car up against the picket fence. Sarah poked her nose out the front door, and, seeing who it was, screeched and flew to the back of the house. But Hattie would not admit surprise when she came in, wiping her hands on her apron front.

"I knowed you was comin'," she said. "I was jist cleanin' a chicken. I told 'em all I'd best git ready, fer I knowed in reason you was comin'."

"How could you possibly have known we were coming?" laughed Mary.

"The old dominecker rooster got plumb up in the door this mornin' an' jist crowed fit to kill. Hit's a sure sign. An' I told 'em all right then — I says, 'Hod an' Mary's acomin' an' I'd best git ready!'"

"How long will it take you to fry that chicken, Ma?" Hod asked.

"Not more'n a few minnits! I'll bound yer hungry, an' I aimed to have it ready. But you come a mite quicker'n I was lookin'."

When they had finished eating, Hod folded the remainder of the chicken and a couple of biscuits in an oiled bread wrapper and stuck it in his pocket. Then he started rummaging through the old corner cupboard. "Ma, you know where there's any fishin' line and stuff? I think I'll go down to the river."

"In that there box on the bottom shelf. Right where you allus kept it. I reckon Tom got so used to you puttin' it there he ain't never thought none o' movin' it. Facts is, I don't reckon hit's been used sincet that time when you was home on furlough."

"I found it," Hod grunted. He turned to Mary and kissed her softly on the cheek. He patted her shoulder. "Don't worry if I'm late. I'll be home for supper, though."

When the screen door slammed behind him, Hattie looked at Mary. "Didn't you want to go with him?"

"Not today."

Mary watched him cross the back lot and lift his long legs over the fence into the tobacco patch. He wasn't going away from her, she knew. But he had some thinking to do today, and he had to do it alone.

Hod eyed the length of the tobacco patch speculatively. Looked pretty good. It was waist-high, greening up from the broad, dark base to the curled edges of pale leaves at the top. Spiking the top were the fragile, creamy petals of the blooms, as delicate as oleander. When he looked back, the acre was a small green sea, crested with amethyst foam. There's nothin' as pretty as tobacco

249

in bloom, he thought.

His feet took the path down the holler, following the purling creek. The stones were white in the sun, and tiny, silver minnows darted frantically from shallow to shallow. On past the schoolhouse he went, across Lem's cornfield, coming finally to the river. He cut a reed and wound the line around it, adjusted the cork for depth, baited the hook, and set the pole in the soft, hot soil of the bank. He leaned back and let his shoulders feel the rough bark through his shirt. He sighed. His eyelids drooped from lack of sleep, and he slid down against the thick mat of leaf mold under the tree. He turned over and laid his face in his arms and dozed dreamily.

The ground was warmly spotted with sun streaks through the leaves, and the river ran a rapid, noisy chatter around the rocks in midstream. Here it eddied in toward the bank in a deep pool, but the edges of the pool were restless with the hurry of the shallows in the middle. Hod listened, and the heat and the noisy talk of the river made him want to strip and become a part of the coolness, the wetness, and the noisiness of the stream. He flung his clothes on a blackberry bush and plunged into the pool, going down deep and opening his eyes in the dimness below. There were the white roots of the big sycamore tree sprangled out in the water, and a frightened fish hiding in their network. He went down to the bottom and laid his hand against the cool pebbles. He clutched a handful of them and came up shouting when his head was clear, " Touched bottom! " Wade and Sandy and Little Wells should have been there on the bank to hear him, and to laugh, and make him open out his hand for proof.

When he tired of splashing and swimming, he eased over on his back and floated, letting the water hold him lightly. He looked down his long length and eyed the whiteness of his stomach and legs. Time was when they were brown as a berry by this time in August. He lifted his arm and let the water run in a thin stream down it, back into the river. He remembered another time when he had lain here on the breast of the river and watched a droplet trickle down his arm and join its source again. And he had traced it on down the stream. Past the Beaver Hole . . . he remembered. Past Old Man Smith's place. Past the covered bridge. On down it had gone to the union with the Ohio . . . to the merging with the Mississippi. To the Gulf and the ocean. And what was it he had thought? O free and searching water! He had wanted to be free as the water, hadn't he? He had wanted to travel with it and see all those places out there, hadn't he? Well, he'd been, now. He'd seen them. Free and searching water! Free, but never staying anywhere . . . free, but always moving. Free, but with no purpose. And what had he done? And what had he seen?

He crawled out on the bank, rubbed himself down with his shirt, and dressed slowly. When he had finished, he sat down, drawing his legs up and lacing his arms around them. He let his mind follow on down the path it had ventured into.

Then freedom had to have a purpose, he thought. It's got to be tied to something, and it's got to be going somewhere. Is it freedom if it's tied to something? Is there really any such thing as freedom? What do men mean by being free? What did I mean by wanting to be free? I thought if I could get off the ridge I'd be free. What was it I wanted to be free of?

He squirmed around and looked back up the valley toward the ridge, humped sullenly against the sky. There it stood, forever and enduring. Was that what he had wanted to get away from? The foreverness?

His mind fringed out his thoughts, tracing each to its frayed end, and somewhere along there he remembered the night when he had made Lily Mae mad with his talk of leaving the ridge. It came back to him how he'd said folks on the ridge always did things the same old way, that they never looked farther ahead than the end of their noses, that they were satisfied to make do. He remembered later that night, after Hattie had forbidden his going to the lumber camp, how he had flung his thoughts wildly to the night sky. He wouldn't be caught in the net of that inertia. He would not settle down in a two-room shack on the edge of Pa's land and doom himself to dark risings and dark sleepings, and nothing beyond but the end of a furrow and sweat for his pains. He had twisted under the weight of seven generations of Pierces on the ridge. The dead weight of it, and the wantlessness of it. That's not for me, he'd said. That's not for me.

That was what he had wanted to be free of, then. That dead weight. That inertia. Troubled, his hand sifted the earth through his fingers. He still didn't want that. He twisted the thoughts round and round in his head. Well, what was it he wanted to be free for, then? I wanted to be free to be myself, he remembered. I wanted to find out who Hod Pierce was. What he could do if he had a chance. Where he belonged, and how big a man he could be, the work and the place that would bring out the most in him. That's a man's right, isn't it?

Yeah, he told himself. You thought if you could get off the ridge, you'd be somebody. You thought folks out there had life sweeter. You thought out there lay freedom. Well, you found out, didn't you? He accused himself. You found out that freedom hasn't any meaning at all over there. You thought there'd be green pastures and wide, lovely spaces, and men would live in those spaces graciously and sweetly. Instead, you crawled over the fence right into a little box. A little box two feet this way, measured by the kind of job you had, how much money you made, the contacts you had. Two feet this way, measured by the kind of place you lived in, the kind of furniture you had in it, the number of gadgets you were able to buy for it. Two feet this way, measured by the sort of friends you had, the kind of clothes you wore, the kind of car you drove. Two feet this way, measured by the time you punched in on a clock, the time you wasted at parties, the time you slept, the time you didn't live.

A little box, walled in on all four sides. At first it wasn't so high but what you could crawl over it and get out for a while. And at first you wanted to get out from time to time. And at first you were certain you were going to make it bigger. Bring into it something fine. At first the top was open, and overhead were skies and the stars, fuzzy clouds and new moons. You could look up and see them. But the longer you stayed in the pen, the less often you wanted to get out. The less often the smallness bothered you. The more satisfied you were with it. Until finally you yourself nailed the last board across the top, closing yourself in, shutting out the skies and the stars, the fuzzy clouds and the new moons. They troubled you. They were too bright and big and far away.

You liked the smallness and coziness, and the space outside frightened you. You crouched in your little pen and felt safe and snug and secure. You didn't have to dare anything in that small space. You didn't have to think. You didn't have to reach for anything. You didn't have to do anything different or brave or honest.

252

You just closed the box around you and made yourself little to fit it. And you dried up inside, contented with the pattern of things. You didn't have to *be* somebody to live in that little box. You only had to be like everybody else.

And what did it cost you? You only had to seal yourself into slavery . . . the slavery of making money, of buying and accumulating possessions, of racing breathlessly toward the pie in the sky . . . success. You only had to punch the time clock and bow and say, "Yes, sir." You only had to forfeit every dream of freedom, every last ounce of dignity, every last inch of self-respect. For how could a man walk tall in liberty caged in a pen!

Hod's hand dropped again to his side, fingering the earth beneath it. He crumbled it and sifted it between his fingers. He lifted it and smelled it, sniffing its dank richness. With the feel of the earth in his hands, suddenly he felt the pull of the plow in his arms. The feel of the furrows under his feet. The hot sun on his back. The fuzzy greenness of new tobacco leaves between his fingers. The clean, winy air in his lungs. His head went back and he took a deep, deep breath. It's good, he thought. It's good.

What was it Grampa said once? I've had me a little piece o' land o' my own . . . an' a roof over my head that belonged to me . . . an' I've raised what I put in my stummick an' it set light there on account of it. I've had me a good woman to go along with me, an' kids that's pleasured me. I've had work to lay my hand to . . . work o' my own choosin'. An' folks around to neighbor with. Don't know what more a man could want. Livin' jist about biles down to that, I'd say.

Suddenly the words were shot through with a new illumination. Like blinding light Hod saw it. There's more, Grampa. You didn't say it, but it was there all the time. It was in everything you said, wasn't it? Living like that a man can be a clod, never lifting his head above it. He can be what I wanted to get away from. Dull, and plodding, and oxlike. He can sink down into the land itself, and never rise above it. There's got to be something else running through it like a scarlet thread . . . giving it color . . . giving it meaning. A man's got to have the knowledge that it's good . . . that it's good and true and beautiful. He's got to have the deep and abiding awareness in him of the dignity of his relationship to the earth, or else it loses its dignity and becomes in its own way another kind of slavery. He's got to hold close to him its beauty. He's got to feel that it's the foundation of pride and strength . . . of dignity and manhood.

Grampa had known how good his life was . . . how right and true. And that's what's got to color life and make it live. That's what makes a man free. That's what lifts the weight of the land from his shoulders and makes him walk tall . . . on his own land, where he can walk on it, smell of it, feel of it, plant it and harvest its growth. That's what freed him, because the land he owned was part of himself and in the last analysis he only owned himself.

And then Hod saw he had answered his own most profound questions: Who is Hod Pierce? And why does he live? He saw that a man could search forever outside of himself for the purpose of his life. But until he turned his eyes inward, he would never find the home he was seeking. It wasn't off somewhere in mansions in the sky. It wasn't in the city or in the country on the face of the earth. It was right down inside of a man.

This thought startled him, and he looked backward timidly. Was he going to have to unthink all he had been thinking now? Start from where? He stood up and felt his tallness reaching up, and his leanness filling out. Start from inside the man. Start from deep down inside. There was no other way. If a man could look at himself and the work he had done at the end of a day, and say, it's been good today . . . it's been as right and as fine and as good as I could make it . . . it's taken the best there is in me to do it, and it's made me bigger and better to do it . . . then that man was at home, wherever he was. Even in the little box? Even there?

Even there. You didn't have to nail the lid down on the box. He looked at that thought, wincing. You didn't have to take the foreman's job. The first time you cheated on a guy you nailed down the first board. But you didn't have to do it. He went farther down this path of thought. You didn't even have to crawl into the box in the first place. Your ideas of being somebody were all wrong. You thought getting ahead on a job, making money, and buying things were amounting to something. All your life you were walking toward that box, and it wasn't the box's fault. It was inside of you all the time.

Standing tall, he felt cleansed and renewed. He tightened his belt a little. He could go back to the city. He could make Hod Pierce's life have meaning there. But he could make it have more meaning here. It would be here. Here on the land where his father and his father's father before him had worked out their own lives. He could take on the full weight of seven generations and it would measure him to his tallest height. It would make him the most somebody he could ever be. By the manner of his living, the way of his work, by his own sense of integrity, he would establish his own proprietorship of himself. Free himself, and walk tall. Who is Hod Pierce? A speck of dust, whirling in a cosmic wind. Yes, but a speck of dust with a purpose, whirling in a wind with a pattern. Part of a timeless whole, which without him would be incomplete!

When Mary saw his face that evening, she knew he had found his answer. It had gone young again, smooth and quiet, and peace spread over it like a healing ointment. And she felt it stealing into her, gentling her fears and calming her. A rising tide of gladness choked her throat. Whatever he had decided, it was right. If it made him look like this, it was right.

After supper he turned to her. " Let's walk awhile. There'll be a moon later on."

They went down the road, scuffling the dust, swinging their joined hands like children. The night mist was crawling up the holler, cooling the heat and dampening the dust. The purpling twilight softened the mass of trees on the rim of the ridge, muting their identity. A dog barked sharply, twice, and then was quiet. Across a hill and a holler a sentinel cowbell tongued the knell of the buried sun. The stars blinked out and came closer. Kentucky stars. Just far enough above so that a man must tiptoe to touch them. Around all the world, Hod thought, there's none so beautiful. The stars over a man's home must always be the loveliest.

He held Mary's hand tighter and guided her into the path that led down into the holler. " Where are we going? " she wanted to know.

" You'll see," he answered. " There's a thing I want to show you."

They followed the trail and came to the foot of the hill, and then they crossed the creek, stepping lightly on the stones. They waded the tall grass up to Grampa's unlighted cabin. Hod let down the gate and went through. Mary followed him. She was afraid to speak. She would break the spell.

When they came up to the old log house, Hod laid his hand against it. " This is it," he said. " This is what I wanted to show you."

" It's Grampa Dow's house, isn't it? "

" It's our house."

Mary was still. There was no mistaking Hod's meaning. This was his answer. She thought she must have known it all the time. Known that this was where they would make out their lives together. Known it even that day long ago when he had boarded a bus and racked his bag above her and sat down beside her. Known that this man would take her by the hand and lead her here. Known it, and wanted it. Something in her was fulfilled now.

Oh, it wouldn't all be as simple as that! She would have to change every habit of her life . . . remake herself . . . strip herself of many small vanities and prides. She would hate it sometimes. She would cry from weariness and ache from the hardness of it. She would feel sorry for herself sometimes, moan for her permanents and manicures and trim, tailored suits. She would be frightened and ill sometimes, borne down by the strangeness. But even as she knew all this, she knew another thing. She had it in her to be that much of a woman. By this man's side, she had it. He would call it out of her . . . expect it of her, and make her be that big. She could take on that stature to walk beside him.

She joined her hand with his against the rough old logs. " It will be a beautiful home," she said.

Hod stopped her by the beech tree at the head of the trail when they climbed out of the holler. " Wait," he said. " Listen to this." He cupped his hands around his mouth and shouted long and loud: " Hey! Hey, you! This here's Hod Pierce ablowin' his horn! "

And the echo rolled up in the holler, reverberated against the cliff, and came back to them, clear and strong. Triumphantly it came back, " This here's Hod Pierce ablowin' his horn! "

256